Contents

Dedication 7 day

To Lance Lindon – thanks for being the organisational psychologist in the family business.

Orders: please contact Bookpoint Ltd, 130 Milton Park, Abingdon, Oxon OX14 4SB. Telephone:+44 (0)1235 827720. Fax: +44 (0)1235 400454. Lines are open from 9.00 to 5.00, Monday to Saturday, with a 24-hour message answering service. You can also order through our website **www.hoddereducation.co.uk**.

British Library Cataloguing in Publication Data
A catalogue record for this title is available from the British Library

ISBN: 978 1 4441 6720 7

First Published 2010

This Edition Published 2012
Impression number 10 9 8 7 6 5 4 3 2 1
Year   2015 2014 2013 2012

Copyright © 2012 Jennie Lindon

Hachette UK's policy is to use papers that are natural, renewable and recyclable products and made from wood grown in sustainable forests. The logging and manufacturing processes are expected to conform to the environmental regulations of the country of origin.

Cover photo © SUDIO 1ONE – Fotolia

Typeset by DC Graphic Design Limited, Swanley Village, Kent

Printed in Great Britain for Hodder Education, an Hachette UK Company, 338 Euston Road, London NW1 3BH by CPI Group (UK) Ltd, Croydon, CR0 4YY

Acknowledgements

I appreciate what I have learned from listening to many experienced practitioners, team leaders, early years advisors and consultants. Special thanks to Anna Batty (Head, Millom Children's Centre, Cumbria); Claire Coughtrey and Tamar Hawkins (Cressex Day Nursery, Bucks); Catherine Croft (early years consultant, Thurrock); Jenny Dexter and Helen Lasko (Christmas Cottage Nursery, Bucks); Mary Jane Drummond (author and consultant); Lesley Dyer (early years consultant, West Sussex); Laura Henry (Childcare Consultancy Ltd); Maureen Lee (Director, Best Practice Network); Kath Mathews (Area SENCO, Gloucester); Sandra Matthews (Acorns Playgroup, Harrogate); Kathy Piercey and the course group completing their foundation degree in Early Years Development and Learning for Reading University, at the Berkshire College of Agriculture, summer 2009; Debbie Shepherd (0–3s Development Officer, Thurrock); Andrea Sully (Learning Research and Development Advisor, North Somerset) and Diane Toms (practitioner).

I appreciate my time with early years professionals, in particular the networks of: Bournemouth, Poole & Dorset; Hampshire, Southampton & the Isle of Wight; and Devon. Thanks also for what I learned in my time with the teams from Buckingham's Nursery School (Leek), Grove House Children's Centre (Southall), Randolph Beresford Children's Centre (White City, London) and Southlands Kindergarten and Crèche (Newcastle-under-Lyme). My thanks to the What Matters To Children team and the opportunity that membership has given me to rethink best practice with children.

My thanks to Lance Lindon (chartered psychologist) for sharing his extensive knowledge of organisational behaviour and managing change, especially for Chapter 7. The diagrams on pages 172 and 176 were developed within his professional practice. Thanks also to Drew Lindon for researching the website and references updates for this edition.

I have created fictional settings for the scenarios within this book and these names – so far as I can establish – are not used by any existing provision. I have woven in my experience with people and places. However, none of these imagined early years provisions represents any of the individuals or teams whom I have thanked earlier.

Photo credits

All photos © Andrew Callaghan, except:

Figures: 3.05 © Terrance Klassen/Alamy; 5.02 © National Geographic Image Collection/Alamy; 5.03 © madjuszka – Fotolia; 7.02 © Pavel Losevsky – Fotolia; 7.06 © Michael Ireland – Fotolia.

1.02, 2.06, 4.01 © Justin O'Hanlon.

Reflective practice – what does it mean?

Reflective practice has become a relatively familiar term for the early years workforce. All practitioners are now expected to be able to reflect on what they do with children and families. The more experienced and senior practitioners explore the concept in greater depth, through the different avenues of their continued professional development. This chapter addresses the general meaning of reflective practice and Chapter 2 explores more theoretical perspectives.

The main sections in this chapter are:
- Best professional practice
- Becoming a reflective practitioner
- Pedagogy and reflective practice.

Best professional practice

In recent years there has been increasing recognition of the need to develop an early years workforce that is able to think about what they do, as well as develop secure practical skills. The more academic approach around pedagogy has reached practitioners through the increasing numbers involved in Foundation degrees and Early Childhood Studies degrees. The different pathways to Early Years Professional Status all emphasise the need for reflective practice in every form of early childhood provision.

A thoughtful early years profession

Reflective practice is presented as an outlook for everyone, not only early years practitioners with greater experience and seniority. In England, the Common Core document (DfES, 2005a) and Key Elements of Effective Practice, KEEP, (DfES, 2005b) stressed a broad base of skills and the necessity to improve practice through reflection and self-evaluation. The first version of the Early Years Foundation Stage (EYFS) (DCSF, 2008) built in the assumption that every practitioner should be able to reflect on what is done and why, and to articulate key values and priorities. The proposed revised version of the EYFS has cut back significantly on supporting materials but the context remains that of reflective practice being best practice.

In Scotland the approach of placing the child at the centre of practice permeates the guidance about self-evaluation (HMIE, 2007), which incorporates reflective practice and guided change for improvement. The Scottish *Pre-birth to Three* (2010) guidance continues the strong value that practitioners will be reflective, seriously considering the impact of their choices of action on the babies and children who are their daily responsibility.

Reflective practice is sometimes discussed almost exclusively as thoughtfulness about one's own practice, and that of your team if you work with colleagues. The sense of challenge is expressed in terms of your existing beliefs, assumptions and practices. However, active reflection about better practice can create an informed challenge to sources of external advice, or pressures in a particular direction. The difficulties arising from examining your practice are then less about internal decisions and much more about the justification for requirements from local and national guidance or statutory requirements. Authentic reflective practice does not generate 'yes-professionals' who, when told to jump, meekly ask 'How high would you like this time?'

The learning journey of reflective practice

This approach of developing a reflective side to how you work is relevant to every member of the workforce. Realistically, this understanding needs to grow as practitioners become more experienced and the more senior team members are responsible for guiding this process. At the time of writing (late 2011) there is considerable uncertainty about the shape of early education and childcare qualifications, and a review is under way, led by Cathy Nutbrown. This section is therefore written with close attention to different levels of experience, but without specific reference to specific qualifications.

The confidence to be thoughtful

Less experienced practitioners will need to be significantly supported – whatever the changes in the qualification structure. Anyone at the beginning of this learning journey should be able to access helpful guidance within their professional life. Many readers of this book will be in that position of responsibility: helping less experienced colleagues to feel confident to voice their wish to know more and gain understanding of the different ways in which adults can continue to learn in their professional life.

Young practitioners, at the very beginning of their working life, are likely to need significant support. Much will depend on the effectiveness of their own educational experiences over the school years. Older practitioners, yet new to the early years profession, may bring valuable skills of thinking and reflection. They will, however, have to apply those to a new professional area. A deeper level of reflective practice later will depend on firm foundations now, including an outlook that values active learning as an adult, in contrast to expecting a checklist telling you what to do on all occasions.

The earliest stage of professional development explicitly includes the beginnings of some self-knowledge, for instance that practitioners have some awareness of how their own experiences and background are likely to affect their practice. They should also have a basic sense of how they are more comfortable learning as an adult – not that they then remain utterly within their comfort zone. Part of being an effective and considerate practitioner with children is that you recognise how your preferred ways to learn, or to deal with confusion, will not match the preferences of every child you encounter.

Building upon a firm foundation of basic knowledge

With guided experience, practitioners should become able to take the initiative in reflecting on their own practice and not be dependent on others to start the process. It is not expected that practitioners manage without support; it is more that they steadily become able to identify the ways in which they need particular support. Different sources of support continue to be essential throughout professional life. The shift for the slightly more experienced practitioners is that they should not sit around waiting for someone else to make suggestions that could extend and improve their practice. The process of initial training should enable practitioners to become more competent, and confident, about turning the spotlight on their own practice. Overall, practitioners need to be able to evaluate their own current practice: how they currently work, what they do and why and how well they achieve what they set out to do.

Genuine reflective practice is underpinned by an outlook of lifelong learning – far removed from the attitude of 'I've been trained, that's it!' Early years practitioners at all levels need to be committed to developing their practice through the means of continuing professional development (CPD). Part of professionalism, even for the most experienced person, is a willingness to continue to learn: an outlook of lifelong learning. CPD may include attendance at suitable training events.

However, reflective practice would not be well supported by this single strand alone. This strand of professional learning is part of ordinary, everyday practice and includes communication with other adults who share the responsibility to create really positive experiences for children over early childhood. With greater understanding of working with young children comes the essential professional outlook of striving for best practice, not being satisfied with meeting only minimum standards and coasting through days by doing just enough.

What does it mean?

Good practice: a standard of behaviour within the early years professional role that will meet the needs of children and families.

Best practice: a term that encompasses the sense of striving to improve, that good practice is not a fixed concept of something to achieve and then take a rest.

Minimum standards: the very basics of what must be offered and that practice must not fall below this level.

Continuing professional development (CPD): an ongoing process of learning, even for the most experienced professionals, through recognising current strengths, addressing areas for improvement and updating knowledge.

Leading others within reflective practice

More experienced and senior practitioners continue to be highly reflective about their own practice. They are also expected to be able to support others in this process. This ability to guide colleagues also rests on an understanding of current policy and the implications of research for good practice as a whole. Their greater experience should enable these lead practitioners and team leaders to introduce ways for others to review and evaluate their practice.

These senior practitioners also promote their own CPD by higher levels of training, some of which will focus on management skills. This higher-level learning should encompass understanding the difference between the role of manager and that of leader, which can be combined within the same individual (Lindon and Lindon, 2012). A professional workforce, encouraged to reflect on their practice, needs leadership for change as well as management for secure daily practice (more on page 164).

What does it mean?

Manager: the role of monitoring and controlling daily practice through past experience and knowledge of effective implementation of systems.

Leader: a role focusing on the possibilities, a vision for the future and ways to harness commitment from the team to strategic changes in practice.

A leadership role may be taken by someone other than the manager, such as a team member with Early Years Professional Status. However, experienced early years practitioners, for instance in the childminding service, can also operate as supportive leaders within their local childminding network. Thoughtfulness for early years practitioners is part of professional interaction with fellow practitioners, within your own team and in a wider local network. The results of reflection, or reflection as a work in progress, need to be shared in communication with others. You work on resolving problems and unclear practice issues, with the overall aim of continuous improvement of practice, for the well-being of children and their families.

Greater experience and the fruits of earlier reflective practice are likely to enable these more senior practitioners to know only too well that current policy, even statutory documents, can include inconsistencies; that research does not necessarily give clear pointers for practice; and on crucial questions, different

Figure 1.1 Reflective practitioners continue to learn through interaction with children

studies have or appear to have produced different answers. It is appropriate to use the skills of reflective practice to challenge inconsistencies and directions that are likely to disrupt the well-being of young children. Undoubtedly some awkward dilemmas can result, because it is neither responsible nor professionally appropriate to ring-fence reflective skills to your own practice and team. Senior practitioners should, if necessary, take the lead in challenging other professionals whose recommendations or requirements threaten to undermine best practice that places children at the centre of any professional decisions.

Becoming a reflective practitioner

This section outlines some of the main strands of thought for developing as a reflective practitioner. All these points are further explored throughout this book.

What does it mean?

Self-evaluation: the process of considering what you do in your practice, including active reflection that considers the possible gap between hope or intentions and what actually happens.

Self-assessment: the practical judgements that are reached as a consequence of an honest and thorough process of self-evaluation. Useful self-assessment leads to some level of observable action.

Reflective practice: the process of serious thought and constructive critical analysis of current practice, leading to an informed judgement about strengths and considered plans for change that will bring about improvements.

Thinking informs choices of action

Undoubtedly, reflective practice is underpinned by thinking about what you do and how. You consider why you make one choice rather than another, or the reasons for holding close to this priority or principle. Reflective practice is also the process by which individuals or whole teams may become more aware of the unspoken values that underlie what they do day by day. Reflective practice is a more straightforward professional development when you are working within an environment that welcomes an open mind. In contrast, reflective practice can be an uphill grind, a lonely task rather than a shared enterprise, when practitioners are based in a work culture with a dismissive, or even an oppressive, atmosphere, with regard to any challenge to the established order and hierarchy.

Early years practitioners are involved in an active role. Done well, work with children is tiring but not only in a physical way. A day or session spent with children should also engage you in emotional and intellectual hard work. An important aspect of reflective practice within any practical profession is that your reflection – in quieter times – has to inform your actions at very busy times. The essence of time with young children in any kind of early years provision is that good practitioners are able to shift track quickly in response to the children and to share out their adult attention between individuals.

For much of the time, early years practitioners – playworkers and schoolteachers too – do not have the option to hit the pause button on what is happening right now and consider what to do for the best. These are not professions in which you can usually say, 'Stop everything. I need to sit and think for ten minutes – and no interruptions!' You do not leave babies or young children in the 'in-tray' while you go away and check something in a book or online, consult a diagram, phone a colleague or any other right-now option. The aim of reflective practice is partly to ensure that your automatic/default reactions are the best option.

Thinking back is the way to reflect on what has happened and to pinpoint what you, or other practitioners, can learn. Like any kind of reflective practice, this focus needs to acknowledge what went well, or better than last time I/we faced this situation. It is very hard to learn from mistakes, if error is all that is highlighted. You cannot change what you did last time, and maybe it was not a serious misjudgement. Perhaps it was just not the best choice you could have made. Reflection, with or without support, is the way to consider 'How do I change?' 'How might I make a better choice next time?' and also 'What tends to get in my way (mentally and emotionally) when I am in the thick of it?'

Make the connection with . . . **a role model for children**

Early years practitioners are expected to support young children over early childhood and actively encourage them to develop their communication and thinking skills. It is impossible for practitioners to support children if those skills are poorly developed within the adults' daily repertoire.

You need to be, as the Steiner Waldorf approach describes, 'worthy of imitation' (Nicol, 2007; Drummond and Jenkinson, 2009). One of the best ways for young children to learn is to see and hear you think out loud, explore how we might solve the problem about. . . and wonder 'What will happen if..?' all for reasons that make sense to children, not as an artificially planned event.

Early years practitioners are expected to support young children to develop positive dispositions towards learning (Lindon, 2012a). How is this possible unless the adults view themselves as lifelong learners?

Emotional self-awareness

Reflective practice is not exclusively intellectual. Some hard work of thinking can enable reflective practitioners to be more self-aware about their own feelings. Best practice for guiding children's behaviour includes the willingness to reflect on our own adult behaviour and contribution to what happens (Lindon, 2012a).

- A thoughtful practitioner will recognise, for instance, that he did not handle very well the three-year-old emotional meltdown in the library today. He was so aware of what felt like disapproving stares from two other adults in the group that had gathered for the storyteller.
- When practitioners can be honest with themselves about their feelings, then there is scope for productive thought about what to do next time. However, it can be difficult to disentangle your own adult feelings from the emotions expressed by a child through their behaviour (Weigand, 2007).
- An increased level of self-honesty also supports greater insight into what other adults might be feeling in a given situation. Perhaps an experienced and confident practitioner realises that she feels intimidated by the forthright style of this trainer on equality practice. Maybe less experienced practitioners on the programme will remain silent, unless given no option. What might be done about this less than ideal situation for professional development?

There can emotional consequences of challenging your own practice, or being challenged. It can be uncomfortable, even emotionally painful, to manage the process of change, especially if cherished assumptions are being taken apart and questioned. This process is supported by constructive comments from colleagues, rather than disruptive fault finding. Early years practitioners are also well supported when guided towards being kind to themselves: nobody benefits from relentless self-criticism.

Take another **perspective**

There is nothing the matter with realising that you have been wrong. The problems arise – sometimes very serious ones – when professionals are resistant to accepting that they have made a mistake, or travelled some way down a less wise route of practice. The risks are multiplied when mistaken beliefs are promoted in a very public way, as Ben Goldacre (2009) documents in his exposure of unsupported claims and examples of 'bad science'.

Stewart Brand (2009), writing about ecology, is refreshingly honest about how his ideas have changed over the decades. He proposed two questions that should always be asked of public figures in any interview. I think these are good questions for all of us:

1. What have you been wrong about?
2. And how did that change your views?

Reflection on values and principles
Reflective practice involves thinking and talking about what sits at the core of your practice. Over time, reflective practitioners become clearer about their values: those beliefs about what is worthwhile, which are often unquestioned. Reflection and open discussion are also the way to revisit principles of best practice, including what is, and is not, a principle.

Any principle worth the time of day should have implications for action. Otherwise the words speak of aspirations and hopes, all of which may be welcome, but do not point towards choices over action. The reverse is also true, that by observing actual practice – in any profession – it is possible to make an informed judgement about the likely principles that inform this practitioner, even if the principles are well below the surface of conscious reflection.

The What Matters to Children approach (WMtC) (Rich et al., 2005, 2008) is led by the key principle that first-hand experience is a necessary and significant element of childhood. This stance is in contrast to the working principle, which has undermined too much early years and school practice, that the adult task is to provide activities for children to do. The principle of first-hand experience(s) is the starting point from which the WMtC materials go into detail about what such experiences look like on a daily basis and the implications for adults' behaviour.

Your guiding principles may not change when you hear about new ideas or research evidence. However, you may adjust the way you put principles into practice in the light of what you have learned.

- Reflective practice should enable thoughtful practitioners to address important questions like 'I believe that my practice is child centred. But what makes me so sure?'
- Individuals or a whole team may struggle to provide specific examples to support the conviction that 'We follow children's personal interests.' The lack of examples does not necessarily undermine the statement of belief. But it does indicate that the team is less than sure about what 'following children's interests' looks like day by day.
- A responsive team may be provoked to serious thought by a leader who is honest enough to admit, 'I've been too focused on "What will make the inspectorate happy?" We need to get back to "What will make the children happy?" Then I'll work hard with all of you on how we'll show the inspector the great work we do here.'

What does it mean?

Value: what you believe to be worthy, of greater importance if you have to make a choice.

Principle: a statement of committed belief, explaining what underlies a pattern of action; the origin or source of decisions and choices.

Since the 1990s early years provision and schools have experienced a constant stream of guidance documents, advisory programmes and initiatives. Even experienced and more senior practitioners can become confused over what is required and what is recommended. When there are further changes, an anxious outlook inclines managers and teams to believe that a wholesale overhaul of existing practice must be required.

At the time of writing (winter 2011) the early years workforce in England is anticipating a revised Early Years Foundation Stage. Managers and other senior practitioners need to be very clear about what does have to change and what does not. A revised framework does not necessarily mean that existing best practice has to change much at all. Sometimes the best response to official change is to revisit what is working really well for the children, or partnership with families, at the moment. Be sure that something needs changing before you take steps.

The Kate Greenaway Children's Centre (2009) took that approach to the changes brought about by the introduction of *Statutory Framework for the Early Years Foundation Stage* (2008). The team, led by Julian Grenier (2010), took the opportunity to identify the strengths of their existing practice (more on page 125).

A significant overhaul of primary education in North Somerset in 2006 went back to the basic recognition that the National Curriculum, for England, was the only statutory document; everything else was guidance. They went back to what was actually required and rediscovered the flexibility that existed. Andrea Sully led the Curriculum Design Learning Network as they developed a creative primary curriculum through a project called *Making learning irresistible*.

The local initiative placed direct, first-hand experiences at the centre and made time a priority, so that children would be able to work in depth. There was a strong focus on an appropriate learning environment and a whole-school approach to what was called 'disciplined innovation'. You can get a flavour of what was done on **www.n-somerset.gov.uk/Education/Learning/thelearningteam/ makinglearningirresistable.htm**. (Note: 'irresistable' is the spelling used in the website address.)

Possible barriers to becoming a reflective practitioner

Early years practitioners with a genuine commitment to young children are willing to consider what is getting in the way of better practice. More experienced and senior practitioners are responsible also for identifying what is blocking less experienced or less committed colleagues. Why do they take the stance that reflection is unwelcome hard work? You will probably admit (if only to yourself) that some of these barriers apply to you, or used to be a block until you tackled them. Also, within a team or local network, some of these sources of resistance will be erected by colleagues. Their unease can make professional life challenging for practitioners who are enthusiastic about the rewards of reflective practice.

It's a practical job – not deep thought

Some practitioners feel that the main point of being in a practical line of work is that you just 'get on with it'. In some cases, this outlook is linked with a reluctance to extend the boundaries to what they believe working with children should entail. The potential problem with this outlook is that practitioners can become focused on what works well for them, perhaps what is efficient in terms of routines. Efficiency – or an easy life – for the adults becomes more important than how babies or children experience these routines. It can be a dangerously short step to the view that the job would be fine were it not for all these annoying children and problem parents.

Practitioners who are open to professional development can still feel some resistance in themselves, or at the very least want to get the balance right between reflection and practical action. The learning journey is tougher if their introduction to reflective practice is overly theoretical and heavy on unexplained, specialist terms.

Other people tell me what to do

Practitioners may take the view that it is up to other people – senior practitioners, trainers, advisors or the inspectorate – to tell them what to do or not to do. There is no point in reflection because 'they' set out the rules. However, practitioners who delegate the thinking responsibility in this way are almost certain to encounter situations in which they hear contradictory advice.

Practitioners need to develop the habit of asking awkward questions in a professional way to deal with unwise advice. One example could be: 'You suggest I deal with unwanted behaviour from young children by cutting back their special time for play at the end of the day. But surely I should deal with behaviour at the time. Also, how can I have a special time of play when their entire day is about learning through play?' Sometimes a clear recommendation goes against a key element of best practice; for instance: 'If I follow your advice to minimise physical contact with young children, surely that will undermine their emotional well-being. They will believe we don't care about them.' Failure to challenge such contradictions leads to practitioners' loss of confidence and feelings of hopeless resentment because 'I'll be wrong whatever I do.'

Undoubtedly, early years practitioners do not have total choice about the details of early years provision. The four nations of the UK each have an early years framework that sets minimum standards and some non-negotiable ground rules about how young children are treated. However, each framework leaves considerable flexibility about how details are put into daily and weekly practice. Some practitioners believe they have no choice, yet the limits have been set by their manager or a firm local directive – and not by the relevant national statutory framework. Active reflective practice is also difficult if a manager insists on an authoritarian interpretation of being in charge. It is important not to underestimate the power of the message 'You have to . . .' for practitioners who are unsure about the answer to 'Who says you have to . . .?' or 'You mustn't . . .'

Everything is fine; why rock the boat?

Practitioners may question the advantage in changing anything, when it all seems to be running fine at the moment. Perhaps they say, 'The children seem happy enough' or 'The parents aren't complaining.'

However, young children usually have no idea that their daily experiences could be different. They have learned that it is just easier if they sit still in this boring registration group time – then it is over quickly. They cannot say to the adults,

'Have you never heard of different ways to offer us self-registration? That would be a much nicer way to start our morning.' Also, when practitioners are very set in their ways, they are not usually receptive to an articulate four-year-old who can reminisce about 'What we did in my old nursery'.

Parents may also lack the experience of alternative approaches within early years provision. They may think that every nursery covers topics about famous artists with two-year-olds. Or else they may be mostly happy with what the nursery offers their child, given other local options. They will not risk annoying staff by challenging whether very young children would not be better occupied finding worms in the garden than painting identical cut-out sunflowers.

I've been doing this for years!

Experience matters but it should bring some level of professional wisdom and not simply encourage stagnation. All those years in the job should have honed a practitioner's ability to articulate possible choices and explain priorities. A more experienced practitioner should be able to share the 'why' within the 'what' of daily practice. Good practice has to get beyond 'I just know' or 'We've always done it this way.' If nothing else, this version of 'just do it' is very likely to be accompanied by the conviction that what practitioners believe to be happening – in terms of children's pattern of behaviour or what they are learning – is the unadorned truth.

This source of resistance to reflective practice sometimes connects with an outlook that you are trained and that covers whatever you need to know. Maybe you get sent on a few courses, but otherwise you are an adult; education is for children and adolescents. This limited view blocks the positive experience of being an adult learner and any sense of lifelong learning. Undoubtedly, there has been a significant change in recent years. The prevailing view now is that early years practitioners make a significant difference to the experience of young children. For this difference to be a positive one, an initial training, however thorough, cannot equip practitioners forever. It is a basis on which you should build, among the many potential strands of continuing professional development.

Anxiety about being criticised

Some practitioners are especially vulnerable to believing that reflective practice is basically about fault finding. A great deal depends on their first experience of a process like peer observation (page 187), or whether senior practitioners have guided the team towards constructive feedback (page 143). Reflective practice should definitely highlight strengths as well as scope for improvement. Anxious practitioners, even relatively senior ones, can be prone to defensive reactions or the retaliation of 'Are you saying I've been wrong up to now?' Reflective practitioners have a more uphill journey if their manager feels intimidated by questions that threaten to disturb the current equilibrium.

Reflective practice does not always lead to change. In some cases, individuals and teams rediscover gems of best practice, such as the power of outdoor learning.

Within my own consultancy business, I have been pleased to spend increasing amounts of time on good practice with under-threes. The reaction of some experienced practitioners has been one of great relief to hear about vigorous support for generous time and respect for care within a nurturing environment.

Pause for reflection

Experienced practitioners, in any profession, may resist significant change because of the perceived, negative implications for what they have done up to now. The change might be in terms of a practical approach or way of thinking. But it might also be the need to reverse up a practice pathway that has been followed for some time. It might be accepting that significant information, or advice on that basis, was wrong or misunderstood.

The rationale goes something like this:

- If I am contemplating serious change in my practice now, then could I have changed in the past; should I have identified and made this particular change?
- If this alternative is obviously better, then what does it say about my professional practice and insights that I did not spot it myself, or much earlier?
- What avoidable troubles have I caused by not realising this sooner, or by promoting an approach or advice that I should have questioned or checked out personally?

How does this relate to your own experiences?

A challenge is necessary if anxiety about the past is not going to block future improvement. The alternative rationale goes like this:

- It is not always true that you could have easily changed in the past. Professionals are trained within the received wisdom of the time.
- Experience sometimes brings the insight and ability to challenge accepted approaches. But this is less likely the more an approach seems to 'work' and fellow professionals agree.
- The professional approach is to remain open, to avoid the temptation to resist change solely because it is uncomfortable.
- Professionals should not be judged on the basis that they have never been wrong; an error-free career is highly unlikely.
- We should judge ourselves, and be judged, by how we handle the recognition that we were mistaken or misled over minor or major issues.

Underdeveloped thinking skills

Wariness about the point of a reflective approach can be fuelled when practitioners have limited experience of being encouraged to voice opinions and the rationale for their stance. For some practitioners, the process of reflection, of active and deliberate thinking, is unfamiliar. A proportion of the early years workforce has not been well served by many years spent in statutory education. Their personal learning journey to a professional outlook can require direct support as young adults, and not so young, on ways to disagree without blunt confrontation or on how to become comfortable to follow a train of thought out loud. It may also be a daunting prospect to get those thoughts down in written form.

This personal journey is greatly helped by experiences with senior practitioners, trainers and consultants who do not feel threatened by being asked 'Why?' Greater experience should bring the ability to share reasons, explanations and a coherent trail of thought – even if this question could have been phrased in a less argumentative way.

Take another **perspective**

Practitioners who are resistant to reflective practice sometimes argue that it is a fad: yet another fancy idea that will be dropped in time. These 'Leave me out of it' potential escapees will not be able to hide until 'normal' life is resumed. Reflective practice is now firmly viewed as part of professional practice in general. An increased awareness of the importance of early childhood will only raise the status and expectations for the workforce.

However, there has to be some sympathy for an outlook of weariness over non-stop early years initiatives, programmes and guidance documents. Some of these developments are very positive, but there are so many. Action for Children (2007) tracked the strategies, policies and initiatives relevant to children and young people launched over the last 21 years across the UK. The period was chosen as representing the age span of what are now regarded as the years before adulthood. England had the highest number of initiatives across the four nations of the UK and the English initiatives tended to have a shorter life before the next document.

Pedagogy and reflective practice

The word 'pedagogy' is now relatively familiar to experienced early years practitioners, especially those involved in further education and training. However, the actual meaning of 'pedagogy' is sometimes less than clear. Many books and articles discuss pedagogy without actually defining the word and associated phrases. We cannot proceed on a vague 'Everybody knows what it means' basis, so I have pulled together here the main features. It is useful to explore what is meant and the value of the concept for reflection about the whole picture of what you do.

The meaning of pedagogy

The word 'pedagogue' has reached the English language via French, Latin and Greek. The term derives from a term used in ancient Greece to refer to the slave who would accompany a boy to school. This attendant, although not of high social status, also had the responsibility to ensure that the child's behaviour on the street and at school was acceptable to the family. The word 'pedagogy' then developed to refer to instruction or a system of training, usually within the context of school. In considerably more recent times, the word has been used with reference to educational practice, meaning an overall approach to supporting children's learning.

What does it mean?

Pedagogy: the details of your approach to the craft of teaching, not exclusively by teachers or in schools. The core values, principles and chosen strategies create the **pedagogical base** to your practice.

Pedagogical thinking: an exploration to enable deeper understanding of what informs your practice and the reasons why you work in particular ways.

Curriculum: a planned programme related to learning, including some or all of the following: underlying principles, recommended or required content, approaches and resources.

In the broadest sense, pedagogy refers to what could be called the craft of helping children to learn and the way in which adults approach the teaching role.

- The word does not exclusively apply to practitioners who have qualified as teachers. Pedagogy applies to anyone who is closely involved with children and their experience of learning throughout childhood and adolescence.
- Once you explore the details of the underlying pedagogical framework, the prevailing values and principles become clearer, along with why, what and how adults are making choices between possible actions.
- The concept of pedagogy offers a well-rounded approach, with equal weight given to understanding how children learn and to understanding how to support that process with the best interests of children to the fore.
- Pedagogy is not the same concept as a 'curriculum'. This term is usually meant to cover a programme related to learning, most often applied to primary and secondary schooling. However, a specific pedagogical approach may well include the detailed vision of an appropriate curriculum for a given age group.

A few discussions of pedagogy claim that it means only a very teacher-directed approach, rather than learner-directed. In these discussions, an additional word, 'andragogy', is brought in to represent the approach that is more respectful of nurturing independent learners. The term originated with Malcolm Knowles, who focused on adult learners' facility and need to determine their own learning programme (Smith, 2009).

Knowles developed his ideas over the 1960s and 1970s and aimed to challenge a view of learning that placed adult, or child, learners as passive recipients of knowledge, an approach he called 'pedagogy'. He stressed the importance of being an active learner, co-learning with others, and of reflection on the appropriate role of the more experienced or knowledgeable partner. He stressed also that individuals' own experiences are a valuable resource for learning and can be helpful in solving problems in their current situation. Over the same period, other theorists and researchers were developing models of experiential learning applied also to adults (page 65).

Knowles's ideas are valuable, and a useful reminder about reflection on how adults learn. However, it is important to note that he developed the concepts over four decades ago. Current usage of the term 'pedagogy' is not the passive-transmission-of-knowledge model described and criticised by Knowles. So it is misleading when that stark contrast is repeated in current discussion of his ideas. The usual meaning now for 'pedagogy' enables a discussion of different approaches, as well as the critical thinking that enables analysis of what works best for children and with which core values in mind.

Understanding what you do and why

Pedagogy can be seen as an interactive process involving adults, child learners and all aspects of the learning environment. In most current uses of the word, pedagogy is used to highlight positive, thoughtful approaches to children. However, the word is non-specific and some adults' pedagogical approach could be highly focused on their own plans, with a role for adults of directing the experiences and outcomes.

A discussion paper from Learning and Teaching Scotland (2005b) uses the phrase 'pedagogical thinking' in ways that are really interchangeable with 'critical thinking' (page 44) as applied to reflective practice with children. The point is made that early years practitioners have a responsibility to articulate what they do: to explain clearly to parents and other interested and involved adults. This communicative aspect of the role applies to every stage of education and 'understanding our pedagogical base will help us to be able to do this. Pedagogy needs explicitly to be seen to encompass a spirit of enquiry and professional dialogue about why we do what we do' (2005: 3–4).

Pedagogy does not simply mean 'teaching' and as such it can be a useful term in the continuing struggle to find inclusive ways of talking about early years practitioners, acknowledging the range of professional backgrounds. A continuing problem within early years practice has been that many guidance documents use a general term such as 'practitioner' to refer to all adults involved in supporting children's learning. However, the words 'teach' and 'teaching' are frequently used to describe those adults' behaviour in interaction with the children. These words carry a weight of 'school' meaning for some readers, which has created difficulties in practice.

As soon as the word 'education' is used, even with 'early' added to the front, some early years practitioners, and parents as well, seem to connect most strongly with their childhood memories of primary school and primary-school teachers. These memories are not from early childhood and risk encouraging unrealistic expectations of children's skill level and inappropriate images of how adults should behave. Uneasy practitioners may conclude that to support early learning they must behave in ways close to their selective memories of what a 'teacher' does. This classroom model is then likely to include greater adult direction of children's activity and an excessive focus on whole-group events, rather than individual exploration and interests. Yet, of course, best practice in nursery school or nursery class has never been identical to primary-school practice. Good nursery-trained teachers do not behave at all like teachers of primary-school-age children.

Janet Moyles et al. (2002) pointed out that early years practitioners, from a range of professional backgrounds, are not necessarily adept at talking about the subtleties of their practice. Practitioners appeared more at ease with describing their practical actions in provision, such as laying out materials for children, than explaining their own impact on children's learning. This report of the Study of Pedagogical Effectiveness in Early Learning (SPEEL) project highlighted that an effective approach within early years could be more complex than in the stages of statutory education. One reason was that an effective adult contribution was sometimes the choice not to intervene, apparently to do nothing. However, the practitioner was very active in watching and listening, recognising how much young children learn by making their own decisions and safe errors.

How inclusive is pedagogy?

Some practitioners in the SPEEL project were also wary about the word 'teaching' precisely because they did not want to embrace a more directive role, which they felt this word would inevitably bring. The SPEEL working definition was that 'Pedagogy is both the behaviour of teaching and being able to talk about and reflect on teaching. Pedagogy encompasses both what practitioners actually DO and THINK and the principles, theories, perceptions and challenges that inform and shape it . . .' (capitals in original; Moyles et al., 2002: 5). The definition goes on to connect practitioner behaviour with values and a shared frame of reference with children and their family.

Figure 1.2 Any definition of pedagogy must include the very youngest children

The early years workforce, and the school staff group too, is not exclusively teacher-trained. Much discussion has attempted to find a word to cover all adults who support learners, especially young children. The word 'educator' or 'early educator' is favoured by some people. There has been some effort to use 'pedagogue', which is more common in some other European countries. I continue to use the word 'practitioner', although it is not ideal, because the word 'educator' still has echoes of school and is less effective in my view to ensure full inclusion of very young children, especially the under-two to threes.

On balance, the written material about pedagogy, as well as quality in early educational settings, is more focused on the traditional nursery education range of three–five years, rather than the full early childhood span. Discussion about educational aims, contents and adults as educators often gives scant acknowledgement for nurture in terms of physical care. In contrast, the Scottish *Pre-Birth to Three* guidance (Learning and Teaching Scotland, 2010) offers a thoughtful analysis of key principles, values and best practice with this very young age group. This guidance is all about making pedagogy explicit without, so far as I could find, using the actual word.

One approach has been to bring the concept of 'social pedagogy' from mainland Europe to the UK (Lepper, 2009 and Smith, 2009). A social pedagogue working with a child or young person will consider everything that matters to this child and forms a close relationship with individuals. In 2009 the Thomas Coram Research Unit in London was commissioned by the government to help pilot this way of working with application to looked-after children and young people. These children are the temporary or longer-term responsibility of their local authority, because their birth or extended family is not able to take care of them. This pilot study focuses only on children in residential care, but in many European countries social pedagogues work across the different types of services for children.

Take another **perspective**

A fully inclusive pedagogy is undermined when much discussion around 'early education' still pays insufficient attention to care and caring (Lindon, 2006). There is further progress to be made in order to reach a genuine merging of what historically has been known as 'education' as distinct from 'care'.

Many early years-trained teachers consider the whole child and regard personal care, such as changing a child, as part of their responsibility. However, the National Union of Teachers (NUT, 2009) issued a statement about a continence policy for schools (which explicitly included the nursery) that, 'the most important issue to cover is that it is not part of the teacher's professional duties to clean up children' (2009: 1). The message is reinforced with bold type in the original and presented within the context of health and safety.

Care of young children needs to be undertaken with close attention to hygiene for everyone. However, toileting accidents in nursery-age children and physical care of younger children in centres are part of the regular flow of the day, not regrettable, out-of-the-ordinary incidents. I accept the complicating factor in primary school of a limited number of adults. However, such a stand goes against the statutory key person role that is part of the Early Years Foundation Stage for every kind of provision for under-fives in England, including nursery and reception classes based in a primary school.

What does it mean?

Social pedagogy: an approach that specifically encompasses a child's whole life, and avoids the possible narrow focus only on education.

Resources

- Brand, S. (2009) *Whole Earth Discipline: An Ecopragmatist Manifesto*. London: Atlantic.
- Department for Children, Schools and Families (2008) *The Early Years Foundation Stage – Setting the Standards for Learning, Development and Care for Children from Birth to Five*. London: DCSF.
- Department for Education and Skills (2005b) *KEEP: Key Elements of Effective Practice*. London: DfES, **www.leics.gov.uk/index/education/childcare/early_years_service/foundationstage/evaluatingandqualityassurance/ai_keep.htm**, **https://www.education.gov.uk/publications/standard/publicationdetail/page1/DCSF-00261-2008**
- Drummond, M.J. and Jenkinson, S. (2009) *Meeting the Child: Approaches to Observation and Assessment in Steiner Kindergartens*. Plymouth: University of Plymouth, **www.steinerwaldorf.org/bookshop_earlyyearsparenting.html**
- Goldacre, B. (2009) *Bad Science*. London: HarperCollins, **www.badscience.net**
- Grenier, J. (2010) 'Planning around core experiences'. *Nursery World*, 4 February.
- HM Inspectorate of Education (2007) *The Child at the Centre: Self-evaluation in the Early Years*. Livingston: HMIE, **www.hmie.gov.uk/documents/publication/catcseey.pdf**
- Kate Greenaway Nursery School and Children's Centre (2009) *Core Experiences for the Early Years Foundation Stage*, distributed by Early Education; also information on **www.coreexperiences.wikia.com**
- Learning and Teaching Scotland (2005b) *Let's Talk About Pedagogy: Towards a Shared Understanding for Early Years Education in Scotland*. Glasgow: Learning and Teaching Scotland. **www.ltscotland.org.uk/publications/l/publication_tcm4617466.asp?strReferringChannel=search&strReferringPageID=tcm:4-615801-64**

- Learning and Teaching Scotland (2010) *Pre-birth to Three: Positive Outcomes for Scotland's Children and Families.* **www.ltscotland.org.uk/earlyyears**
- Lepper, J. (2009) 'Social Pedagogy Demystified'. *Children and Young People Now*, 2–8 April.
- Lindon, J. (2006) *Care and Caring Matter: Young Children Learning Through Care.* London: Early Education.
- Lindon, J. (2012a, third edition) *Understanding Child Development: 0–8 Years.* London: Hodder Education.
- Lindon, J. (2012c) *Understanding Children's Behaviour: 0–11 Years.* London: Hodder Education.
- Lindon, J. and Lindon, L. (2012) *Leadership and Early Years Professionalism.* London: Hodder Education.
- Moyles, J., Adams, S. and Musgrove, A. (2002) *Study of Pedagogical Effectiveness in Early Learning Brief No. 363.* **www.education.gov.uk/publications/standard/publicationDetail/Page1/RR363**
- National Union of Teachers (2009) *Continence and Toilet Issues in Schools: Advice to NUT Members, School Representatives and Health and Safety Representatives.* **www.teachers.org.uk/node/12506**
- Nicol, J. (2007) *Bringing the Steiner Waldorf Approach to Your Early Years Practice.* Abingdon: Routledge.
- Rich, D., Casanova, D., Dixon, A., Drummond, M.J., Durrant, A. and Myer, C. (2005) *First Hand Experience: What Matters to Children.* Clopton: Rich Learning Opportunities. **www.richlearningopportunities.co.uk**
- Rich, D., Drummond, M.J. and Myer, C. (2008) *Learning: What Matters to Children.* Clopton: Rich Learning Opportunities.
- Smith, M. (2009) 'Social pedagogy', *The Encyclopaedia of Informal Education.* **http://www.infed.org/biblio/b-socped.htm**
- Weigand, R. (2007) *Reflective Supervision in Child Care: The Discoveries of an Accidental Tourist.* Access this and other articles at **http://main.zerotothree.org/site/DocServer/ZTT28-2_nov_07.pdf?docID=7244**

Theoretical perspectives on reflective practice

Reflective practice in action for early years, and other practical professions, has been shaped by key theoretical perspectives, some of which have emerged from other disciplines of study. This chapter describes and explains significant ideas that have influenced current approaches to being a reflective professional in work with children and families.

The main sections of this chapter are:
- Reflection as part of professionalism
- Professional practice as a learning journey
- Critical thinking.

Reflection as part of professionalism

If you put 'reflective practice' into a search engine such as Google, the practical papers and reports that are brought up are linked strongly with the teaching profession, health including nursing and, to a lesser extent, social work. These are all lines of work with a significant practical side, driven by face-to-face contact with people, adults or children, and with observable consequences, positive as well as negative, for those people on the receiving end. The application of reflective practice has reached the early years workforce through a high profile for these ideas for teaching in schools and strong academic interest as the discipline of early childhood studies expanded.

A focus on behaviour within professional practice

The key names associated with influential perspectives for reflective practice were interested in aspects of professional behaviour, but often not the three professions given above. Some of the main concepts and models were developed as part of the study of organisations, usually commercial and with a view of how best to intervene to order to improve organisational effectiveness. Some of the names that you will read in the following section were those of trailblazers in organisational theory. It is a useful reminder of how much any area of professional practice, in this case for early childhood provision, can learn from other disciplines and professions. We will perhaps have reached a benchmark of respect for children and early years practice when theoretical insights from early childhood professionalism travel regularly in the opposite direction and are embraced by other professions.

Chris Argyris (1970), for instance, made a radical shift to look in detail at the behaviour of people in the workplace, and to use a clear focus on what they did as the way to identify levers for organisational change. He remained interested in the structures of an organisation but through the lens of the impact on what employees actually did. Suppose an organisation wanted a staff team that was willing to take risks to follow through new ideas. Then it was deeply unwise for a senior management team to hold tight to administrative systems that put hurdles in the way of anything except the safe option. Argyris was clear, writing as a consultant to organisations, that it was not his role to tell senior management to change the administrative system. It was his job to show the consequences of the system and how it undermined what this organisation purported to value and really want.

Theories, personal beliefs and behaviour

Donald Schön's ideas appear regularly in discussion of reflective practice for the early years workforce. However, Schön co-wrote influential books with Argyris, and their 1974 book about theory within professional practice was an important forerunner to the much-quoted Schön (1983).

Argyris and Schön (1974) were interested in the contradictions that could be observed within professional practice in many different lines of work. Part of the contradiction, which could also be viewed as an inconsistency, was that there could be a noticeable gap between what was assumed to happen within daily practice and what actually did happen. Perhaps some readers are already thinking that the statement about contradictions seems very obvious. Of course, everyone tidies around the odd mismatch between good intentions and actual events today. However, the theoretical perspective was, and is, worth bringing to the forefront of thinking honestly about what we do.

Argyris and Schön took the stance that few people were genuinely aware of this kind of thinking within their professional life. The underlying point was also that an increased awareness would improve the work of individuals and the organisations of which they were a part. Their key ideas were that:

- People hold 'maps' in their head and these personal formats guide them in terms of planning ahead, implementing and reviewing their actions within professional life.
- However, the internal mental maps that people *actually use* to make practical decisions and take action are not necessarily the same maps, or theories, that they *claim to use* in order to guide their actions.
- Few people are aware of this gap between assertion and reality.
- Additionally, many people are unaware of, or perhaps unable to articulate, the maps that actually do guide them.

Espoused theory and theory-in-use

The contradictions between 'maps' are not entirely about the difference between what people say and what people do, although the situation might sometimes be accurately described in that way. Argyris and Schön suggest that people may comfortably hold a theory consistent with what they say and a different theory that is consistent with what they do. They may not be aware of this pattern of thinking but their actions are deliberate, not accidental or random. These ideas apply to all deliberate human behaviour, although the discussion here, and in much of the literature, is about people in their working life.

- Argyris and Schön use the term 'espoused theory' for the outlook and values on which people believe they base their behaviour. You will hear professionals' espoused theory when they are invited to talk in general about what they do and what is most important in their line of work.
- Argyris and Schön use 'theory-in-use' to cover the outlook and values that are strongly implied by the way that professionals behave in practice. You will gain an insight into someone's theory-in-use by observing them within their daily work routine or making a recording. In consultancy work, careful observation is frequently a crucial first step before making any informed, and therefore useful, comments and suggestions.
- Argyris et al. (1985) also suggested that people operate with what they called 'nested theories'. The idea is that, once you start to unpack someone's theories and how they operate in action, it becomes clear that some ideas are linked, tucked inside one another. I think a handy image (not used by Argyris) would be that of nesting dolls. You have to take the set apart fully to discover just how much is contained within the outer doll.

What does it mean?

Espoused theory: the outlook and values on which people believe they base their behaviour.

Theory-in-use: the outlook and values that are strongly implied by the way that people behave in practice.

Perhaps there will always be some gap between espoused theory and theory-in-use for any individual or organisation. Human beings are not always consistent. However, a wide gap, combined with a lack of awareness of that gap, could create difficulties in working life. A professional might be less than honest in communication with colleagues or users of the service. When those other people notice the gap, they may express disappointment, frustration or annoyance at being misled.

People in organisations

It is worth recalling that Chris Argyris and Donald Schön developed these theoretical concepts in the 1970s, when there was far less emphasis on continuing professional development. Their approach was a significant lever for change in accepted views about learning within professional life. However, they also had a major impact on management development training and managing change in business organisations.

Figure 2.1 Do we really support lively physical activity for children?

Scenario

FineStart Nursery

Simone, an early years consultant, is offering regular support to FineStart, a large day nursery. The manager, Katy, was taken aback by a lukewarm inspection report and is keen to make progress with identified areas for improvement. Simone has agreed to attend the staff meetings. She has realised part of the problem is that Katy and her staff have not reflected on the gap between what they say they value and how they actually behave.

Katy has been clear in conversation with Simone that 'If we have a disagreement here, then we work it out together in a staff meeting.' Katy's espoused theory is that of joint problem solving in an equal partnership with other staff. But Simone has observed a pattern – not just one staff meeting – that, when Katy's own views are questioned, she appears to listen. However, after a short silence, she simply restates her position or asserts her preference. When individual staff disagree, Katy's strategy is to allow a brief exchange, which she calls 'clearing of the air'. Then she proposes the solution for how any conflict will be resolved.

So Katy's theory-in-use is to allow others to speak, but she retains control and actually imposes her perspective or solution. In talking with some of the staff, Simone realises that they too have observed this pattern and are now irritated by Katy's assertion that 'The FineStart way is we talk things through properly.' Theo, the most outspoken practitioner, seems to speak for the others when he says, 'Katy means well. But the FineStart way is actually that she talks and we listen.'

Pause and reflect

Simone discusses her observations with Katy, who justifies her theory-in-use on the grounds that 'Well, if nobody can agree on what to do, I have to decide' and 'I have more experience than my staff, so I need to guide them.' Simone starts the process of explaining how Katy could support genuine problem solving when there is a disagreement and exploring in specific instances how her good ideas could be even better with suggestions from her staff.

Comments

1. Everyone has some gap between an espoused theory and their theory-in-use.
2. In a similar way, there is sometimes a gap between what practitioners are sure they do and the actual patterns of behaviour seen by an impartial observer.
3. What gaps have caught your attention in the practice of other people? In your own practice?

Pause for reflection

You may like to reflect on how 'saying' and 'doing' can feel internally consistent: to yourself if you are honest and the way in which you have realised a colleague, or team leader, makes choices in practice. Human beings sometimes use their thinking power to build bridges between logically inconsistent statements. If the gap is challenged, there is some kind of 'Ah but. . .' explanation or justification.

I have a very strong focus within my training on giving time and attention to the personal care needs of babies and very young children. I sometimes encounter individuals or teams whose *espoused theory* is that 'we want every child to feel valued as an individual'. However, discussion around personal physical care highlights that the established pattern is to give limited time to care.

Further discussion to bring out practitioners' *theory-in-use* leads to their using phrases such as 'Well, in an ideal world, we would spend time chatting and singing to a baby.' A well-intentioned team, whose theory-in-use revolves around 'There is just never enough time in the day,' is open to supportive discussion to explore how time is used at the moment. They recognise that their current choices are not the only options. Perhaps the team needs to be reminded of the extent to which changing and feeding times are crucial, personal events for babies and toddlers.

On the other hand, it is more difficult work for a trainer or consultant if the theory-in-use is: 'Nappy changing and feeding are boring and we have the right to organise the routine efficiently, so it's over quickly.' In this case, the well-being of young children has definitely slipped down the list of priorities, in favour of how practitioners feel.

Chris Argyris was an innovative thinker about organisational change and his ideas informed both internal and external change agents: individuals with the explicit role to bring about change for improvement. Argyris built a theory of intervention that focused on the human processes that are crucial for improving how organisations worked. This approach was significantly different from previous models based on 'fit': that is, fitting the man to the job and the job to the man.

(The model did use the word 'man'.) It was previously believed that changing structures or systems would be sufficient for lasting change in an organisation.

Argyris led the movement to refocus on people. Imposed system change does not work if the human element is discounted. People may agree to a change, or feel they are given no choice, and then find creative ways to avoid the new procedures in their corner of an organisation. Exclusively rational system change may be some way along the agreed timescale before somebody realises that individuals are far from committed to the change. They may even be engaged in sabotaging the process, by their actions or deliberate inaction.

Single- and double-loop learning

Human beings are not always logical, nor apparently consistent. They sometimes juggle several lines of competing logic. Professional practice will not develop so long as people remain largely unaware of their espoused theory, their theory-in-use and the gap between the two stances. Developments by Argyris and Schön in their initial theoretical perspective were aimed at helping professionals to understand the process in general and to put the spotlight on their own theories. The purpose of that kind of exploration is then that professionals can make more active and better-informed choices.

Argyris and Schön (1974) developed a theoretical model to support discussion of this process and to help make the less visible human reasoning element clear enough to support action. They identified three main parts to their model, explaining theories-in-use and how they develop: governing variables, action strategies and consequences. I describe their ideas now, in my own words, with examples that are relevant to early years practice. The basic ideas, the first level of discussion, are shown in Figure 2.2.

Figure 2.2 Working with your theory-in-use: basic process (developed from Argyris and Schön, 1974)

Governing variables

These are the issues that matter to people and which they are trying to keep within acceptable limits or boundaries. The concept of a governing variable is a very broad one and will vary depending on the nature of the work. Any profession will have a host of governing variables. Some will be important principles or key values. They might be agreed rules or commitments to a plan. They may be assumptions and beliefs about this kind of work. Some variables will be personal to this individual and people may be more or less aware of these personal dimensions. Governing variables will usually operate along a continuum, an acceptable range for this person or group.

Scenario

FineStart Nursery

Many governing variables will be on a continuum, that is to say, they will not be on a yes–no basis. Even something that appears to be the same value or principle, when expressed in words, will not be identical for what it means to this person or team.

Katy, manager of FineStart, wants to be kept up to date, but within boundaries. With too little information, from her perspective Katy feels ill-prepared and in the dark about recent developments. However, with too much information she feels overwhelmed, unable to judge what is important and what can be shelved, and definitely outside her comfort zone.

Katy is feeling vulnerable since the recent inspection and criticises herself to Simone in their session. However, Simone has the perspective to reassure Katy that her comfort zone is broad, in terms of striving to keep up to date. Katy reads widely, given her limited spare time, and follows up projects that she believes will be of interest to the staff. Simone suggests that Katy may need to focus more on a few points of interest, so that she can reflect more on how to make the ideas directly relevant and understandable, especially for her less experienced practitioners.

Comments

1. Think about possible governing variables for your practice. What are they and what is the span in which you feel comfortable?
2. Perhaps return to this question after reading further in this chapter.

Action strategies

This part of the model refers to what people do, or plan to do, in order to keep their governing variables within the acceptable range. Another way of expressing the process is 'the chosen strategies to implement this value'. Any action, or sequence of actions, is most likely to have an impact on more than one governing variable. So any situation can lead to the need to set one variable against another. But this balancing act may only become clear on reflection.

Consequences

Any action will have consequences and what follows on from action may be intended (expected and to an extent planned) or it may be unintended: a pleasant surprise, something to make you stop and think, or more like a shock. The consequences could be for the person who has made the choice about the strategy for action or the consequences could apply to other people.

When the consequences of the action strategies are what was wanted (intended), then the person's theory-in-use is confirmed: their professional life is working consistently with their beliefs. However, if the consequences are unexpected, then there is a mismatch between intention or expectation and outcome. The experience may be positive or negative, but either way the theory-in-use has been challenged by events.

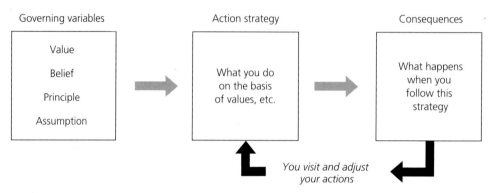

Figure 2.3 Working with your theory-in-use: single-loop reflective practice (developed from Argyris and Schön, 1974)

Chris Argyris and Donald Schön suggest that there are two main responses to the experience of unexpected or negative consequences: their concept of single-loop or double-loop learning in professional life. Faced with a mismatch, some people remain on the single loop – shown diagrammatically in Figure 2.3.

- They take for granted the value, assumption, ruling, and so on, assuming they are not open to change, or discussion.
- Also, they are possibly not familiar with the option of going right back to basics.
- They stick in the single loop and try a variation in their action strategy, to see if this will work and bring about the consequences they expected and wanted.
- Or else they wish to reduce the unintended consequences to a more manageable level.
- The focus here can be about finding alternative techniques or redoubling efforts on a strategy that 'should' work.

Figure 2.4 Working with your theory-in-use: double-loop reflective practice (developed from Argyris and Schön, 1974)

Alternatively, some people go back a step and return to examine the governing variable or variables that are central to the current situation.

- Double-loop learning confronts the assumption, goes back to the meaning of this key value or questions what exactly is meant by this ruling or broad guideline. This approach, shown visually in Figure 2.4, is a typical element of reflective practice.

- This kind of exploration sometimes reveals that individuals, or a group, are balancing one managing variable against another. They may have another value 'hidden' within the more obvious expressed value: the concept of nested theories.

What does it mean?

Single-loop learning: making changes in action strategies in the face of unexpected or unwanted consequences to previous actions.

Double-loop learning: returning to basic values or assumptions in the face of unexpected consequences, before considering alternative action strategies.

Nested theories: values or key beliefs that are hidden inside another governing variable, until that variable is directly examined.

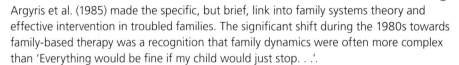

Take another **perspective**

Argyris et al. (1985) made the specific, but brief, link into family systems theory and effective intervention in troubled families. The significant shift during the 1980s towards family-based therapy was a recognition that family dynamics were often more complex than 'Everything would be fine if my child would just stop. . .'.

- In families, as in unreflective early years teams, it is less challenging for the adults to focus on the behaviour of the child or adolescent. Continued requests for ideas to control or manage the child are an effective way to 'paper over the cracks' in family life or early years practice on guiding children's behaviour.
- A family therapist, or early years advisor, will work with people to move from the single-loop circling and into a double loop that goes back to the governing variables. These may be a conviction that adults are never wrong or that it is emotionally inconvenient to look at your own adult behaviour.
- Many models of counselling (Lindon and Lindon, 2007) operate so as to support individuals to step back and reconsider their governing variables, although that is not the term used within the models.

Scenario

Crocus Playgroup

The Crocus team are committed to the value that young children need to feel a sense of belonging: that they are welcome here and come to feel it is 'my playgroup' (governing variable). A regular part of the morning and the afternoon sessions is that everyone comes together, early in the session, for a full-group time (action strategy). The aim is to greet every child as an individual, to hear their news and to manage their expectations for what will happen today.

So far, this action strategy of a full-group time appeared to work well: children sat, listened and joined in the greetings (expected consequences). For the next term, however, the playgroup started to take two-year-olds, when previously their youngest children were rising threes. Also, in response to local needs, some children now attend all day, bringing a packed lunch. The playgroup team – Natalie (the manager), Janice and Felicity – have noticed that the two-year-olds struggle to sit still in the group time. Also, the full-day children object to 'having to do it again' in the afternoon (unexpected and negative consequences).

The Crocus team discuss the negative impact that children who fidget or object have on the group. The team agree (single-loop thinking) to try a different version of the group time. The youngest children are encouraged to sit for a very short while and then allowed to go and play elsewhere. The full-day children are given the option just to join the morning group time.

However, after a week of this alternative strategy, other children ask, 'Why can't I go and play too?' and some just get up and leave the group. Janice, who has been especially committed to a 'proper whole-group time' wants to go back to insisting that every child is involved. Her view is that the opt-out strategy has disrupted those children who enjoyed the time and were able to sit nicely and listen.

Pause and reflect

Natalie decides that a thorough discussion is needed and organises a team meeting. She starts by suggesting that they all go back to the basics of what they hoped the group time would achieve (double-loop thinking). The three practitioners revisit their commitment to making children feel welcome and 'at home' in Crocus playgroup. They all judge that it is important to let children know what will happen today. The playgroup has flexible planning, so it is not a long list: one or two special adult-initiated activities or special experiences, such as meeting a visitor to the playgroup.

They start to discuss how else they could achieve those aims; a whole-group time is not the only possible strategy. They could greet children, and their parents, individually as they arrive. They could create a 'What's on today?' board with simple visuals and writing – aimed again at parents as well as children. Natalie and Felicity are positive about trying these alternatives. Janice is reluctant and it becomes clear that, for her, the whole-group time meets an additional belief, so far not voiced (nested theory). Janice believes strongly that all the playgroup children need to learn to sit in a large group because 'they'll have to do that when they go to school'.

Questions

1. How should the Crocus Playgroup discussion continue? What are the main issues?

2. Recall experiences within your professional life that fit something of the pattern here.

A model to support double-loop learning

Double-loop learning and exploration can feel more risky, especially in any organisation that does not welcome the questioning of basics. A great deal of Argyris's subsequent work with business organisations was aimed at exploring how they could increase the capacity in their workforce for double-loop thinking and learning. The rationale was that in a rapidly changing world, organisations would become less efficient if the established approach was to keep trying variations around the same basic theme. Argyris and Schön (1974) proposed two models about theory-in-use to explain the way in which one kind of thinking (Model I) inclined people towards single-loop learning and another (Model II) made them more receptive to double-loop learning.

Argyris et al. (1985) went on to explore these concepts in depth. The main message of his subsequent research was that most people operate on Model I, and that this theory-in-use fits in the prevailing social pressures in the USA and the UK. However, when asked, most people will say they are committed to Model II, that is, this approach is their espoused theory. These ideas support reflection about practice, but it is important to realise that the vast majority of research around these models has been undertaken by Argyris and his research associates. The details of the two broad models are also more in tune with the commercial/business world in which they were developed. This section considers what the concepts could offer to the early years professional world.

Model I theory-in-use

Argyris and Schön (1974) and Argyris et al. (1985) proposed that the key characteristics of this model were as follows, and again I have expressed this in my own words:

- The goals are defined and you strive to achieve them, but the goals themselves are not open to discussion. The details of the working environment are designed to fit those ends and any misfit is controlled rather than viewed as information that needs consideration. Argyris et al. describe the consequence as a 'self-sealing' system, which blocks constructive learning and change.

- The overall aim is to maximise winning, whatever that means in practice given this theory-in-use, and to minimise losing. In order to hold tight to this governing variable an individual acts so as to retain control of a task, the final statement about what matters round here, or who has the final say. The consequence is that relations with other people can be self-protective; the aim can be to defend oneself against loss of certainty or of status.

- There is a strong motivation to downplay any negative feelings or contrary information that would shake the security of the system as defined. Contradictions are brushed over, uneasy feelings are denied and people who question are sidelined at best. Doubts or careful checking are done more in private than in open discussion.

- There is an emphasis on the rational, perhaps with plausible explanations why it is better to withhold information or leave someone out of the loop of discussion. This focus on rationality further ignores the dynamics of the actual situation, including the feelings that underpin some of the behaviour. Errors of judgement and misuse of information persist, with further defensive actions, when lifting the lid threatens unquestioned goals to an even greater extent.

The theory-in-use that supports single-loop processing can include defensive reactions to protect oneself and allegedly to protect other people. Unreflective defence of unquestioned goals can lead to a distortion of reality, or be a self-fulfilling prophecy. Once individuals are stuck in the loop, it can be a struggle to step back mentally and resolve the problems.

Scenario

Greyhorse Road Early Years Unit

In Greyhorse Road Primary School the nursery and reception classes have been brought together this year to form a combined early years unit. Chloe is the teacher leading the group of four practitioners. She very much wants a contented team, which she defines as 'We're all one big happy family.' But she senses that Pippa and Maryam still feel like the 'nursery pair', with her and Marsha as 'reception'. Chloe's main action strategy to bring them all together is to smooth over any disagreements. Her preferred tactic is to use low-key, rather obscure ways of letting colleagues know that their practice is not quite right.

For instance, Chloe has been trying, clearly yet unsuccessfully in her view, to get Maryam to allow children more control over their paintings and other creative endeavours. In exasperation, today Chloe has taken a more direct approach. Maryam retorts with, 'If you think I'm doing this wrong, why didn't you tell me before?' Chloe is sure that she had told Maryam.

A mild disagreement between the nursery and reception 'pairs' of practitioners about shared responsibility for tidying up outdoors has not been resolved within team meetings. The resentment has come to the surface and hurt feelings of 'us two and you two' are expressed by Pippa. Later, Chloe thinks back over both incidents and decides this only goes to prove that disagreement is so disruptive in the team. How can she prevent it happening again?

Questions

1. What is likely to happen if Chloe continues in this way?
2. Chloe is offered regular supervision by Heena, the deputy of the primary school. How could Heena support Chloe? Look at some ideas in the section about supervision on page 156.

Model II theory-in-use

In contrast, a different outlook takes people more towards a double-loop approach.

- The goals are open to question but also the values that form a governing variable set the scene for reflection and questioning. For instance, a key belief is that best practice needs good-quality information and insights can come from any source. No single source is judged to be automatically reliable. Any idea can be questioned and any recommendation has to be given with an explanation or clear reasons.
- Because there is less emphasis on control and protection, there is far more of an atmosphere of shared control, although there will usually be someone who carries more responsibility or who is in charge. Everyone can contribute to the double-loop process.
- There is a shared commitment to bringing discussion and choices out into the open. It is expected, and welcomed, that disagreement will be voiced, although in a constructive way, and that confusion will not be judged as personal failure to grasp the obvious.
- Problems are there to be resolved and not hidden. Risk is something to be faced and managed, not avoided as a threat to the established order.

Professional practice as a learning journey

The distinction made between espoused theory and theory-in-use is also useful to highlight the gap that can emerge between training and practice.

Training and professional practice

Argyris and Schön describe espoused theory as the details of what is presented and taught in professional training, especially at the early, 'novice' stage. The details could be seen as a map, describing the appropriate way for a given profession to operate. The map created by the espoused theory may be significantly different from the theory-in-use, which more accurately describes what typically happens within the daily life of this profession. The details of the theory-in-use are the actual patterns of behaviour that novice professionals learn and those habits will strengthen with repetition.

Schön (1983, 1987) went on to challenge a dominant, and unwise, model of professional training, which he called 'technical rationality'. This approach takes the line that students are charged-up with knowledge, rather like a battery, during their training. They can then discharge that knowledge when they are engaged in the working world of practice. It never has been an accurate description of how good professionals think on their feet and has become ever less appropriate in a world in which some aspects change very fast. A significant push to placing a high value on reflective practice has been the social changes that mean that even within one profession nobody can expect to use the discharge battery model, with only the mildest of top-ups, over their working life.

What does it mean?

Technical rationality: an unwise model of training that presumes professionals are adequately equipped by transmission of a finite body of knowledge and techniques.

Indeterminate zones of practice: inevitable areas within professional practice when the appropriate knowledge or best approach is not immediately obvious.

Pause for reflection

Donald Schön's ideas were developed almost three decades ago. (I am writing this section in 2011.) But I think his concepts are still very relevant. In the preface, Schön (1983) made the following points, which I invite you to consider.

- Schön judged that some academic institutions held 'a view of knowledge that fosters selective inattention to practical competence and professional artistry' (1983: vii). Under these circumstances, training or potentially useful research might be disconnected from genuine practical value.
- On the other hand, Schön also argued that in a range of professions that had a 'mystique of practical competence', the consequence of this outlook could be that experienced professionals would be resistant to describing what they knew. Some were even convinced that trying to pin down an intuitive feel would somehow weaken a vital contribution to professional ability.

- Schön was convinced that key elements of professional competence had to be voiced and shared effectively. He collected many examples of practice for the book, in which a senior practitioner aimed to help a less experienced or junior colleague. Schön's observation was that the more senior individuals usually knew more than they seemed able to express: what Schön called 'a kind of "knowing-in-action", most of which is tacit' (1983: viii).

Questions

1. In your view and experience, to what extent are these three points still applicable?
2. Do you feel that the professional atmosphere has changed significantly? If so, in what ways?

It may feel reassuring to believe that there is a fund of rigorous professional knowledge that, once grasped, will provide techniques for all professional occasions. However, this outlook is not a realistic perspective. Schön did not dismiss the value of appropriate knowledge, only stating that there were serious limitations to an approach that viewed professionals as well-informed technicians. He drew attention to the reality that effective professional life has to include 'awareness of indeterminate, swampy zones of practice' (1987: 3). Schön goes on to apply that splendid phrase to the uncertainties of working life for civil engineers building roads, some of whom presumably encounter actual swamps.

Does your 'map' allow for 'swamps'?

Practitioners working with young children do not feature in the earlier literature about reflective practice, although case studies are offered from the teaching profession in schools. The early years workforce undoubtedly faces a range of these indeterminate situations when there is no clear-cut answer. Schön's analysis of professional life has many applications to practitioners working with children across the age range of early childhood and in any of the different kinds of provision.

- The problems and potential confusions of taking responsibility for young children often do not present themselves in a neat way. They do not easily fit ready-made templates of 'what to do when'. Effective early years practice needs to be prepared for the 'swampy zones', not least because the nature of daily life with young children is that a situation can change very swiftly.
- Even well-supported ideas, for instance about how to guide children's behaviour, do not 'work' every time. In fact, an approach that is wise in theory can be effectively derailed by an application in practice that views the approach as a technique to apply. The mechanistic models for 'managing children's behaviour' can backfire with unexpected consequences (Lindon, 2012c). They also usually sideline a key value about building relationships with children.

- Schön offers the insight that the more challenging areas of professional practice may not even present themselves as a clear-cut problem, demanding a solution, but as 'messy, indeterminate situations' (1987: 4).
- If something is not viewed as a problem, then practitioners are unlikely to engage in behaviour that could resolve the situation. Of course, all professionals also need to have a thorough grasp of problem-solving skills (more on page 98). However, that particular button for skills will not even be pressed if the prevailing outlook is that this is yet another of those 'grin and bear it' times.

Figure 2.5 You can never be certain what exactly will engage a young child

Schön (1987) suggested that the indeterminate zones of practice, the potential swamps, were characterised by three aspects. Here are his key terms, but my form of explanation, with special reference to early years practice.

1. *Uncertainty:* there is no easy way forward and it is doubtful that a set technique can be applied this time, with much hope of success. Maybe there are areas of ignorance that disrupt the basis of an approach that assumes you have all the information at your disposal. An inflexible ten-point plan to partnership with families can leave serious areas of uncertainty, not least over what these parents would welcome from your service.

2. *Uniqueness:* the situation has specific features that mean that existing knowledge or techniques do not seem to apply, or the fit is very uneven.

Professionals in an area such as early years are faced by many individual babies and children, who respond in personal ways to apparently similar treatment. Individual children also react with an apparent lack of internal consistency. Only ten minutes ago these two children were playing happily together; now they are shouting 'I'm not your friend!' at each other.

3. *Value conflict:* application of your knowledge or a familiar technique will go in direct opposition to a clear value of your service. Perhaps even harder to face is a situation where doing nothing is not an option and yet two equally promoted strategies each contravene a view of good practice. For example, unreflective interpretations of safeguarding practice have led to pronouncements that no early years practitioner should be alone with a child. Then settings that have instituted witnessing procedures for personal care have been challenged on the basis of disregard for children's privacy.

Some professional uncertainty is certain

Schön (1987) suggested that the struggle between espoused theory and theory-in-use was especially sharp for professions such as teachers or social workers, because of the lack of a secure body of knowledge to guide practice. Undoubtedly, educating children or supporting vulnerable people will never be the same kind of work as designing a building or standing up in court as a lawyer. However, even those professions which appear to be supported by a relatively certain framework can find themselves in a turbulent period, because previous certainties have been overturned. In the decades following Schön's book there has been a significant attempt through research and reviews to provide reliable evidence, which can support choices in practice – for teaching, social work and also early years provision.

Nevertheless, professionals within early years, such as schoolteachers and playworkers, will always face some level of uncertainty within their daily working life. Best practice within early years provision is to be flexible and alert to what interests children today. The nature of children's play includes a level of uncertainty. A significant shift in the model for genuinely good practice has meant that practitioners who were taught an adult-dominated model have needed to find ways to tolerate, ideally embrace, the shared control and uncertainty of young learning. Donald Schön's concept of 'artistry' in professional life applies to exactly this situation. He uses the word to mean that professional competence and confidence are also needed to handle the inevitable uncertainties, the indeterminate zones of practice. Even with increased practical direction from the evidence of research, there will always be aspects of practice that are uncertain.

What does it mean?

Artistry: a flexible and innovative approach to areas of professional practice, blending possible information and strategies – a contrasting alternative to mechanistic application of techniques.

Professionalism is more than techniques

Ghaye and Ghaye (1998) considered Schön's critique of technical rationality with particular application to teaching in school. In later books they applied the concepts to healthcare professionals: a reminder that these same ideas have affected a broad spectrum of professional life.

In their exploration of reflective practice in teaching, Ghaye and Ghaye highlight the risks of a pattern where one group of people develop theoretical perspectives and/or undertake research to generate evidence. Then this group passes on the digested practical applications to a different group: the people who actually deliver the service. In teaching, as in early years practice, these people are in contact with children and their families. Several problems can arise from putting teachers (or early years practitioners) into the role of technician: someone who should apply allegedly tried and tested techniques.

In the model, no offence is meant to technicians. There are some professions in which secure, technical competence is crucial for effective practice. Taking X-rays is not an enterprise to approach in the spirit of 'We'll just see how this goes.' There are important, technical points about how to do this procedure. However, since healthcare professionals take an X-ray of a person, best practice also includes their communication with that adult or child, and not treating them like an inanimate object.

Early years practitioners, or playworkers and schoolteachers, are potentially undermined if they are placed exclusively on the receiving end of other people's ideas for good practice. Such an outlook undervalues what can be learned from the considered experience and informed opinions of practitioners. The stark role division also risks creating a 'feed me' outlook in a body of practitioners. Of course, children benefit from practitioners who are keen to learn about new experiences and ways to use resources to enhance children's learning environment. But problems arise when all training sessions are judged from the perspective of 'Have I got new activities that I can do?' Areas of practice, such as ways to involve parents and family carers, benefit from discussion around the issues – not yet another 'to-do' suggestion for a small corner of involvement.

A high profile for reflective practice does not, and should not, undermine the importance of gaining firm foundations of knowledge and practical skills. In the early years profession, this basis includes a sound grasp of child development to enable practitioners to hold realistic expectations and challenge unrealistic approaches or required outcomes (Lindon, 2012a, 2012e). The point of establishing a reflective workforce is to benefit children. The end result is also likely to be a more interesting, enjoyable and personally satisfying work life for the adults in the enterprise.

Reflection-in-action and reflection-on-action

Donald Schön (1983) progressed his particular interests in the behaviour of professionals by exploring aspects of reflective practice along two main strands:

reflection-in-action and reflection-on-action. He brought the concept of reflection on to centre stage for an understanding of what professionals should be enabled to do. Schön acknowledged that some professionals were resistant to thinking about what they did and why. The expressed rationale for this wariness was that thinking – or thinking too much – would inevitably paralyse action and therefore effective practice. His view was that this belief was mistaken, although it was necessary to recognise what could hold back the necessary reflection.

What does it mean?

Reflection-in-action: professional thoughtfulness, keeping key values to the front of your mind, recognising choice points and using even limited time to make the best decision for the moment.

Reflection-on-action: thinking and talking over what has happened with the aim of learning what went well, what might be changed another time and why. The term is usually applied to past events, but can be used for forward thinking.

Reflection-in-action

This process is also called 'thinking on your feet' or 'keeping your wits about you'. The reflection is, inevitably in a hands-on profession such as early years, an experience of thinking swiftly at the time, but sometimes with slightly more breathing space for thought.

Van Manen (1995: 35), writing about the role of a teacher in the school classroom, questions how reflective it is possible to be when the teacher is 'live' and thirty pairs of eyes are watching closely. He continues to refer to a 'quality of engaged immediacy', which explains why the job – done well – is tiring. There are immediate parallels with early years practice. Van Manen describes experienced teachers who may find it hard to explain to others what they do, but who nevertheless 'thinkingly act and often do things with immediate insight' (1995: 36). I agree that this kind of reflection should be counted as such, and not demoted to some kind of lower-level status of reflection.

In early years practice just as much as in the school classroom, sensitive practitioners make many small, of-the-moment decisions and some of these are active in thought and action. You decide, within a short thinking time, whether to join a child's play. Without over-thinking this situation, you consider whether it looks as if that child would rather be alone or you could sit quietly and play alongside. At a slightly later point you may comment or suggest, because that feels like the right move now. So long as you take it one step at a time, you are unlikely to make a seriously wrong move. Equally important, children who are confident you respect them, and their interests, will feel able to decline your offer. It is actually a measure of how much young children feel genuinely at ease with you that they do not worry about saying, 'Not now' or 'I'm busy, please be quiet.'

Reflective practice for professionals with high levels of contact with other people, whether with adults or children, includes this kind of brief stop-and-think and at-the-time awareness of the choices you are making. Van Manen calls this 'contemporaneous reflection'. Perhaps one of the more challenging, and crucial, tasks for an experienced team member is to be able to share this ongoing thoughtfulness with a less experienced colleague or one who is confused.

It requires self-insight to express in words the thoughts that ran through your mind within a sequence of many small decisions. Honest communication with someone else also requires confidence not to tidy up those thoughts in order to appear neater or more rational.

Pause for reflection

The High/Scope approach to conflict resolution is a very positive set of strategies, which are underpinned by adult awareness of their own reactions and feelings just as much as wise suggestions about what you actually do, faced with squabbling children (Evans, 2002). However, their visual material also demonstrates the power of linked reflection-on-action with using the small windows of opportunity for reflection-in-action.

In the DVD *Supporting children in resolving conflicts* (High/Scope, 1988) you can watch and listen as one practitioner, accompanied by a consultant, watches a recording of how she handled a recent argument between two boys in the nursery. The practitioner voices the small yet important decisions she made during the incident, including her decision to wait a short while to see if the boys were going to be able to resolve the conflict without her intervention.

The consultant acknowledges the decisions that the practitioner made and affirms the positive thinking behind those choices. For instance, there is no solution to this particular disagreement that will leave both boys equally happy. But the practitioner does not try to apply the social superglue and insist on a way to 'play nicely together'. She accepts that one boy will leave the interaction to follow his preferred interests for now. She will keep company with the second boy, who looks very crestfallen and in need of a play partner.

Reflection-on-action

This type of reflection is the thoughtful work that can operate on either side of immediate actions. The discussion of reflection-on-action frequently focuses on thoughtfulness after something has happened. However, it is equally possible that some of this kind of reflection can happen before an event that will benefit from forethought. Van Manen calls the forward thinking 'anticipatory reflection' and the after-the-event thoughtfulness 'retrospective reflection'.

This process is ongoing and not a single sit-down session. This kind of reflection could follow a single-loop process (look back at page 28). There is nothing inherently wrong in the single-loop process; sometimes it makes complete sense to fine-tune what you do, in the light of information from what has happened. However, valuable reflective practice is willing to go back to assumptions and values and to engage in the double-loop process (look back at page 29), when that is needed.

Reflection-on-action may be undertaken on your own, with your own thoughts – or talking out loud, if that helps. However, full reflective practice is best supported by help from other people and a range of techniques that support that reflection. Other chapters in this book explore those possibilities and what is needed to make any technique work well. This kind of reflection can increase self-awareness, as well as extend a practitioner's repertoire of possible strategies. With self-awareness, and the motivation to try alternatives, the reflection in a quieter moment can help to inject that vital moment of forethought into an active situation.

Ghaye and Ghaye (1998) also talk about knowing-in-action, for which they describe two elements. One part is reflection on what you actually do to reach a secure knowledge base that rests on practice. The second part is to use this understanding to transform and improve what you do. The challenge, and the hard work of thinking, is to make this knowledge audible and visible. Practitioners, and anyone supporting them in CPD, need to get beyond 'I just know,' 'It's all common sense' or the fancier version, 'Experienced practitioners have an intuitive grasp of . . .' which is not then accompanied by further explanation.

The process of reflection-on-action usually happens on the basis of memory – sometimes the shared recall of practitioners who were also present. It is very helpful to be able to explore on the basis of an accurate written or visual record of events. The High/Scope example reminds us how valuable it can be to watch oneself on video, however uncomfortable it may feel at the outset. This option is further discussed on page 88 of this book.

Make the connection with. . . **the ideas of Jean Piaget**

In some discussions of reflection-in-action, there is the suggestion that this aspect of reflective practice is provoked by a turn of events that surprises the practitioner or by a problem that needs attention. Possibly, in a busy working life, people are more inclined to reflect when the flow is somewhat disturbed. Much of the discussion around reflective practice stresses that the whole point is to integrate thoughtfulness into daily working life.

The notion that mismatch and misfit provoke thought raises a useful connection with the theoretical perspective of Jean Piaget on how children learn. He proposed that, when possible, children incorporate new experiences in their existing ways of acting upon and understanding the world. This process is assimilation. However, children steadily encounter experiences that will not fit their existing mental processes. Through a process of accommodation, children then develop a fresh way of looking at and acting upon the world.

Adults have gathered a much larger body of knowledge than young children. The lifelong-learner outlook is compatible with a continued process of accommodation: rethinking and reorganising the mental maps in the face of new insights. It is not a professional outlook to shove inconvenient new ideas into an existing framework, claiming that somehow they do fit.

The MIT Teacher Project

Schön (1983) describes the Teacher Project at the Massachusetts Institute of Technology. The researchers had encouraged a small group of teachers to explore their own intuitive thinking about apparently simple tasks in a range of subjects. A key point was that the teachers had permitted themselves, 'to become confused about subjects they are supposed to "know"; and they have tried to work their way out of their confusion' (1983: 67). A significant turning point for the group had been watching and discussing a filmed exchange between two boys sitting at a table, separated from one another by an opaque screen.

One boy had a pattern of blocks of various colours, shapes and sizes, and it was his task to explain the layout in words so that the other boy could create the same pattern on his side. After only a few instructions it became clear that the second boy was building a very different layout of blocks. The initial interpretation by the group of teachers was that the first boy had 'well-developed verbal skills' and the second boy was 'unable to follow directions'. However, the researcher pointed out the first boy's exact words in an early instruction: he had confused colour and shape in his choice of words. From that moment on, the second boy had shown perseverance and ingenuity in trying to reconcile instructions with the pattern in front of him. The teachers could now see a logical reason for his behaviour and his errors could no longer be interpreted as an inability to follow instructions.

In this example, the teachers watched a filmed exchange in which they had not themselves taken part. The reflection was on how easily they came to interpretations and conclusions about what was happening and why. As the project evolved, the teachers were swifter to challenge themselves to avoid assumptions and, instead, to discover the meaning of a child's behaviour that was puzzling to them. They described this process as 'giving him reason' – a respect for behaviour that was reasonable, when it was better understood.

Reflection on shared and non-shared reference

Careful observation of young children shows that they can become very confused if adults do not connect abstract ideas clearly to a familiar context. Ridler (2002) observed different strategies by teachers of five-year-olds in lessons that aimed to extend the mathematical understanding of these young children. The key point was that adult and children need to have a shared reference point; they need to be 'talking about the same thing'. If adults – teachers or practitioners from another professional background – do not consider this issue, then confusion for children and frustration for adults can follow.

This research offers another perspective on reflection-on-action, eased because Ridler observed and transcribed the classroom exchanges. She gives four specific examples: two when the adults and children were talking about the same thing; and two when they were not and the adult did not realise and react. (These are described in detail, with permission, from the unpublished paper.)

First teacher

In the first example, the children had number lines on their desks from 1 to 10, and their teacher instructed the children to point to numbers on their line. She asked them to 'find the one with the hat on' and the children all pointed to the number 5. The teacher then asked, 'How do you make a number 5 again?' And the children used the formula of 'Down and round and put the hat on'. In this case, the adults and children were both talking about the same thing. First of all, they were referring to the written symbol 5. Then they were talking about how to make/write the symbol 5.

In the second example, the same teacher started her lesson by holding up numbers and getting the children to say the number name each time. Then she alerted the children to a shift by saying, 'Stop there. Now we'll make it harder for you. If I show you number 4, I want you to tell me what comes next. So if I show you 4, you'll say . . .?' And the children said correctly 5. Adult and children were again talking about the same thing. The children understood that first the task was to name the number and then the task was to think and say which number came next in the order of numbers.

Second teacher

In the first example, this teacher wanted to explain how many more cubes child B had than child A. The teacher took four cubes from A (all the cubes that A had). She said to child A, indicating B, 'What do I have to do to make it fair?' Child A replied, 'Take all of her cubes.' Child A seems to be thinking of the situation in terms of fairness and social equivalence. Child A had no cubes, so fairness meant taking away child B's cubes as well. But the teacher was thinking about removing the same number of cubes from B's pile and was then going to ask how many were left in B's pile of cubes. But the teacher's words do not indicate a number operation.

In the second example, this same teacher was aiming to explain addition. The children had sheets of paper with boxes drawn on them and the teacher held up two cards with written numerals (2 and 1). She said, 'You're going to make the sum on your board.' The objective from the adult point of view was that the children were supposed to use plastic bears to represent the number in each box on their paper. But they did not understand that the first number went into the left-hand box with the bears and the next number into the middle box.

Confusion reigned, but the teacher did not stop and explain the whole idea behind creating this visual sum. She understood the standard way to construct an addition sum but the children did not, and were confused between written number, plastic bears and the symbolic nature of the sum on their sheet of paper. The teacher carried on with getting the children to create the visual sum. Then, later in the same discussion, she asked, 'What do 2 and 1 make?' One child at least showed the confusion by answering 6, which was the total number of bears on the paper sheet (2 and then 1 and then the 'answer' of three separate bears). The teacher saw the boxes as a clear representation of a sum with an answer, but the children did not share that understanding.

On reflection – what is happening?

These examples from Scottish classrooms show shared reference (adults and children are talking about the same thing) and non-shared reference (talking about something different) between the teacher and five-year-olds during a mathematical activity and discussion. The examples are also a useful spotlight on the importance of reflection-in-action. The second teacher carried on despite evidence from the children's responses that they most likely did not share the reference of the teacher. In the first example of this pair, the child thinks the teacher is talking about fairness and not number. In the second example, the children do not understand what they are supposed to be doing and why.

Time given to ensure that young children understand is invaluable; it is not an optional extra to check properly, 'Are we talking about the same thing?' There is no point in continuing to speak about anything if children do not understand. They have not learned the concept which is clear in the adult's mind. Children have learned that maths (or whatever) is confusing and they just have to put up with not understanding. Another way of looking at these examples is to say that, used reflectively, they show the importance of critical thinking and critical analysis of events and experiences for children.

Pause for reflection

Non-shared reference, in mathematics or any other subject area, is not a problem so long as the adult recognises it, stops, asks open questions and listens. Adults can then explain properly because they have now grasped what it is that some or most of the children do not understand.

The confusion of today may be cleared up tomorrow, so long as practitioners recognise there has been misunderstanding, think about how to redress the situation and do more effective tell-and-show with the children. Practitioners have then usefully explored reflection-on-action. It is valuable for children to realise that, firstly, adults have given time to thinking about how to help and secondly, that being confused as a child is not your fault.

Questions

1. Can you recall a time, as an older child, adolescent or adult, when you did not understand a key point and the person teaching you failed to grasp your confusion, or brushed it aside?
2. Maybe it only became clear to you later, perhaps much later, what you had not known or understood.

Critical thinking

The phrase 'critical thinking' is regularly used within materials to support and promote reflective professional practice. Too often the term is not defined. There seems to be an assumption that 'Everybody knows' what is meant by this particular use of two words. The meaning of the phrase is not obvious and I plan to unpack it in this section.

The meaning of 'critical'

Moon (1999, 2008) describes the problems created for students by language experienced as 'jargon' words. Unfamiliar terms complicate a currently unfamiliar process: of mentally stepping back from what they have learned, or are in the process of learning. The phrase 'critical thinking' was used in the first version of the Early Years Foundation Stage (2008) in the Principles into Practice card 4.3, *Creativity and Critical Thinking*. The term was not explained within the card nor did I ever find a working definition elsewhere within that EYFS guidance. There seemed to be an assumption that 'everyone' would know what the phrase meant; in my professional experience that was not the case. Practitioners need to have confidence in understanding the phrase applied to their own reflective processes. Without this grounding, it is hard to see how even experienced practitioners will be able to consider what critical thinking will look like in a version that is meaningful for young children. I return to this point later in this chapter on page 51.

Sometimes it is useful to look at the dictionary. In my *Shorter Oxford English Dictionary*, the word 'critical' has two main, alternative meanings, listed in this order:

1. 'Given to judging, fault finding, censorious.'

2. 'Involving or exercising careful judgement or observation, nice, exact, punctual.'

The phrase 'critical thinking' within discussion of reflective practice embraces the second definition. This usage developed significantly towards the end of the 20th century, led by discussion in academic circles.

Words matter and I believe that the first definition is the one most often used in social communication. So, a responsible approach to professional development should start with acknowledging that discussion of reflective practice has chosen the less familiar definition, from the perspective of the general population. It is irrelevant that this second meaning has now become commonplace within academic circles. The closest, common usage elsewhere would be saying something like 'This meeting will be a critical turning point.' In this instance, the person speaking would not mean that everyone at the meeting is going to list other people's faults. The message is: 'The events of this meeting will make a significant difference for where we go from here.'

Aspects of critical thinking

The basic ideas of critical thinking have historical roots back to the early 20th century with the ideas of John Dewey. There is good reason to say that the origins go even further back to Socrates, a philosopher who lived in Greece in ancient times, some 2,400 years ago, and established a form of philosophical enquiry through questioning. John Dewey promoted an active process of what he called 'reflective thinking' and contrasted that with a passive process of simply accepting knowledge as given. It was important to uncover reasons and the implications of applying given knowledge or suggestions for action.

> ## What does it mean?
>
> **Critical thinking:** focused thought on a subject, event or aspect of practice in order to consider seriously all the details and reach careful and well-supported judgements.

Thinking about a familiar area

The term 'critical thinking' refers to purposeful and reflective judgement around something that is meaningful and relevant to you and which is familiar, at least to an extent. You cannot think deeply about an area in which you feel you are at the very beginnings of your competence. Critical thinking rests upon a foundation of knowledge and awareness of a secure range of skills. Individuals vary and some people want a more substantial foundation than others before they feel confident to apply the range of techniques for supporting critical thinking.

Moon (2008) developed the phrase 'tools for the manipulation of knowledge', by which she means 'techniques for working with knowledge in order to create new knowledge or to communicate it to others in an altered form – such as in the construction of an argument '(2008: 15). You cannot effectively use the tools until you have a comfortable base of knowledge. Jennifer Moon also makes the useful distinction between what is taught and what is learned. She highlights the risks of behaving as if these are one and the same thing.

Learning the skills of thinking

Reflective practice requires that early years practitioners are willing and able to think about what they do, and not rest upon the details of 'what I'm told to do'. Critical thinking will especially be applied to situations when everything is not clear-cut: the swampy zones of indeterminate practice (look back at page 35). You explore questions about, as well as possible solutions for, issues that are not clearly defined and for which there may be no single, right answer.

A useful reflective approach is to consider how thinking skills can evolve over childhood and adolescence, along with an honest appraisal of how far some young, and not so young, adults have been supported in this development. An influential paper by McGuinness (1999) was the beginning of a considerable range of projects exploring ways to encourage a breadth of thinking skills over the years of childhood and adolescence.

Active thinking depends on a learning environment in which the habits of busy thinking are welcome to the adults and modelled by them day by day. Commitment to fostering thinking skills has implications for adult behaviour and the role of being a teacher in school. McGuiness stresses that if teachers accept the responsibility to help children develop well-honed thinking and reasoning skills, then the adult contribution is not exclusively about getting children to understand and use specific strategies, such as for problem solving. Strategies are useful, but the adult responsibility is just as much about creating dispositions for active thinking. The working definition of pedagogy has to move away from a passive learner-and-transmission model (read more on page 65).

Pause for reflection

McGuinness concludes her key point about dispositions as well as skills by saying, 'For this reason classrooms need to have open-minded attitudes about the nature of knowledge and thinking and to create an educational atmosphere where talking about thinking – questioning, predicting, contradicting, doubting – is not only tolerated but actively pursued.' (1999: page 2 of the summary brief)

Comments

1. Apply this statement to reflective practice within early years settings, network discussion groups and course or study groups.
2. Are these strands of thinking actively pursued by the adults within your daily and weekly professional experience?

Figure 2.6 You will learn a great deal through observing how children choose to spend their time

Resources

- Argyris, C. (1970) *Intervention Theory and Method: A Behavioural Science View*. Reading, MA: Addison-Wesley.
- Argyris, C. and Schön, D. (1974) *Theory in Practice*. San Francisco: Jossey-Bass.
- Argyris, C., Putnam, R. and McLain Smith, D. (1985) *Action Science: Concepts, Methods and Skills for Research and Intervention*. San Francisco: Jossey-Bass. The authors have made the entire book available online at **www.actiondesign. com/resources/research/action-science**
- Department for Children, Schools and Families (2008) *The Early Years Foundation Stage – Setting the Standards for Learning, Development and Care for Children from Birth to Five*. London: DCSF, **https://www.education. gov.uk/publications/standard/publicationdetail/page1/DCSF-00261-2008**
- Evans, B. (2002) *You Can't Come To My Birthday Party: Conflict Resolution with Young Children*. Ypsilanti: High Scope Press.
- Ghaye, A. and Ghaye, K. (1998) *Teaching and Learning through Critical Reflective Practice*. London: David Fulton.
- High/Scope UK (1988) *Supporting Children in Resolving Conflicts* (DVD). **www.high-scope.org.uk**
- Lindon, J. (2012a, third edition) *Understanding Child Development: 0–8 Years*. London: Hodder Education.
- Lindon, J. (2012c) *Understanding Children's Behaviour: 0–11 Years*. London: Hodder Education.
- Lindon, J. (2012e, third edition) *What Does It Mean to Be Four? A Practical Guide to Child Development in the Early Years Foundation Stage*. London: Practical Pre-School Books.
- Lindon, J. and Lindon, L. (2007) *Mastering Counselling Skills*. Basingstoke: Palgrave Macmillan.
- McGuinness, C. (1999) *From Thinking Skills to Thinking Classrooms*. London: Department for Education and Employment. **www. sustainablethinkingclassrooms.qub.ac.uk/DFEE_Brief_115.pdf**
- Moon, J. (1999) *Reflection in Learning and Professional Development: Theory and Practice*. Abingdon: RoutledgeFalmer.
- Moon, J. (2008) *Critical Thinking: An Exploration of Theory and Practice*. London: Routledge.
- Ridler, C. (2002) 'Teachers, Children and Number Understanding', Conference paper, British Psychological Society Psychology of Education Conference, University College, Worcester.
- Schön, D. (1983) *The Reflective Practitioner: How Professionals Think in Action*. London: Routledge.
- Schön, D. (1987) *Educating the Reflective Practitioner: Towards a New Design for Teaching and Learning in the Professions*. San Francisco: Jossey-Bass.
- van Manen, M. (1995) 'On the epistemology of reflective practice', *Teachers and Teaching: Theory and Practice*, volume 1, no 1; available online at **www.maxvanmanen.com/category/articles/**

Developing as a reflective practitioner

Developing your reflective practice is a personal journey but should not be a lonely one. Other people, their ideas and insights, are valuable for guiding that journey. This chapter focuses especially on the process of developing as a reflective practitioner yourself. But many of the ideas are directly relevant to the relationships you develop with fellow practitioners, as part of a team or other professional contacts.

The main sections of this chapter are:
- A personal learning journey
- The process of learning.

A personal learning journey

The concept of a flow of learning has become central to ways of looking at how young children learn. The overall aim is to follow the individual story of what interests a child and to document in ways that show the unique nature of this personal narrative. In a similar way, the objective in developing as a reflective practitioner is to become more aware of your own learning journey and find ways to sharpen your awareness and ability to learn from direct experiences.

The value of reflection for practice

Joy Amulya writes about the purposeful learning that can emerge from 'an active process of witnessing one's own experience in order to take a closer look' (undated: 1). The aim of reflective practice as a whole is to examine our own experience, rather than simply let it flow on past us. Specific confusions or the dilemmas that provoke active problem solving can motivate practitioners to make the time for serious thought and discussion. However, the more general approach about reflective practice aims to establish ongoing habits of thoughtfulness that are not only provoked in times of struggle.

- Joy Amulya makes the fundamental point that reflective practice is organised around inquiry, a curiosity about aspects of practice.
- She suggests that reflective practice is basically the effort to make relevant experiences more visible and that this process is driven most usefully by questions, dialogue and narrative accounts of experiences.
- Questions and dialogue can be with other people, but keeping a professional journal is one way to open and continue that kind of dialogue with yourself.

- Thoughtfulness and critical thinking skills help individuals and groups to unpack the descriptive story of experiences and events. It then becomes possible to identify what Joy Amulya calls 'the learning edges', by which she means specific questions or issues that an individual or team needs to understand in order to take their practice forward.

It is worth reflecting on the point made by Joy Amulya that reflective practice emerges from an outlook of inquiry and a curiosity. Miller and Sambell (2003) quote from students on their early childhood studies programme, who describe the experience as a kind of waking up from a non-reflective outlook. They looked at their world in a different way and continued to question whenever an approach or idea was taken for granted. Drummond (1996) describes teachers who felt there was no turning back once they had started to question and think deeply about their practice.

Getting used to reflection

Use of a reflective diary is discussed later in this section. However, it is often helpful to explore ways of looking below the immediate surface that do not initially ask practitioners to go into details of their current early years practice. Here are some possible ideas:

- What does a familiar situation look like literally from the perspective of someone else? Ask practitioners to spend some time at the eye level of a typical three-year-old. What does the early years setting look like – indoors and in the garden? What does the local high street or the library look like?
- What does it feel like as an adult to make personal contact with a service with which you are unfamiliar? Discussion needs to follow from actual experiences of going into a health centre, for example, or somewhere similar. Or the reflection could be from the first visit to a local leisure centre.
- What were your first impressions of the reception area? What caught your attention? How were you treated by the first staff member you encountered? To what extent did you feel at ease, or uncomfortable; what contributed to those feelings?
- Reflect on a recent event, perhaps a relatively dramatic event such as a scuffle between people in the street. How did the incident look from your perspective? How did it probably look from the perspectives of other people, those directly involved and onlookers? What would you consider was the range of feelings that different people were experiencing?

A reflective learning diary

Moon (2003) points out that terms such as reflective diary, learning log or learning journal are often used as if they are interchangeable. She suggests that all of the approaches include some level of reflection. However, each approach is slightly different in that:

- Reflective diaries are focused on demonstrating reflection on an experience.

- Learning logs are mostly a record of events that have happened, which are relevant to this person's learning (further discussion from page 109).
- A learning journal is a record of learning but more focused on bringing out specifics of that process.

Different kinds of personal learning records have become prominent in many higher-education programmes. However, the approach of a learning log is increasingly used to support children in primary and secondary school. They use a personal learning log to document what they have learned and how. The log is then often used, with adult encouragement and guidance, for children to act as independent learners and determine the implications for their next steps in a learning journey for a specific area of knowledge or skills.

For this section, I have decided to use a combination term, reflective learning diary: RLD for short. I hope the use of this term will capture the situation of reflective practice for early years practitioners, who keep a record in a format that is more like that of a diary, but who are also bringing in what they have learned through reflection.

What does it look like?

Starting a reflective diary is usually a first step when early years practitioners start a degree, the Early Years Professional Status track or become involved in a programme of more than one or two days to support continuing professional development. Under these circumstances, you may be offered a possible layout for your reflective account.

- There is no single, correct format, because different layouts will serve different purposes.
- There is also scope for a format and style to be tailored to individual preferences, but not so much as to lose the rigour of detailed description and serious thought about the meaning of what has been written.
- It is often useful to have some guiding questions, definitely when practitioners are at an early stage of understanding the process of reflection. However, some key questions can be valuable for the most experienced practitioners.
- To some people, in any line of work, a generous spread of plain paper is a welcome invitation to fill it. Yet, to others, the blank page is an empty space that threatens 'Have you really got something that's worth writing here?'
- People vary in terms of personal style and some practitioners may work better with a more free-flow approach. Others may welcome more of a guiding structure. Part of reflective practice is to become more aware of your personal style: the opportunities it brings and the possible drawbacks.
- The more free-flow individuals may need to realise that pages of description will become overwhelming. You do not undermine the integrity of experience by bringing skills of critical thinking to bear on the information. On the other hand, individuals who work better with some guiding questions or boxes may need to ensure that completing the format does not squeeze authentic experiences into categories.

Many practitioners, whose ideas were invaluable as I wrote this book, had chosen to continue different types of written, reflective accounts after the completion of their study. As you integrate the approach into your regular practice, it makes sense to adjust any format so that it works best for yourself and your colleagues if you work in a team. Certainly, a reflective diary or log approach is not exclusively for personal learning within a course or other form of CPD.

Is it the same as making observations?

A reflective account has some features in common with making accurate observations, for instance of children or the approach of peer observation (further discussion page 187). However, there are key differences.

- Observations are usually made within a limited time frame and with some framework around what is being observed and for what purpose.
- An RLD is more open-ended, even when there is more specific focus than reflecting back over the day. The advantage of an RLD is that it encourages practitioners to consider the apparently random events of a day or to bring some sense through thinking around what Jennifer Moon calls 'messy information' (2003: 7).
- Observations are designed to be shared with relevant other people, such as a room colleague, the child's parent and in some cases children themselves.
- The RLD is a personal, confidential record that is not designed to be shared. An exception is when the RLD is part of a portfolio for study.
- Practitioners are sometimes told to avoid the personal pronoun 'I' when they are writing observations of children or summary reports. The rationale is usually that a more impersonal written style is more objective. The name of the invisible 'I' should be given on any written account.
- However, an RLD is definitely written in the first-person style; you write as 'I'. This grammatical style is important to show that the entire process supported by an RLD is a personal exploration. This learning journey can still be very thoroughly considered.

Common features are the care that needs to be taken over accuracy for actual events and the courtesy of explaining to anyone else present why you are making a written record. If you work with other people, it will become clear to colleagues that you are keeping an RLD.

What is my focus?

The focus of an RLD varies. However, it is not a personal 'Dear diary', so it will never be a simple invitation to empty the contents of your head onto the page.

- In some cases you may build an account of the flow to the day.
- You may write up, and then reflect upon, a conversation with an individual child or a small group, when that conversation ran for some time and had many twists and turns.
- Or you might be especially interested in particular kinds of events, such as any event within the day that is related to parents or other family carers.
- You might put energy into reflecting on how team meetings operate.

- Or you may home in on all the examples within a day of dealing with young children's personal care needs.
- You could reflect on a specific experience, such as making a short presentation to a staff or network meeting, or to a group of fellow students.

Is it all written?

Most discussion of reflective accounts assumes they are written. However, there is no reason why you could not include different kinds of material, for example visual, when that is an appropriate way to capture an event or experience. If your RLD forms part of your portfolio for degree study, then the entire set of material will include more than exclusively written accounts. Practitioners who use an RLD within their daily practice, or as part of a shorter programme of CPD, need to recall that any visual information is used for a good reason, never just to fill out your RLD.

- Perhaps your account of contact with parents throughout a day is enhanced by marking up where these conversations took place, using a rough plan of your setting. You might add this feature to your RLD because you are wondering whether some parents feel uneasy about 'interrupting' you and only talk if you are standing up and relatively close to the door of your room.
- Perhaps you have chosen to reflect in detail on a specific experience that you enjoyed today with the children. You have taken a photo and that image has captured the feelings that you have so far written in words. The photo definitely adds to your account.

Make the connection with... **documenting children's learning**

In each of the above examples the visual image is added to the RLD because it enhances the reflection. They are not added because the practitioner, or anyone else, thinks that some kind of visual 'should' be in the RLD, or that it will make the account look more detailed or in some way better.

There is a direct connection here to wise practice in documenting children's learning in their personal portfolio, in a wall display or A3-size book. You need to select photos, with the children's input, because visuals 'say' something relevant. There has to be a good reason to add this photo to the documentation and reflection on 'What does this image add?' leads to relevant words being written to accompany the photo.

The point about keeping an RLD, and using it as a prompt for active thought, is to seek improvements in your practice. It is not unusual for practitioners to feel uneasy when they are first invited to set up a reflective account. Are you being expected to criticise yourself in a negative way? Is this request an implied criticism that you were not very thoughtful up to now? The main points are:

- Reflection through using an RLD is about finding positives, the strengths of your practice. In some cases, you will recognise the quality of aspects of what you do. Perhaps you are not giving yourself full credit.

- Even in areas where your practice is strong, the RLD may help you to generate more, good reasons for continuing in this way. You shine a light on what it is that works so well; this is very useful if you have a responsibility to share those insights or approaches with other people.
- Applying critical thinking skills to the content of your RLD will sometimes identify areas in which you feel stagnant, are struggling or feel that you have made a wrong turning in your choices over practice.
- This exercise is not all about fault finding; it is about constructive criticism. Your aim is to become clearer about the scope for improvement, which can feel like a friendlier phrase than talking about your 'weaknesses'.
- Everybody can be reflective, but some practitioners may not have had much encouragement so far to think about their experiences. So it can help to be given specific suggestions on a focus at the outset.

You will find many sets of questions in this and other chapters. They are all suggestions and, if you are involved in study or other forms of CPD, your tutor will have suggestions. There is no fixed set of questions that you should ask; see what works best to encourage you to be very thoughtful about your practice.

A personal record yet careful

Whatever you call this open-ended document, it is personal to you. The material is not an essay that you hand in to someone else, although as a student your RLD may provide some insights for your other written work. Additionally, as a student, your reflections on different aspects of your practice are very likely to contribute to your course portfolio.

A great deal of the content of your RLD will be about your own choices, actions and thoughts. However, even if you work alone as a sole practitioner, such as a childminder in your own home, some entries will include reference to other people. It is a good habit to establish, even with personal notes and considered reflections, that you never write offhand remarks that would be embarrassing if someone else inadvertently read them. It is important that your RLD is an honest and detailed account; otherwise there is little point in putting in the effort. However, there is a difference between a blunt note that 'Toni's mum hasn't a clue about how to talk with her daughter' and exploring in a more descriptive way, 'What I learned this afternoon about how Toni's mum usually talks with her daughter . . .'.

Make the connection with... **confidentiality**

Your RLD should remain in a secure, confidential context. You may choose to write it by hand or you may prefer typing your account, perhaps into a template format. Although a personal account, it is still about professional matters. By implication or clear connections, your RLD will carry information about other people besides yourself: your colleagues if you work together with other practitioners, children, their family and maybe other professionals with whom you have contact.

It would never be responsible, professional behaviour to put the record into the public space of online communication. Your RLD should not be entered into, nor transferred to, a personal blog, social networking site, or any other similar online forum. Maybe this prohibition seems very obvious to some readers. However, it is far from obvious to every practitioner, especially some (not all) younger members of the workforce who have grown up with familiarity and technical expertise in using different forms of online sharing of information.

Questions

1. Please consider, and ideally discuss, this issue about the boundary between personal and professional.
2. Use of social networking sites now needs to be part of a clear discussion about partnership with parents and the distinction between a friendly working relationship and being friends (Lindon, 2009). Have you addressed this issue in your work?

Becoming more adept at reflection

Some early years practitioners, or other professionals from practical fields such as playwork or teaching, may start with a strongly reflective outlook. Maybe your temperament and personal style incline you towards pondering or mulling things over in general. Maybe you have experiences, from your own schooling and learning within adult life, that have created a positive outlook for what can be gained by allowing time for focused reflection. Anyone can sharpen up their own skills, but also some readers will be in the position of supporting fellow adults towards reflection. It is valuable to consider what is involved, perhaps looking at the process in terms of levels, going deeper into the reflective process.

Accurate description

Accuracy is an important basis for reflecting on events and experiences. In fact, some focused reflection is often useful when tightening up description. Practitioners need to spot the difference between descriptions of what happened, which is as close to fact as you can manage, and the sense that you can make of it, your interpretations. There is a close connection here to the skills of making and writing up observations of children within your daily practice. In fact, the skills of reflective practice can make a noticeable difference to the quality of observations, and related, meaningful plans for children. Catherine Croft (personal communication and 2009) highlights the importance of distinguishing the different elements of reflective observation, whether for your own direct use or to guide reflective supervision of a colleague (more about this approach from page 159).

Figure 3.1 What exactly did the children do over time?

Sometimes it will be on your return to a written account that you can tease out the separate strands:

● What you have observed Leila do, such as play with the blocks for ten minutes and what she has built.

● The expression on her face that 'looks serious but not unhappy', which leads you to think that she was concentrating on her building. Until young children can tell you how they feel, you can only go by what their body language may be saying.

● The fact that Leila kept looking towards the door, and then left the blocks as soon as Ian, her key person, entered. Leila seized Ian's hand and went with him out into the garden.

● You wonder then if Leila feels less at ease when Ian is out of sight. Does Ian reassure Leila that he will be back soon and should he reassure Leila?

Even if you know a child very well, you are still making a considered guess. Look at the visual of the iceberg on page 63. The discussion in that section is about adults; consider a child version of the visual. What can you directly observe of children and what is hidden under the surface?

Scenario

Daleside After-School Club

The team at Daleside are working their way through two key issues. One is a rolling problem about expectations from some parents that the club is an extension to the actual school day, with issues about who is responsible for ensuring that children do the homework set by primary schools. The introduction of the Early Years Foundation Stage has also raised worries over how much they are supposed to do in order to fit that framework.

Alicia, the club manager, is keen to involve everyone properly in discussions and to spread helpful information. Her deputy, Ronan, is doing his foundation degree and his current focus is to be reflective about what happens in team meetings. He is pleased to share his ideas with Alicia.

Pause and reflect

What happened on Tuesday when we discussed how to work together with the local nursery classes on what the under-three–fives are learning?

Did I actually give enough space, and friendly silence, for everyone to contribute? Or is it more that I really want to believe I did?

I was left with the impression that Sheila is being judgemental about some parents' expectation that we complete homework with the older children. How much is my irritation caused by the fact that Sheila will insist on generalising from a few instances to making sweeping statements about 'the parents'? Am I missing important points because I am annoyed with how she expresses a real issue?

Comments

1. Ronan is working hard in his RLD to distinguish between his account of what actually happened, his feelings about events and the sense he makes of them. He is experimenting with highlighter pens: red to highlight what he was feeling and green for written comments that are his interpretation, not factual description.
2. What strategy do you use to make this kind of distinction in your RLD?

....

Reflecting on the descriptive account

Reflection about the accuracy of your description, and wondering about possible gaps, can help move you towards a deeper thoughtfulness about what is happening.

- This reflection can take you towards 'What could I do differently?' but it is unwise to rush to 'Next time, I'll . . .'. With this deeper level of reflection, you experience the difference between single-loop and double-loop learning (pages 28–9). If there are sensible changes to make in how you behave, then stepping back to think more deeply about what is happening will support you to make a much better-informed choice over changes.
- Reflection is a process of 'What sense do I make of this event, experience or incident?' When you reflect back on an experience with children, you may ask yourself 'What did I learn from their reactions to our trip to the museum?'
- One question might be 'What was I thinking when . . .?' But reflection is not only about the thoughts that were going through your head. The process is also about emotions. Sometimes what you were feeling during this time will be the most significant aspect for making sense of what you did.
- Maybe you need to check key assumptions and beliefs. Are you assuming that you know the motives or feelings of a colleague who was involved at the time? What makes you sure of this knowledge?

Once you develop the habit of reflection, you begin to be more insightful about yourself, although this self-awareness may bring some level of discomfort. It can be valuable to review several reflective accounts of similar aspects of your practice and consider whether there are any themes in common.

Does this account within your RLD shine a light on to those parts of your practice in which you feel confident?

- What do you consider is the source of that confidence and can you tap that insight to support you in areas of practice in which you feel less sure?
- Are you spending enough time feeling pleased with your skills or understanding in this instance? Enjoy feeling pride in your work.
- Or are you brushing over that part of your reflective account, maybe with 'I should be doing that anyway'?
- Do you tend to spend more time on berating yourself over a reflective account in which you can see significant need for improvement?

Can you identify key themes that enable you to continue to get to know yourself better?

- Are you usually so keen to feel 'I'm doing something' that you risk not gathering enough information?
- Or are you usually so concerned about gaps in your information that you are tempted to keep postponing action 'in case . . .'?
- Perhaps you put together an account from last week of your support for Donna's mother with reflecting on your conversation today with Wendy, a member of your team. You realise that you are prone to assuming that what you believe to be happening is the whole story, and that can stop you asking open-ended questions and listening to the answers.
- A recent event has made you reflect on whether you do not allow enough for different perspectives on the same event.
- Alternatively, you may begin to speculate on whether you are so committed to finding out how other people view a past event or future plan that you can lose sight of your own perspective.

The point of reflection on your diary account is to evaluate what may be recurring themes – in what you do or do not do. It is easy for some choices to become habitual; you no longer think about an action as a choice.

- You can home in on elements in your diary of 'I always' or 'I hardly ever . . .' and reflect on your reasons.
- The result of that thinking is not always that you change that choice. Perhaps it is a sound strategy that a manager starts each day by going into each room in the nursery and greeting adults and children.

A reflective approach is open-ended; you do not assume quickly that you have explored all the possibilities. You are ready to approach an account from another angle and to revise your first ideas. Students using an RLD within a degree programme course of study are also likely to be expected to make connections with theoretical perspectives discussed within the programme.

Take another **perspective**

You can learn from reflection on a past event, gaining practical insights about your assumptions, what you could do differently next time or how you could stop yourself from making less-wise choices in behaviour.

Reflection has gone awry if it becomes a regular habit of fault finding, in either yourself or someone with whom you are working. It is also deeply unhelpful if you slide into blaming yourself for the kind of person you are. The point about reflection is that it enables you to be more honest with yourself:

- 'I do find it hard to let go of a plan when I have already put a lot of thought into it'; or
- 'Probably I will always struggle to put my alternative point of view, when a colleague is very forthright about their views.'

The point is that you work to accept yourself as you are. Change what can realistically be changed; improve yourself in ways that work with your strengths. Learn to accept what cannot be altered and do your level best to continue to like yourself. There is a strong connection here with taking a responsible and positive approach to guiding children's behaviour.

A key theme in interaction with children is that you keep their behaviour separate from them as a person. You help them to understand that you are annoyed or frustrated about what they did. Be equally kind to yourself: be irritated or disappointed over what you did, but avoid disliking yourself.

Making sense of the behaviour of other people

Inevitably some of your reflection will be about what other people have done and their reactions. Wise reflection about others has to allow that all you can directly observe is what they say and do: their visible and audible behaviour. Everything else is hidden from your direct observation. This reality about interpersonal communication has been visually represented by the iceberg image, as shown in Figure 3.2. This image has been used in different contexts for at least three decades. It is not at all clear who first developed the idea.

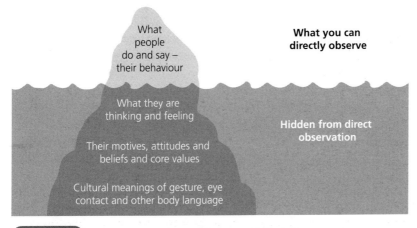

Figure 3.2 Behaviour as the visible part of the iceberg

The application to behaviour here is a useful reminder that:

- Even with people you know well, it can be a risky business to make firm statements about what the other person is thinking, but has not said out loud, or what he or she is feeling.
- The hidden parts may emerge in response to direct invitations to tell: 'What do you think about . . .?' or 'How are you feeling about . . .?'
- Body language, including facial expression and gesture, is a visible part of behaviour, so can be directly observed. The issues arise over how you interpret that visual message.
- Personal differences in body language are overlaid by family experience, which in turn is influenced by broad social and cultural traditions about appropriate behaviour – for anybody – and possible differences between individuals on the basis of gender.
- Beliefs, values and motivations can emerge as individuals feel able to express their personal stance or 'what really matters to me'. However, some core beliefs may be less than obvious – see the idea of nested theories discussed on page 29.
- It is just as important for you to realise that other people cannot know your hidden part of the iceberg unless you express it.

Scenario

Daleside After-School Club

Ronan has become frustrated by Katya's silence in the last two team meetings. He realises it often helps to ask yourself questions about any description, but especially when you are sharpening your awareness of the difference between events and the sense you make of them. Ronan considers:

- I have just written the sentence, 'Katya doesn't want to contribute.' But I do not know that 'not wanting' is the reason, or the only reason, for Katya's silence.
- I do not know what Katya is thinking or feeling about this whole business of how we fit into the EYFS documentation. I only know that today, like last time, I cannot recall anything that Katya said out loud.
- I am beginning to believe that Katya is worried and unable to express her concern. But, now I recall, she frowns that way sometimes when she is concentrating.
- I cannot know what is in Katya's head, unless I ask.

What might Ronan do? On his own initiative or in discussion with Alicia, the club leader?

Pause and reflect

Katya is not directly involved in reflective practice. If she were, then perhaps she might reflect along the lines of 'What did I think about in that meeting, yet not say?' 'What did I want to say, but didn't?' 'What got in my way?' Katya might think that her colleagues were quick with their ideas, and she feels intimidated by Sheila's forthright manner. But maybe Katya is honest with herself: that if she has not spoken

REFLECTIVE PRACTICE AND EARLY YEARS PROFESSIONALISM

by about halfway through a staff meeting, then she loses the motivation to try. 'Are they stopping me, or am I stopping myself? Has this now become a habit that I just accept?'

The process of learning

The point of developing the outlook and skills of reflective practice is to become a more active and aware learner throughout adulthood. Two broad theoretical perspectives offer further support to this aim: the concept of a cycle of learning with related differences in personal style, and the concept of stages of competence in the process of learning.

Cycles of learning through reflection

Working from the 1970s, Kolb (1984) developed a model that shows the process of experiential learning, presented as a cycle, shown in Figure 3.3.

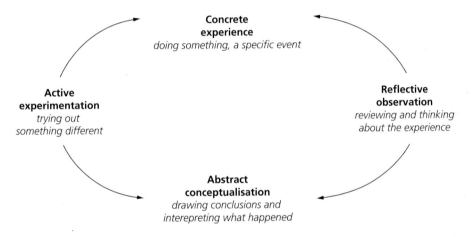

Figure 3.3 David Kolb's basic learning cycle

Kolb's model describes an active process of learning that is in sharp contrast to a pattern in which more knowledgeable or experienced people pass on information to others or direct them what to do. This approach, sometimes called a transmission model, places learners in a passive role until they are sufficiently equipped to start telling other people what to know or do. (Look back also at Knowles's concept of andragogy, on page 15). The underlying principle of promoting experiential learning is that what is learned is then more secure. The basic idea is sometimes traced back to what was allegedly said by the philosopher, Confucius, in China around 450 BCE: 'Tell me and I will forget. Show me and I may remember. Involve me and I will understand.' The four parts of the learning cycle include:

1. *Concrete experience*: you do something specific, are part of an event, or someone more experienced in this area shares a key idea or important technique with you. This experience could be an event such as a training day, but could also be something significant within the daily flow of your practice.

2. *Reflective observation*: you take some time or are given the specific opportunity to review what has happened or what you have done. In some circumstances, this part of the cycle could be relatively brief; on other occasions, it may be longer and more complex. Here is where you apply skills of critical thinking (page 44) and other thinking tools that enable you to step back from the experience.

3. *Abstract conceptualisation or conceptualising*: on the basis of that reflection, you reach some ideas about what you have learned, which could be a continuing process relevant to this skill. These concepts, what you have drawn out of the experience, should help you to apply what you have learned to a different, but relevant, situation. A grasp of the underlying concepts should help you to make an appropriate adjustment to the details of a new situation, rather than imposing a one-size-fits-all template. You may also weave in theoretical perspectives or useful concepts that you have learned on other occasions, and which are appropriate here. Your concepts may lead to specific plans on the basis of your new insights.

4. *Active experimentation*: you put into action your plan of what you could do, or do differently, on the basis of what you have learned. You actually try something. Sensible practice is to try a new approach for a reasonable amount of time before final review. However, you then have direct experience of this new approach or applying knowledge and the cycle continues.

Figure 3.4 Young children learn through first-hand experiences

David Kolb, often writing with Roger Fry, presents the model as a cycle in which you can conceivably start at any point. It is important that people pass through the different stages, so that they are aware of these different aspects to full, active learning. When you are progressing within a specific area of skill or knowledge, your later learning rests upon the earlier. In this situation, the image of the cycle can be more like a spiral of linked circles as your learning goes deeper. In developing his model, Kolb acknowledged the ideas of John Dewey, Kurt Lewin and also Jean Piaget, all of whom in different ways focused on an active process of learning from direct experiences.

However, Kolb also became interested in individual differences and the existence of personal learning styles that reflected preferences between the four broad parts of his model. David Kolb worked with a short questionnaire that aimed to identify the four types or inclinations, each of which combined two of the four parts of the cycle. This typology was criticised on the grounds that the brevity of the questionnaire did not give a sound basis for assigning anyone to the four types. Additionally, the information was derived from people's own self-reports, with no independent evidence to support the claim that they did, or did not, behave in that way.

During the 1970s, Peter Honey and Alan Mumford (Honey, 2006) developed a longer questionnaire and the ideas were applied across a wide range of organisations, with the aim of improving the details of individual CPD plans. Honey and Mumford identified four types of learning styles, which link relatively loosely to each of the four parts of the model: Activists, Reflectors, Theorists and Pragmatists. This typology and the questionnaire are generally viewed as having a more secure basis than David Kolb's analysis.

For every keen supporter of a focus on learning styles you are likely to find someone who advises caution. There is not the support for an unquestioning acceptance of the model, nor a justification for using the typology to place oneself or others in a closed category. A general criticism of the cycle as a whole is that it is not an accurate portrayal of how people actually learn. However, the usefulness of the model is probably more in terms of aspirations: that the full cycle is likely to be a more effective way of learning. The model has mainly been applied to the world of work in countries such as the UK and USA, so there is very limited acknowledgement of the likely impact of cultural context. I agree with caution, alongside finding the model and implications useful for raising issues around the process of learning and reflective practice in work with children.

Be aware of the process of learning

An advantage of the model for early years and related professions is the emphasis on first-hand experience being something that happens to you. There is a direct connection with the importance of enabling children to relish first-hand experiences, indeed literally ones they can get their hands onto, rather than events that have been pre-packaged by adults (Rich et al., 2005 and 2008; Lindon, 2010a). The need for direct experience on which children are able to act, make choices and experiment is also highlighted by Gopnik (2009) with reference to how their brains develop throughout early childhood.

A drawback is that discussion of this learning cycle is usually tipped towards the rational, to cognitive processes; there is limited acknowledgement of emotional content. Feelings can play a significant part in the learning process, as both a supporting and an undermining factor. There is no reason why one cannot use the reflective and conceptualising parts of the cycle to create a fuller picture of learning. It just does not seem to happen in much of the relevant literature about the cycle or learning styles.

Wise application of the model of experiential learning definitely does not exclude sharing important information or techniques with less experienced others. However, it places that passing over of accumulated wisdom within the context of enabling others to be genuinely active and integrate new learning into what they already know. With adults, as with children, there are times when experiential learning needs some informed input. Otherwise you can emerge very frustrated: someone could have given you a timely hint, yet left you to spend precious time finding out the long and hard way. There are also experiences in which clear direction about safe technique or unexpected risks have to be part of any responsible guidance from a more experienced person.

Awareness of individual differences

You can sidestep the arguments around methodology in order to reflect on possible differences in a practical way. Look again at the model (page 65) and think about yourself and people you know well. Be honest: are you more comfortable with one aspect of the cycle than another? The more general idea about learning styles is that individual adults will have a preferred part of the cyclical model.

- Some people, for instance, prefer to be active in doing something, but are progressively out of their comfort zone when invited, or pressed, to reflect on what had happened.
- Others are keen to reflect on experiences but less enthusiastic about moving on from the fruits of reflection. Perhaps they also feel that there is always something else to consider and it is risky to proceed without this complete picture.
- Other people, in contrast, are content to draw out and build on abstract ideas, yet are considerably less at ease when invited to make some definite plans on the basis of those concepts.
- Yet other individuals are so happy to try out new ideas and strategies that they devote much less time to learning from a given approach. Maybe they find it hard to stop tweaking aspects to practice.

You may already recognise yourself, or colleagues, in the brief descriptions above.

There is no style that is absolutely better than the others. However, there can be styles that are a better fit for particular jobs and professional endeavours.

REFLECTIVE PRACTICE AND EARLY YEARS PROFESSIONALISM

Certainly, early years practitioners need to be at ease with practical action and not so keen on reflection that important to-do decisions are forever postponed 'until we've thought about . . .'.

Another practical aspect of learning styles is about what happens within a group of people who need to work together. An early years team needs a mix of styles, of individual strengths within the cycle.

- What could happen within a nursery team if the majority of the group were most comfortable with either 'getting on with the job' or 'trying out new activities'? Maybe team meetings would be very practical and people would be busy.
- But perhaps the team would in the end wonder why all their parent-involvement initiatives did not seem to bring more of a sense of partnership with families. They have not woven in that it takes at least two sides to form a partnership and asked 'What is the perspective of the parents in this case?'
- In contrast, what could happen if most of the team – or the most outspoken practitioners – were very enthusiastic about reflecting on 'what we are really doing here' or 'the deeper meaning of this disagreement'?
- The team may have detailed discussions, some of which are positive for their practice as a whole. But in the meantime, no progress has been made on visual improvement of the outdoor space as a welcoming learning environment.

Equally important, the team as a whole needs to respect different contributions. In either of these imaginary settings, the lone voices – those out of step with their colleagues' preferred style – might be given anything from a mild to a very hard time.

- In the first setting, the lone voice speaks up with 'Can we at least talk a bit about what partnership actually means?' She is met with 'We're not writing an essay. The inspector wants to see evidence of partnership. We have to do something.'
- In the second setting the lone voice offers: 'I've done a rough plan of how we could improve the area in the garden that's full of weeds.' He is met with amused looks and a rather patronising 'Another of your little sketches?'

Either of these teams will be less effective and their practice will be weakened, because they sideline the team member with the less favoured style. An important perspective is lost with the dismissal of that member's contribution.

Links with other concepts

Argyris and Schön (1974) developed the concept of single-loop and double-loop learning (pages 28–9). This model is sometimes presented as adding another layer to Kolb's cycle. The four-part cycle is seen as single-loop learning, because it is assumed that, in the standard model, any assumptions and values – Schön and Argyris's concept of governing variables – are taken for granted. The double-loop learning includes an extra mental step back and consideration. This cognitive activity leads to reconsidering, reconnecting and reframing the key questions.

The cycle of learning is sometimes discussed as a single-loop process. However, there seems to be no inbuilt reason why the reflection and conceptualising stages should not include deeper thought about underlying principles. The cycle could then be better presented visually as a spiral. The learning cycle is not only about doing something different within the active experimentation stage; it is also about your reasons for making this change. The abstract conceptualisation stage can include a re-evaluation of what and why, relevant to this event or aspect of practice. In the end, the test of any conceptual model, like the learning cycle, is whether you find it useful as a tool for practical thinking about your process of learning.

In terms of the ideas of Schön (1983, 1987), the learning cycle of David Kolb is much more of reflection-on-action (look back at page 38). A swift progress round the four parts of the cycle could possibly be fitted into reflection-in-action, but it is not a good fit, especially for the usual timescale for practitioners responsible for children.

Stages of competence in learning

Another practical model focuses on the stages of competence as an individual becomes more adept at a given skill or area of knowledge. The four stages of competence model has been used in psychology and related applied fields since at least the 1970s. It is not certain who originally developed it. However, the Gordon Training International organisation in the USA says that one of their team developed the key ideas, applied initially to the teaching profession. Certainly this organisation has been active in promoting the concepts and practical uses. Other theorists and consultants have worked on the ideas and wording.

The four stages are: unconscious incompetence, conscious incompetence, conscious competence and unconscious competence. The process of learning is that on any new area of skill or knowledge a learner will spend at least some time at each stage. There are practical implications from the model for self-awareness of your own learning and also for gaining practical insights into your role when you are responsible for supporting someone else to learn (page 151). My way of expressing this model is given below and, compared with some writers, I build in a greater role for feelings alongside the cognitive process and for individual differences.

Unconscious incompetence

This is the stage of blissful ignorance: you are unaware that you do not know about this area. Even the most knowledgeable or experienced of adults will have remaining areas of potential learning for which the door is shut. In many cases, this lack of knowledge or skill may not be a problem; nobody needs to know everything.

Sometimes, the door of possible learning may open a fraction and an individual makes a more conscious choice that they do not want to learn in this area. However, sometimes in professional life it becomes clear that the door is going to have to open. This beginning may trigger feelings of excitement, but the emotion may be more of unease or a wish to find any way out of the inevitable task of learning. There may be an attempt at resistance with arguments that learning this skill or area of knowledge is a waste of time and not genuinely relevant to the job.

The wording used with this level and the next stage causes difficulties for some people, who object to being called 'incompetent' under any circumstances. Alternative suggestions have been to talk about being 'unaware' or 'ignorant' or 'unmotivated to learn'. In discussing the ideas of the model, you could bring in these alternatives without relabelling everything.

Conscious incompetence

At this stage learners are only too aware of what they do not know, struggle to understand or wonder if they will ever be able to do. They recognise the gap in their competence and begin to address it, but may have a more difficult learning journey than necessary if they are without suitable help. Individual differences can be seen here. Some individuals may be more tolerant of the struggle and confusion. Others may give up, or attempt to give up, before there is any realistic chance that they could experience some improvement.

Previous experiences of learning will be a factor in how resilient someone feels during this stage. Can they access supportive memories of previous learning and think positively? Helpful self-talk could include 'This stage is uncomfortable. I will make mistakes or forget key information. But I'm not stupid; I just don't know much about this. I will improve.' Negative self-talk may be 'This is horrible. I keep making mistakes. I'll never understand what I'm supposed to do. I feel stupid. How can I get out of this?'

For adults, as well as for children, continued experiences of struggle, without suitable help, can mean that tactics for escape and excuse become their main strategy. A sense of learned helplessness can become the strongest feeling (Lindon, 2012a) and this outlook undermines further learning. However, with support and constructive feedback (more on page 143) individuals can develop an outlook of mastery that aims for unravelling confusion and realising that practice is necessary to improve. A positive outlook also includes the expectation that more knowledgeable and experienced people should help.

Conscious competence

With appropriate support, handy hints and focused practice you steadily improve. You no longer need active help and that feeling of being utterly confused has faded. However, you have to keep your mind on what you are doing or what your next step is. Maybe you have strategies that help you to focus, such as talking out loud or a low-level mutter. Maybe you make notes. Whatever helps you, the situation is that you have to concentrate and not let your mind wander, or try to do something else in parallel. You feel more comfortable, more able and you can envisage the time when this skill or area of knowledge will be fully part of you.

Unconscious competence

You are so adept at this skill that you do not have to think 'What do I do next?' You can talk at the same time, or perhaps let yourself daydream. Occasionally, it occurs to you that perhaps you should keep your mind on this task in a more active way. For instance, once you are a very competent driver, you may travel a familiar route and, looking back, cannot recall the detail. Would you, and other drivers or pedestrians, still have been safe if something out of the ordinary had happened?

Making sense of this area of knowledge seems like second nature, as if you have always known this information and meaningful connections. This stage can feel very satisfying. However, if you remain in this state of mind, then it is unlikely that you will be able to share the skill or knowledge with someone else. It is tempting to say that a skill is 'obvious' or 'easy'. However, that is only the case because you have had sufficient practice, or have now forgotten what it was like not to be so clear about this area of knowledge. Even individuals who are sensitive to the feelings of others may genuinely struggle to be clear in explaining or demonstrating something that is now automatic to them.

Figure 3.5 Sometimes you need to explain your judgement that an experience is worthwhile to children

Helping other people to learn

It is just about impossible to share skills and help people who are less experienced than you unless you make your knowledge and skill level more accessible to yourself and therefore to someone else. My approach in using, and sharing, this model has been to describe the need to recapture the feelings of being at the conscious competence stage for this skill. This process aims to bring back to full awareness the sequence of steps you take in a task. If you have become very adept, and perhaps fast, in carrying out a physical task, it can be necessary to slow down so that the steps once again become clear to you. It is then more possible to explain, show and if necessary break large steps down into finer steps for this process. You will find more on page 151 about the coaching process and helping fellow adults to learn.

Another issue in sharing a skill with other people is the clear message that the impressively competent person was not always at this stage. Even adults or older children who are exceptionally gifted have put in the work. Possibly some people have a flair, a nascent talent that just needed nurturing, but they have not zoomed straight to the level of unconscious competence. Personal stories show that 'prodigies' in chess, music, tennis, maths or any other area have spent significant amounts of time in focused and repetitious practice.

This concept of improvement through practice is important within the early years workforce for the adults within any team, as part of their lifelong learning. However, the opportunity should not be lost to show a role model of continuous learning day by day to the children. They have a considerable learning journey ahead of them. They need to learn within an emotionally safe environment that 'having a go' and practice definitely make your skill level 'better', although not necessarily 'perfect'.

Scenario

Meerkats Day Nursery

Shoshana is close to attaining her Early Years Professional Status. Becky and Joe, owner/managers of the nursery, have been keen for Shoshana to share ideas with the team within meetings. Last month Shoshana explained the stages of the competence learning model. Becky has been provoked to think about individual staff, as well as herself, and how tempting it is to stay inside your personal comfort zone.

The team is planning the programme for their summer family fun day, which has been a great success in previous years. Last year, Joe and some of the older siblings started an impromptu dance session. He suggests that maybe they could organise something this year such as simple, beginner line dances. Immediately, there is a mental shuffling in the team and Corinne announces, 'You'll do a wonderful job. I'll organise the face painting.' Then Alastair adds, 'Joe, you're a natural-born dancer. I've got two left feet.' Becky comes to a swift decision and says, 'Me too, Alastair. But this time we are all going to have a go. We'll practise with the children here. It's important for them to see that we can learn something new.'

Questions

1. This may seem like a minor issue, but what can be the consequence if practitioners are always allowed to stay within their comfort zone?

2. Can you recall examples of when children saw you learn something new or struggle with a skill that did not come easily? What do you think they learned from that experience?

A fifth stage to the model?

There has been a lot of discussion within consultancy and teaching about how to deal with the dilemma around unconscious competence and sharing skills. Chapman (2009) brings together a wide spectrum of ideas – do look at this online resource (details on page 75). Some contributors resist any sense of return to the level of conscious competence, seeing it as dropping a level, somehow regressing. In fact, the stages of competence are not a hierarchical model with associated higher status for the later stages. Adult learning continues to cycle through the stages; they are not better or worse.

Suggestions reported by Chapman include a fifth stage to the competence model. The possible ideas focus on a heightened sense of awareness of a skill or area of knowledge, so that the person is alert to how that skill may be passed on to someone who is at an earlier stage. Suggestions for what to call this fifth stage include reflective competence (David Baume), enlightened competence (Lorgene Mata), and chosen conscious competence (Andrew Dyckhoff). In the same resource Will Taylor offers a model to incorporate this stage, which also captures the cyclical nature of learning. I found this alternative the most workable and, following the invitation offered on the website, have taken Taylor's model and made my own modifications.

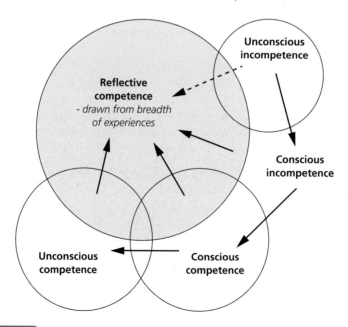

Figure 3.6 The continuing process of reflective competence from the ideas of Will Taylor

REFLECTIVE PRACTICE AND EARLY YEARS PROFESSIONALISM

The advantage of Will Taylor's model is that it represents a continuing process of learning and avoids the (wrong) impression that the four stages of competence are a closed, hierarchical model. The alternative visual image shows continued learning for individuals who have gathered some experience, perhaps a great deal. I have added my own ideas to the description here.

The central circle gives prominence to reflective competence: an ability to consider what you know and understand. There are connections here with the concept of metacognition (page 45). Reflective competence may also be supported by communication with and feedback from other people. This whole process does not have to be a solitary enterprise. In fact, learning is likely to be less full and effective if other people's contributions are unwelcome to the learner. Experiences all support that central store.

Mature and confident learners are characterised by the open recognition that there will always be some areas of which you are ignorant. Will Taylor suggests that the aware, experienced people are comfortable to revisit the accessible areas of their personal area of unconscious competence. I think that reflective competence is, in time, also fed by at least some level of awareness of one's own area of unconscious incompetence. For that reason I have added the dotted line into the central circle. Mature learners experience a regular rediscovery of what is called 'beginner's mind' as you face your areas of ignorance, recognise that you have made errors based on misunderstandings and avoid being complacent.

Adults who embrace the idea of lifelong learning realise that there will be a stage of at least mild discomfort as they tackle a new area. They may even have insights into how they personally react within this stage. Perhaps you know that you get annoyed with your own incompetence and also that this emotion is not helpful. So, perhaps it is better to show the same patience and kindliness to yourself that you offer to others whom you are helping.

Resources

- Amulya, J. (undated) *What is Reflective Practice?* The Center for Reflective Community Practice, Massachusetts Institute of Technology. **www.itslifejimbutnotasweknowit.org.uk/files/whatisreflectivepractice.pdf**
- Argyris, C. and Schön, D. (1974) *Theory in Practice.* San Francisco: Jossey-Bass.
- Chapman, A. (2009) *Conscious Competence Learning Model.* **www.businessballs.com/consciouscompetencelearningmodel.htm**
- Drummond, M.J. (1996) 'Teachers Asking Questions'. *Education 3-13*, volume 24, no 3, 8–17.
- Gopnik, A. (2009) *The Philosophical Baby: What Children's Minds Tell Us About Truth, Love and the Meaning of Life.* London: Bodley Head. Also a conversational feature on **www.edge.org/3rd_culture/gopnik09/gopnik09_index.html**

- Honey, P. (2006) *The Learning Styles Questionnaire.* **www.peterhoney.com/ documents/Learning-Styles-Questionnaire-80-item_QuickPeek.pdf**
- Kolb, D. (1984) *Experiential Learning: Experience as the Source of Learning and Development.* New Jersey: Prentice Hall.
- Lindon, J. (2009) *Parents as Partners.* London: Practical Pre-School Books.
- Lindon, J. (2010a) *Child-Initiated Learning.* London: Practical Pre-School Books.
- Lindon, J. (2012a, third edition) *Understanding Child Development: 0–8 Years.* London: Hodder Education.
- Miller, S. and Sambell, K. (eds) (2003) *Contemporary Issues in Childhood: Approaches to Teaching and Learning,* Newcastle upon Tyne: Northumbria University Press.
- Moon, J. (2003) *Learning Journals and Logs, Reflective Diaries.* Dublin: Centre for Teaching and Learning, University College Dublin. **www.ucd.ie/t4cms/ ucdtla0035.pdf**
- Rich, D., Casanova, D., Dixon, A., Drummond, M.J., Durrant, A. and Myer, C. (2005) *First Hand Experience: What Matters to Children.* Clopton: Rich Learning Opportunities. **www.richlearningopportunities.co.uk**
- Rich, D., Drummond, M.J. and Myer, C. (2008) *Learning: What Matters to Children.* Clopton: Rich Learning Opportunities.
- Schön, D. (1983) *The Reflective Practitioner: How Professionals Think in Action,* London: Routledge.
- Schön, D. (1987) *Educating the Reflective Practitioner: Towards a New Design for Teaching and Learning in the Professions.* San Francisco: Jossey-Bass.

The reflective practitioner in action

This chapter focuses on personal exploration and learning, along with practical approaches to how reflection can be encouraged. Many of these ideas are equally useful for sharing with colleagues and other ideas are discussed for shared reflection within a team or working group.

The main sections of this chapter are:
- Tools for reflection
- Critical thinking as a reflective team.

Tools for reflection

Reflective practice is both a personal and a shared enterprise. It is personal because you cannot be a reflective and actively thoughtful practitioner if this process is completely dependent on the presence of another fellow adult. The support of other people can be invaluable for encouraging any professionals to be self-aware, as well as for sharing good ideas for provoking and extending reflection. However, reflective practitioners need to operate in this way because they are convinced and confident of the value of thoughtfulness and not because somebody says to them 'Think about what you do!'

Reflection in context

The practical ideas in this section all revolve around information processing and decision making. By this comment I mean that:
- Reflective practitioners are thoughtful and active learners, ready to consider 'What information do I have?' 'Is that enough?' or 'Do I need to find out more?'
- Practitioners are aware that they are making a decision, choosing between alternatives and consider 'Where does this information lead me?' or 'I've done it this way, but is there another or better choice to make here?'

The whole process is mentally active and individuals experience the shifts of perspective that come with being an active learner. However, that phrase itself sometimes needs further descriptive explanation.

Active learning

Farmer (2009) drew from his training experience to point out that, in reference to children, some practitioners define 'active learning' as physically active: learning while and from being on the move and outdoors. A limited working definition applied to children can also mean that practitioners do not apply the full meaning of 'active learning' to themselves.

As Farmer explains, it is accurate to say that active learning can be physical and can be supported by direct involvement in experiences. It is certainly important that no practitioner defines learning as something that children only, or mainly, do when they are sitting nicely and listening to an adult talk. Yet for children, as for adults, active learning is emotional and intellectual, as well as sometimes active in the physical sense, including 'Can I get my hands on it?' The Early Years Foundation Stage, along with other guidance documents around the UK, places a significant emphasis on providing generous opportunities that offer active learning for young children. It is possible to approach this focus also from the perspective of information processing and decision making.

When young children have opportunities for active learning, they are able to extend their own basis of information, driven by what interests them today or over this week. They discover what works, what else they want to know and the questions they want to ask. Children also have many opportunities to consider genuine choices and to reach decisions about what, when or how. They have the support of familiar practitioners who help them to think out loud and to voice those options. Those adults are also honest and do not offer pretend choices in which the adult has really already decided and is therefore committed to talking children around to what is going to happen anyway.

For children, as for adults, the process of active learning stands in contrast to passive learning, when individuals wait for information and direction from someone else. Children, or adults for that matter, may be given limited options other than to be a passive learner and habits can then be formed of 'I wait till somebody shows me what to do' and 'Why isn't anyone telling me what to do?'

The reasoning process and learning

Practical tools to encourage and help thinking are divided roughly by whether they use an inductive or a deductive approach. Both approaches are suitable at different times; one is not 'better' than the other. However, adult reflection is fuller when practitioners feel confident to use both kinds of reasoning.

- Inductive reasoning works with what you already know or have experienced and moves towards conclusions, decisions or plans based on this foundation. Tools for thinking that help to lay out information and make thinking visible tend to work in this way. You organise the information you have, maybe see the gaps and spot new connections.
- Deductive reasoning starts from a principle or core value – and idea – and the hard thinking work is to consider 'Where does that take me (or us)?' The aim is to avoid being limited by 'What we do at the moment' and to provoke a fresh rethink. The shift from single-loop thinking into double-loop (pages 28–9) can reset a train of thought or group discussion and set you off in a very different direction. This kind of thinking can be done alone, but it is often provoked and supported in the company of fellow professionals.

Scenario

Meerkats Day Nursery

The team of Meerkats Day Nursery have benefited from the ideas that Shoshana has brought back as she has progressed towards her Early Years Professional Status. The discussions have not always been easy but, supported by owner/managers Becky and Joe, Shoshana has been able to support much more of a 'stop and think' outlook in the whole team.

For some years, forward planning at Meerkats was led through broad topics for the over-threes. A set of topic resource folders, created by Corinne, the deputy, were the starting point of planning. The staff in the three–fives room were familiar with using a spider diagram format to weave in new ideas for activities. The format has become more responsive to the interests of the current group of children than was previously the pattern.

In the most recent team meeting, Siobhan explains a recent development. James and Danny, four-year-old twins, had arrived in the nursery on Monday morning with news of how they had been on 'the train that goes under water', during a long-weekend family trip to Paris using the Channel Tunnel. Conversation had flowed with questions, and some incredulity, from other children, about how any train could 'go under the water' and what a 'chunnel' was. Siobhan had no doubt that this now shared interest should be encouraged to grow. But what about the existing plans for the coming week and was this yet another spider diagram that would end up as scrap paper?

Pause and reflect

Shoshana linked back this discussion to the team's exploration a few weeks ago around 'We need to be sure that a topic is the best way to support an area of children's learning' and 'We should question if this is a good time for children to explore an avenue that we have pre-planned.' Further discussion is not only linked into developing the open-ended documentation of children's personal learning journey, but also considers whether a shared 'research board' or 'Our Big Question this week' should now be implemented.

Questions

1. It takes time to change ways of working, and teams need good reasons for adjusting patterns that have seemed to work well. What do you think is important for continued change in Meerkats Day Nursery?

2. What do you think should be a next step for Shoshana and for Siobhan?

3. Should anyone check how Corinne feels, since she invested time and energy in a resource that now looks redundant?

What does it mean?

Active learning: a process, for children as well as adults, when individuals engage in thinking about what they know and how they can extend their understanding.

Inductive reasoning: working from experiences and known information to reach the underlying idea or principle.

Deductive reasoning: working from an idea, principle or theoretical perspective in order to reach a supported understanding of what should happen.

'Telling' the story

One way of bringing out the story of practice with young children is through the reflective diary approach described in Chapter 3. Another approach is to read accounts of sustained involvement of children in an enterprise that intrigued them. For instance, Marsden and Woodbridge (2005) describe how a reception-class teacher and four children developed and tested a range of maths games. An additional example is provided below.

An informal approach can be for another person, perhaps a colleague, to invite you to describe events in words and then reflect on what can be learned. The invitation may be 'Please talk me through how you decided to . . .' or 'Can you explain to me your reasons for . . .'. Once practitioners feel at ease with reflecting on their practice, they may need minimal encouragement to restart the process. However, it takes time to develop the habits of reflections and starter questions can be central to building that useful experience. The next section describes one set of questions that has worked well, as a guide to bringing out the narrative of what has been observed.

Pause for reflection

Best Practice Network has collected examples of early years professionals' reflection on aspects of their practice. Some accounts have been published in *Early Years Educator* magazine. For example, Godfrey (2009) offers the reflective account that was provoked by a four-year-old who very firmly stated, 'Worms turn into butterflies, you know.'

Godfrey was surprised by this young child's conviction, but made the swift decision not to disagree out loud. She asked two questions: 'Are you sure about that?' and 'What else do you know about butterflies?' All the children close by were keen to talk and it was clear that they knew a lot about the life cycle of the butterfly. They were, however, uncertain about what happened to worms. The four-year-old who started the lively conversation remained convinced on that day that worms definitely did turn into butterflies. The conversation lasted until the children's interest moved elsewhere.

Godfrey documents her reflection-in-action – thinking whilst surrounded by the children – but she also shares her reflection-on-action, her thinking after the event and talking with her colleagues in the nursery. She considers that maybe there is scope for more discussion and exploration around the concept that some creatures do not change dramatically; for them, growing up just means getting bigger, yet looking much the same.

Comments

1. Access the article online (details on page 104) and use this account made by a thoughtful practitioner to further your understanding of reflection. The example would also support discussion within your own team or network.
2. Think about how this example demonstrates the power of sharing a narrative: all that followed from a confident, although factually inaccurate, statement from a four-year-old.

Figure 4.1 An enjoyable experience for children will provide adults with food for thought

Simple questions – complex answers

This section is all about asking 'awkward' questions: posing and listening to questions that put you usefully on the spot and give a handy push away from complacency. It is not about being awkward for the sake of it, or being argumentative. Thinking tools for this kind of reflection are often simple questions, or apparently simple until you start to consider the answers. The most useful sets of questions are often not long and the questions themselves are phrased in a straightforward way. I have used one particular set of questions in this section to highlight key features of the process. The majority of my comments will be relevant, regardless of the exact questions you find to be most helpful.

These questions can support individual reflection, so could be used by practitioners working alone, such as childminders, or by individuals who currently experience very limited joint commitment from fellow practitioners. However, this process of reflection is likely to be fuller when it can include discussion, collaboration and constructive comments from other people.

The first set of reflective questions I encountered was developed by the Open University for a course on Curriculum in Action (1981) and was further described by Mary Jane Drummond within a resource developed by a working group for the Early Childhood Unit of the National Children's Bureau (Drummond, Lally and Pugh, 1989). The materials were developed in work with teachers and focused on experiences in the primary classroom. However, the aim was always that the approach could be used with other professional groups and settings. In a different context, Drummond (2003) wrote that the process of assessment is all about how, day by day, adults observe children's learning, strive to understand it and then put that understanding to good use.

Take another **perspective**

At the time of writing (2011) the set of questions used in this section is 30 years old. This 'historical' resource is a timely reminder that the concept and practice of reflection are not an invention of the 21st century.

The Early Childhood Unit working group was brought together in the late 1980s, out of concern that a prescriptive framework like the newly required National Curriculum could be imposed on early years practice. I was a member of the working group and our aim was to create a resource to support reflection and practical thinking for early years practitioners. The anxiety about an outcomes-driven model proved to be realistic, as successive frameworks for early years, especially in England, directed the attention of practitioners increasingly to adult-determined goals and simplistic forms of 'evidence'.

The wheel has turned once again to focus considerably more on children's experiences, rather than pre-packaged activities. The spotlight is back, or coming back, to observation of what children are actually learning, rather than adult plans and intentions.

This basic process, from the original Open University course, starts with individual practitioners making one or two short observations of children who are busy in their setting. The observation may be made by a practitioner who is not directly involved and is able to watch, listen and note at the time. However, observations may also emerge from direct involvement and, in that case, will most likely be written up as soon as possible after the experience is complete. Any account of an observation is guided by the following questions:

1. What were the children actually doing?

2. What were they learning?

3. How worthwhile was it?

4. What did you (the adult) do?

5. What did you learn?

6. What will you do next?

The process of reflection starts at this point as individual practitioners consider what they have written or are able to discuss with colleagues in a team or group. A next step can be to take each question in turn and look more deeply at actual events with this focus in mind. Another possibility is that two practitioners watch the same event and make independent observations, which they then discuss together.

In the original Open University course there was continued opportunity to explore ideas within the group. In this context, the reflective process moved from description of observed events to critical analysis and to framing further questions. The questions can provoke serious thought when practitioners are willing to go beyond the surface of what has happened. In any formal or informal group there needs to be effective support, maybe firm encouragement, to avoid any tendency to treat the questions lightly. Otherwise, the questions, and other similar sets, risk being used to confirm current practice and resist any change. The adult conviction can be that what practitioners want to believe is happening is the accurate account and right interpretation.

The commentary that follows offers ideas of how reflection can develop practitioners' understanding and lead to insights about current practice. These are possibilities and not a fixed list of further questions that everyone should ask of themselves. However, they should help to extend reflection and be options to keep in mind when you are supporting a colleague in this process of observation plus reflection.

1. What were the children actually doing?

This question is about observation but, for practitioners who are willing to reflect, the situation is not simply that of 'I will look carefully and I will then know exactly what is happening.'

- How open-minded do you manage to be? Do you notice more of what you expect to see and hear? Can you replay the period of observation in your mind – especially if you were directly involved and are writing your notes later? Have you missed anything, or any child who was present?
- Is your attention best caught by examples of what you hoped the children would be doing at this time or in this part of your setting? Can you begin to spot a possible gap between what you intended would happen and how the children actually used the resources? Is this gap something that makes you uneasy and want to tighten up on in your forward planning? Or do you find the gap exciting, in that children are able to engage with the resources and make active decisions themselves? Are you pleased to be surprised?
- Is your answer to this question already anticipating the answers to other questions in the set? Are you tempted to think, if not to write, 'The children are not doing much'? In discussion with a colleague, are words like 'just' and 'only' hanging over an observational account?
- Have the interpretation and evaluation, maybe negative, started alongside the observing?

2. What were the children learning?

If practitioners value certainty, then this question can be an uncomfortable experience. Best practice when working with young children is to avoid making assumptions about what children will learn, or are learning, from a particular experience. In some cases, your expectations may be confirmed about what will engage individual children and in what way they have taken their learning a step or two further.

- You can never be sure what young children are learning within a given experience that you observe. You can reach a supported, very good judgement based on careful watching and listening and then making sense of what you have observed.

- The answer for an adult-initiated experience cannot simply be 'What I wrote down as the intended learning outcome on my planner'. Even with children you know very well, you cannot predict what they will actually seize, mentally and physically, from an experience organised by an adult. Nor can any reflective practitioner depend on a hit list of the perceived learning potential of this resource.

- You may have well-based, reasonable hopes for what familiar children could learn from an experience. You may have set up an open-ended activity on the basis of what you have observed greatly interests them this week. But still, you will not be able to predict what children will learn at the time, nor – just as importantly – what it later becomes clear they did learn. Bear in mind always that young children also learn successfully from their own self-chosen play and conversations.

- The answers have to be reached from different angles, which in turn raises issues around 'What leads me to believe that the children were learning this or in this way?' There is also the key question of 'On what timescale am I working?' when I ask myself what children have learned? Do I allow for the possibility that some children take their time: thinking over an experience and then later showing or sharing in words what they gained?

- A more open-ended, and accurate, approach has to be through 'What might the children have been learning while I was observing?' This leads to another question: 'What makes me think this?' This question circles back to the first question and to how did the children actually behave in their play, their snacktime, the conversation – whatever was the focus of the short observation. Also, how did they look in terms of facial expression and body language?

Scenario

Princes Children's Centre

Harriet, the centre deputy, has supported practitioners to rethink why they make observations of children and how making sense of any observation will depend on the thought that has gone into watching and listening. In her conversation today with Ravinder, Harriet feels that greater understanding is in process.

Ravinder explains how she has been keeping a closer eye on one of her key children. She has been concerned that Kieran 'flits' between activities and was close to interpreting this behaviour as 'poor concentration'. This morning Ravinder observed Kieran at regular intervals and not a single period of time.

In the first part of the morning, Kieran had stood and stared at the Christmas card workshop corner, but there was no 'just' about it. Ravinder noticed that Kieran's eyes were scanning the whole workshop area and he looked long and hard at some of the cards underway. He then walked away from the workshop corner and back to his construction in the block area. Kieran returned half an hour later and organised himself to make three cards using different materials. Kieran then set his productions carefully on the 'work done' shelf. He noticed Ravinder and invited her to look at his work, saying 'D'you want to see my special cards?'

Questions

1. What do you think Kieran was doing – from his perspective?
2. What has he probably learned today?
3. What has Ravinder probably learned?

Scenario

Kerry, Accredited Childminder

Kerry has always been committed to following children's interests and what she has learned during her study for Early Years Professional Status has provided theoretical concepts to support her existing practice. She feels more confident now to consider 'How do I know that?' or 'What leads me to that conclusion?'

Kerry has been adding to the children's learning journey folders and thinks back to what happened this afternoon to support her confident belief that 'Ivan and Rashid were exploring the concept of speed.' Kerry is able to support that summary statement with observational evidence that both Ivan (nearly four years old) and Rashid (nearly five years old) made their cars go at different speeds around the track they had built. Ivan used words like 'fast' and 'really fast – the red car's going to crash!' Rashid made his car go more and more slowly, saying, 'Oh no! Daddy's run out of petrol again! Mummy will say, "I told you so!"'

Pause and reflect

Kerry thinks about the last comment and her insight into how this young child is almost certainly linking actual events into his pretend play. She has built a friendly working relationship with Rashid's parents and is sure that this learning story will be equally fascinating to them.

One child's learning story will often include details about other children, who are their chosen play companions. Practitioners need to reflect on how they write up examples, which could include information about another child or family.

Questions

1. What would have been lost if Kerry had been tempted to overlook and disrespect the play with 'Ivan and Rashid are playing with the cars, yet again. I'll have to get them to do something else'?
2. What do you think Kerry should do, regarding the learning stories for Ivan and Rashid?
3. Have you faced this situation? What kind of details could be inappropriate to put into a learning story, when the description is personal about another child?

3. How worthwhile was it?

As you read through this section, your own questions are almost certainly forming in your mind. Perhaps you look at this third question and already think about not moving too fast towards making a decision.

- What leads you to decide or suggest that what the children were doing was worthwhile? What is the basis for saying that what they learned was valuable? Who judges 'worthwhile', 'worth the time' or 'worth the effort'? Is it adults, children or a combination of both?

- Adult-initiated experiences are often linked at the planning stage with hope for what children will gain from this event or activity. However, there will be unexpected and unpredicted consequences from such an experience.

- Is there a temptation for practitioners to count their learning intentions as more important? So, is an activity regarded as more successful when children's learning has fitted that track? In contrast, is the observer keen to notice, and value, whatever focus of engagement has been chosen by the children?

- Is there a gap between what you expected and what actually happened? These are young children learning within early childhood. Does this gap matter? Is the difference a matter of interest? Or are adults tempted to judge that the children were distracted into play or conversation that was 'irrelevant or lacking purpose'? How can young children possibly be 'off task'?

- Practitioners need to have a good reason to regret that children have learned something other than what was hoped or anticipated. One such good reason would be adults' honesty that their approach to, for example, a planned activity around emergent writing had inadvertently reduced children's motivation to explore this important skill.

- How do the children look: are they intrigued, absorbed, keen to do or find out more? Or do they look bored, waiting to be released from this activity, doing the minimum to satisfy the adult? How worthwhile does this experience appear to be in their eyes?

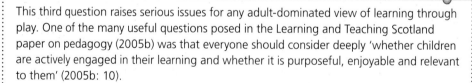

Take another **perspective**

This third question raises serious issues for any adult-dominated view of learning through play. One of the many useful questions posed in the Learning and Teaching Scotland paper on pedagogy (2005b) was that everyone should consider deeply 'whether children are actively engaged in their learning and whether it is purposeful, enjoyable and relevant to them' (2005b: 10).

The Early Years Foundation Stage (for England) has a strong focus on following children's interests. However, the statutory and guidance materials embraced the phrase, 'planned, purposeful play': a choice of words that has sometimes excused a significant amount of pre-packaging of children's experiences in the name of early learning. The question about 'how worthwhile' was the children's play and learning goes to the heart of whose plans, whose purposes within play and who gets to judge that time has been well spent (Lindon, 2001).

4. What did you (the adult) do?

This question starts with a focus on description: the behaviour of the adult in the situation. The question is about what was done and how; but it is also about choices not to say or do something, or the timing of a friendly intervention. The aim of this reflection is to make those choices more transparent and to increase self-awareness. Whether you are reflecting on your own practice, or helping someone else, the aim is not to find faults and list the 'You should have . . .' moments with the benefit of hindsight.

- In some cases, the answer may be that the adult remained at a slight distance and observed. But even then, did the children look up and did you smile or show interest and acknowledgement?
- Are the children interested in the fact that you were observing, or show their interest through questions or imitation then or at a later date?
- Some observations will be made by practitioners who are directly involved in the experience. In that case, the written account includes actions taken at the time which were actually choices. Looking back now, what led to those choices?

5. What did you learn?

Practitioners should learn something from observation and the subsequent reflection. But what is the focus?

- What have you learned about the children? What do you know now, or understand better, because you have taken the time to reflect on what you saw and heard?
- What have you learned about yourself? Have you gained a stronger sense of your tendency to intervene too swiftly in play, or to hold back too long out of fear of being an interfering adult? Or have you, in this instance, realised that you are now comfortable in supporting children to use the conflict-resolution skills that seemed rather awkward to you a few months ago?
- What have you learned about the routines of your setting, about use of time and space, about resources within your learning environment? Have you noticed that the more relaxed lunchtime routine does seem to have created the space for more conversation?
- What have you learned about the gaps in your knowledge and understanding of the children? In your observation, and reflection on the content, did you include what children might be feeling? What emotions did you consider they might be experiencing and how did you judge that?
- To what extent did you explore what was the likely perspective of the children themselves, how they might view the activity, outing or experience? How do you reach a judgement on what they are probably thinking if they do not express their thoughts in words?

6. What will you do next?

This sixth question is both the last in the set and the first in the next cycle of observe, describe, analyse and reflect. The answers to next steps have to be securely based in what you have observed and learned this time.

- Is the focus on what it is that you now judge the children are ready and enthused to explore? What you do may range from providing further resources, working with children to create more space, organising an activity or experience yourself and making it available in an open-ended way.
- If there are next steps for an individual child, then these need to be linked closely to what you have observed. Next steps in terms of resources or experiences should be connected to current interests. It should be easy for another early years practitioner to see the link to items of interest or a child's self-chosen exploration.

Scenarios

Kerry, Accredited Childminder

Kerry looks back on her observation of Ivan and Rashid playing with the cars. She spent most of the time watching and listening. There was a point when it seemed to make sense to get closer and add her comment to their explorations. However, not long after she started to talk with the boys, they asked to get their outdoor shoes and headed for the garden.

Pause and reflect

Kerry realises that she does not know if Ivan and Rashid had come to a natural end in their play. Should she have kept silent? Did she actually interrupt their play? On balance, Kerry thinks that the boys made a genuine choice to go outside. But she will keep an open mind about when and whether to make a verbal contribution to the boys' play. Kerry also considers what could be appropriate next steps in what she makes available for Ivan and Rashid. They may be interested in exploring other ways of experiencing fast and slow. But they may be more motivated to extend their focus on cars, perhaps with a bigger racetrack, and maybe a source of pretend petrol to avoid further breakdowns. Kerry plans that their next local walk will include the petrol station and going into the supermarket on the same site to ask for any spare cardboard boxes. There will be a possibility for Ivan and Rashid to build a garage with a petrol station.

FineStart Nursery

Simone, an early years consultant, is offering medium-term support to FineStart, following a less than favourable inspection report. Currently in the staff group, Theo has been the most responsive to reflection on how the adults choose to behave. This week he describes two examples, which highlight for him good reasons for being thoughtful.

- Yesterday Theo judged there was a rolling choice point about whether he should make a suggestion to extend Sukey's play in the water tray. She was playing alongside Grace and initially there seemed to be no social interaction. However, Theo decided to hold back from saying anything. On reflection he thinks that his choice not to intervene in any way meant that he actually noticed how Sukey was glancing across at Grace. After a few minutes, Sukey began to pile up her boat with pebbles just as Grace had been doing.
- Theo has also reflected back on the argument that broke out last week between Alfie and Ruby. He considers his choice points again. Overall, Theo feels satisfied that he made

the right choice to wait and see if the two children could sort out their disagreement about stocking their pretend shop. He moved closer when their voices started to rise and Alfie began to look very unhappy. Theo is concerned that perhaps he left his friendly support a bit too late.

Questions

1. What have Kerry or Theo probably learned about their own interaction with children and the individual children themselves?

2. Sometimes practitioners can become over-concerned about making the right choice every time, when the best option may only appear 'obvious' with hindsight. If Theo appears anxious 'not to get it wrong', how should Simone support him?

Reflective dialogue and recordings

Practitioners are often daunted about the prospect of being filmed or even sound-recorded. However, so long as the feedback is constructive (see page 143), then a chance to watch yourself on film can provide a step shift in your practice. It is sobering to keep in mind that other people see and hear you in action all the time. You are the only one excluded from this observational knowledge, until you accept the opportunity to watch or listen to yourself. The other approach is through peer observation (see page 187).

Early years settings are busy places and this opportunity, especially filming, is unlikely to be possible unless you have an extra person; this may be as a result of consultancy or because you are involved with a research project.

- It is definitely unwise to organise film or tape recordings unless you can also organise sufficient time to listen to and look at your efforts at least once; ideally more than once.
- You then really need some time to reflect, but not too much time or a long delay, before you look or listen again, with someone by your side.
- After filming, the practitioner who has been recorded should have time to view themselves in private. Then it is appropriate to watch the film again with a view to receiving comments, questions and maybe feedback.
- You watch the recording as an opportunity to comment as the action progresses. The SPEEL team (Moyles et al., 2002) called this process a 'reflective dialogue', which was a blend of commenting and reflecting on the what, how and why of events.

What does it mean?

Reflective dialogue: a commentary on what has happened, or what can be viewed in a filmed sequence, and further thought about what was happening and why.

Learning from being recorded

The aim is that your colleague, or in projects a member of the research team, supports you in moving on from descriptive comments arising directly from what can be seen and heard in the film.

- They may ask open-ended questions and guide the person who has been recorded towards a well-rounded reflection about strengths in practice and scope for improvement.
- If you are involved in a research project, or your setting has employed a consultant for the purpose of recording, then the researcher or consultant may have a set of open-ended questions to guide discussion.
- Alternatively, the previous set of six questions may work well. The set could be a starting point or raise other questions from within the commentary on each of the key questions (see page 83).
- Have a clear agreement about what happens to the recording. Does the person who was recorded keep the CD or DVD?
- If you are part of a research project, then that team should have explained clearly how they will use and store the recorded materials.

A reflective dialogue needs to be a chance to recognise good practice; the aim is not all about spotting what could have been done better. The best of early years practitioners can find scope for improvement. But that development can be about understanding more clearly the good reasons for behaving in this way with children. The significant opportunity of watching something that has been recorded is that it is possible to point to actual examples, even to rerun a sequence. You can say, 'That's what I mean when I say you follow the children's lead. You acted like a proper customer for Amelia in her pretend café.' You can suggest, 'Here's where you asked Sergio three questions, one after another. He went quiet after that. What do you think happened?'

Take another **perspective**

It is important that practitioners who are filmed are as open to constructive feedback about less positive aspects as much as on what has gone well. Certainly, it is unwise to try to undermine the constructive criticism with 'That doesn't usually happen' or 'I was just so busy at that moment.'

- Think about it. If you are keen to find 'excuses' to undermine comments implying scope for improvement, then any positive comments are vulnerable to the same dismissal. Do you wish to undermine feedback on examples of current good practice with 'That doesn't happen all the time, so it doesn't count'?
- The same point applies to the constructive feedback that is part of the role of a consultant with any kind of provision.

You can understand how this kind of reflection could work by reading the information given in the following three resources: the High/Scope work on conflict resolution (discussed on page 40); the SPEEL project; and the National Children's Bureau resource of *Everyday Stories*.

SPEEL project

Moyles et al. (2002) filmed sequences in early years settings as part of the Study of Pedagogical Effectiveness in Early Learning. The SPEEL team used video recording as a way of bringing pedagogical choices more into the open. The team gave practitioners the chance to choose when they would be filmed, in order to create a recording of about 20 minutes. The aim was that the practitioners could judge what would show their own effective practice.

Each practitioner watched their recording before viewing it again with a member of the research team. Then open-ended questions from the researcher aimed to support individual practitioners to reflect on their own actions, and reasons for these choices: the process of 'reflective dialogue'.

- The SPEEL report describes that many of the practitioners were most comfortable talking about the resources they laid out for children and the activity which they had chosen to have filmed. In conversation with the researcher, practitioners tended to focus on the children's behaviour in the sequence, rather than what they, the adults, were doing.
- The practitioners came from the full range of types of early years provision. Many practitioners did not find it at all easy to articulate choices and get behind their intuitive feel that the approach just seemed to be right.
- Some struggled to explain their grounds for saying that the recorded exchange was effective practice. This was a fair question, since they had been invited to showcase what they judged was best practice. The explanation offered was often along the lines of the answer given by one early years teacher who said, 'How do we know? We just know – we just do' (Moyles et al., 2002: 3).

Figure 4.2 Sometimes you decide to watch; it is not a good time to comment

The researchers' questions highlighted that many practitioners' view of what was their most effective practice included a very directive adult role with the children. One of the practical conclusions of the SPEEL report related to a focus on helping children with 'thinking skills'. The team concluded that many practitioners were sure that they offered the kind of open-ended questioning that would be effective in a friendly challenge to children to think further, or in a different direction. However, many of the recorded examples of adult contribution to the conversation were questions that checked children's understanding of vocabulary or information to which the adult already knew the answer. From practitioners' own reflections, it was clear that some questions were largely predetermined by the adult's planned learning outcomes for this activity.

Pause for reflection

Read the transcripts of two recordings and the reflective dialogue that followed between the practitioner and researcher. Access these in the SPEEL report **www.dcsf.gov.uk/ research/**. Type RB363 into the open search and you reach the summary and full report. Go into the full report and scroll down to pages 80–92.

Ideally, use the material as the focus for discussion with colleagues or fellow students. The point, of course, is to reflect and learn for yourself and not to find fault with these practitioners, who have given permission to share their thinking in this helpful way.

- Consider the six questions, given earlier in this book on page 82, to support reflection on observation. To what extent does the SPEEL reflective dialogue transcript show an exploration in any of these areas?
- What are the gaps and where does the confusion start?
- To what extent do you think that either practitioner has been provoked to rethink her practice (they are both female)?
- What can you take away as learning to apply to your own practice? For instance, both practitioners ask children many questions or make questioning comments. What do you think were the consequences for the children of those adult verbal contributions?

Everyday stories

This resource provides the observational materials gathered in 1996–7 by Elfer and Selleck in a research project for the Early Childhood Unit of the National Children's Bureau. The site, at **www.everydaystories.org.uk**, gives the written observations on 15 young children over a full day in their nursery. You can access the stories of those children, some with an assessment within the original research framework and comments from the practitioners.

The stories are useful for your own reflection, ideally again in combination with the chance to discuss your views with colleagues or fellow students. For instance, you could read the story of Angelina, who was 31 months old.

- How do you think Angelina experienced this day? What were the highlights for her; what were the down points?

- What was the perspective of the practitioners involved in Angelina's day? How do you judge that – from the observation itself and from the commentaries also provided?
- The research team was especially interested to explore practitioners' outlook on attachment. What do you take away from how individual practitioners respond to these questions, or to those about Angelina's personal care needs?
- What other professional issues catch your attention, for instance the different outlooks about how to address links between nursery and the cultural background of a family?
- My attention was caught by the practitioners' outlook on the importance of getting a child younger than three years of age to say 'sorry'. What do you think?

This research was undertaken in the 1990s, but all of the issues raised are as live as ever. Reflective practice about the role of the key person has developed further, supported significantly by this research team (Elfer et al., 2003). The English Early Years Foundation Stage statutory guidance made it a requirement that provision was organised with a key person system. However, many of the practical issues and uncertainties, reflected in these stories, still need to be unpacked and resolved through careful professional dialogue (see also Lindon, 2010b).

Critical thinking as a reflective team

Thoughtful early years practice is both an individual and a group experience. Many of the approaches discussed in terms of individuals, in other sections of this book, are relevant to critical thinking within a group context, such as a team meeting. There is no reason why the approaches discussed in this section could not be useful to individuals or pairs of practitioners supporting each other.

Being heard

A practical issue about discussion within a group can be that contributions from practitioners are uneven. Facilitating a discussion with a group of very quiet practitioners can be as challenging as dealing with a group of individuals who compete vigorously to be heard. Many staff groups are a mixture of more outspoken and less forthcoming individuals. A team will not progress in joint critical thinking if discussion is dominated by only the few, or if a senior practitioner ends up talking to fill a lengthy silence. In a large staff team, or regular network, it may be better to organise a series of smaller subgroups, so that everyone has a realistic chance to be heard. Undoubtedly, the team leader or network facilitator has to bring together the different discussions and issues.

Speaking up in a team or network meeting is a shared responsibility, with obligations for the person who leads or chairs the meeting and everyone who is involved. In any kind of meeting, it often helps to have some ground rules for communication. These should ideally be agreed with everyone, at the beginning of a meeting or to become a 'way that works best for us'. Confident speakers need to listen properly to others and resist filling every silence. Equally, the person who facilitates discussion has to be ready to hold back the keen contributors in a courteous way.

In groups where there is no shortage of contributions some possible ground rules could be:

- 'Only one person talks at a time.' The person facilitating the discussion must enforce this rule courteously yet firmly and, of course, follow the rule themselves. Some early years settings have a talking stick or talker's teddy, which is used to help the eldest children to take turns in small-group discussion. The same item could be introduced into the adult discussion. Done with friendliness and good humour, this strategy should feel appropriate.
- 'Say three good things' is a tactic that asks everyone to focus on the benefits of someone else's contribution before taking the floor with their own idea, suggestion or even constructive objection. (This tactic can be very useful for groups who have developed a habit of frequently saying 'Yes, but . . .'.)
- Another option that can work well is to adopt a ground rule for part, if not all, of the discussion that everyone must accurately summarise what the previous person has said before starting their own contribution. This rule helps people to listen to others. However, it also sometimes enables the person who originally made that contribution to reflect, 'Was that what I meant to say?' or 'That doesn't connect with what I proposed earlier.'

Possible suggestions for very quiet groups include:

- An understood, and so an expected, strategy that early on within any discussion the practitioner who is facilitating the session will start a 'round robin'. At this point everyone in turn says something, however briefly, about the issue or the topic.
- Senior practitioners should have become familiar with individual practitioners and know whether writing down ideas in advance may help colleagues who have difficulty speaking up in front of others. They could be encouraged to make a few notes for themselves to guide their contribution. Another possibility is that suggestions are invited in written form and given to the facilitator before the meeting. This option really needs to be an interim measure to ease more direct contribution.
- It is possible for the facilitator of the discussion to ask quieter members to comment – before that person has been silent for too long. The chair could tell the individual before the meeting that his or her contribution will be invited on a specific topic.
- Less confident team members could be helped by a senior practitioner who directly brings them into the discussion. Everyone then needs to make that effort; it is not all right to sit in silence thinking 'Why doesn't anybody ask me?'

Shared issues: shared discussion

A staff group becomes more of a team when a habit of discussion is established. Team leaders, or facilitators in a regular network, need to create the space and maybe ask the open-ended questions that encourage reflection over what is otherwise not questioned.

Anna Batty, head of Millom Children's Centre, described (personal communication) how the team had a thorough discussion around whether a poster communicating 'Don't smack' was the best way to deal with this issue for parenting within the centre. An underpinning theme within their discussion was that it was not all right to have a poster – any statement relating to centre values – unless everyone was in agreement over what they understood by the message and, just as important, what they would actually do in a relevant situation.

The decision was made that the centre would not have this kind of notice any more. They needed to find constructive ways to challenge any individual parents who dealt with their children with physical, or verbal, rough handling. The judgement was that a poster on the wall did not help one way or another.

The Millom team also explored this issue for the details of meaning from a poster about equality and diversity.

Pause for reflection

I think that this example from the Millom team provokes thoughtfulness about any kind of written directive about behaviour. I invite you to consider:

- Do you have a poster of this kind? The message may be about your centre being a no-smoking or no-mobile-phone zone. Perhaps the message is about other kinds of behaviour that are 'unwelcome here'.
- What job do you think the poster, or other kind of notice, does? Do parents, or anyone else, read it? Do they understand what you ask them to do or not do?
- How do you deal with incidents that happen in front of you – at the time, or having a private word with parents later?
- You may decide that a poster will do a good job, or you want to try this approach. Part of this plan has to be that everyone is confident to explain if a parent asks, 'What's that all about?'

Within your team or network you could collect experiences of notices that you see as a user of a service elsewhere. Does your leisure centre or health clinic have one of the now common notices along the lines that aggressive behaviour towards the staff will not be tolerated? Assuming that this place is not full of shouting and shoving adults, how do you feel, as a service user, about a notice that fails to acknowledge that most service users behave well?

Making your thinking visible

One way to share thoughts and ideas is to say them out loud. An alternative is to capture ideas or interim plans in a written format.

- Early years practitioners may think of flip charts and using large sheets of paper as an approach used within training days. But there is no reason why shared critical thinking should not be written out or placed in diagrammatic format, if that helps to clarify ideas and move the process forward.
- Ideally, any diagram does not become too complex. Otherwise there is a risk that the plotting of the spider web or flow chart – and perhaps making it look beautiful – becomes more important than the thinking or problem solving that it was supposed to illuminate.
- Another possibility is to combine a diagrammatic format with appropriate items or figures. This approach to making your thinking visible can work well when you are reflecting on effective use of the environment or people.
- Warden's (2006) idea of the Talking and Thinking Floorbooks™ evolved as a creative way of consulting with young children. But the approach of combining visuals and words in a large-scale format can be very freeing for adults, in order to relax and let the ideas flow.

Edward de Bono's Thinking Hats

Edward de Bono has a long track record in developing ways to support and provoke creative thinking. His approach of the Six Thinking Hats® was a way to enable adults in many different professional contexts to avoid using only argument and counter-argument to explore a subject or reach a decision. Under those circumstances groups, teams or working committees spend a great deal of time with individuals putting their views ever more forcibly and trying to undermine the views of other people, because other perspectives are a threat.

Edward de Bono's alternative was to offer a way for thinking in parallel and to bring in different, equally important, angles on discussion and well-rounded decision making. The ideas have been used in many different contexts in business and also to support and extend thinking skills for children in school. The approach of the Six Thinking Hats® is usually applied within a group situation and is relevant to the options for reflection. The hats can be imaginary, although some people with whom I have spoken in early years welcome using actual hats.

The White Hat represents the necessary logical input: the information that is available and how accurate it is. Is more information needed and how do we get that? This input is about facts and figures in one way or another, and some discussions and reflections can really need a strong dose of 'What do we actually know? What are we assuming?'

The Black Hat represents the voice for possible difficulties and risks. What are the potential problems, in what ways should we be cautious and what could go wrong?

This hat needs to be heard but not to dominate, nor to be the justification of 'why we won't ever risk anything'.

The Yellow Hat is the voice of why something could well work and the potential benefits. This hat represents the strand of thinking about the advantages, the positives of following this route and what is attractive about this idea.

The Red Hat is the entry point of feelings, of intuition and gut feel. This hat needs to be heard, because unexpressed feelings may well emerge in other ways that could derail a good idea. Feelings can be expressed without a need to justify or explain; emotions expressed honestly are valid in their own right. Some discussion around the Six Hats idea suggests that this hat should be limited to a short time. Certainly, even in professional contexts that value a nurturing atmosphere, there will be a boundary to how much time is given exclusively to how people feel about a practice issue.

The Green Hat is the thinking strand that brings in alternatives. The Green Hat takes an innovatory approach. What else could we consider, think about or do? Are we just throwing out some ideas without a second glance before considering why and why not? Full discussion needs Green Hat thinking but also the input of White, Black and Yellow Hat thinking.

The Blue Hat represents the voice, the person who will manage the thinking process and oversee the discussion. Blue Hat guidance is needed to facilitate, to focus and refocus, to ensure that the discussion does not become an argument and that all the strands are given hearing time and respect.

It is worth thinking about whether your team or network meetings are dominated by one or two hats. For instance:

- Is there a great deal of Red Hat thinking, along the lines of 'I just have this feeling that I'm doing the right thing. And no, I can't explain it.' Have carefully explained changes been met again and again with 'No, it doesn't feel right. You want me to do whatever the children want. It'll be chaos.'
- Or is there such a strong support for Green Hat thinking that new ways and constant change are embraced without much thought about the consequences, or whether there is really good reason to change yet again?

The Six Thinking Hats® approach can be used as intended as a way to make team discussion and reflection more rounded and productive. It is also valuable as a way to reflect on the balance in a team as well as personal preferences and habits. Edward de Bono's approach is introduced through training courses and supporting resources. An internet search brings up a range of materials that briefly show the ideas and process. A useful short resource can be watched on this site, where each hat is discussed in turn: **www.youtube.com/watch?v=cjVxSk1Mq 04&feature=related**.

What could we do?

The second diamond opens up with exploring what could be done. If you have taken time to reach an agreement on what the problem is, then you can have a meaningful discussion about what you could do about it. You need to generate a range of possible solutions to the problem – ideally always more than one – rather than jumping at the first proposal. Effective problem solving is regularly derailed because people want to find an answer quickly, often without much discussion of the actual problem. There may also be competitive solution giving and commitment to personal favourite answers. The diamond closes on to a clear and shared agreement about the best idea, the way forward.

Figure 4.4 Sometimes you need to address adults' reservations in order for children to play in ways they clearly relish

What exactly is the plan?

You have decided on the best, broad strategy out of those discussed. You now need to talk through the details, as the third diamond opens. Key questions are:

- 'Exactly how will this solution work?'
- 'What would we need to be prepared to do to make it work well?'
- 'What's on our side to make it work?'

- 'What might get in the way of this solution?'
- 'How can we deal with those possible blocks?'

You reach an agreement on the best way forward, and deal with any persistent confusion about who is going to do what, where and by when. The third diamond closes with the agreed plan. Again, everyone needs to be committed to this solution and their responsibility within the approach. A problem or problematic situation will not change for the better if a group leader imposes the solution or lets one subgroup impose on another in terms of responsibilities for making this approach a success.

Put that idea into action

If you have a proper discussion, then there is a much better chance that the agreed solution will work for improvement. The fourth diamond opens to encompass the agreed action(s), along with any agreed support for people to fulfil their role. You all need to work to a realistic timescale; even good ideas do not necessarily work straightaway. Remind yourself and your colleagues of the need to persevere and be patient.

Review

You revisit what has happened within conversations but also the same group context in which the problem solving was undertaken. What has happened? Are the consequences as expected and positive? Are there unexpected consequences and are these a source of further problems? Address any issues, if necessary by returning to an earlier diamond, maybe as far back as the question of 'What exactly was the problem?' You will see the connections here with the model of single- and double-loop thinking (pages 28–9). Sometimes your agreed solution to the agreed problem has worked smoothly. So take time to be pleased, before you tackle the next stage of a complex problem, or a different issue altogether.

Scenario

Meerkats Day Nursery

The team has been at ease with touch and cuddling. But locally there have been some conflicting messages from different workshops and trainers.

This week, Alastair attended a training day where a local safeguarding specialist made a forceful presentation about the obligation to justify direct physical contact with children. One participant had become distressed when challenged over her commitment to helping three- and four-year-olds with the intimate aspects of toileting. The only other male practitioner in the group said that the policy in his nursery was that men did not provide intimate physical care. He expressed surprise that Alastair was 'allowed' to change the nappies of his key babies – if only for his own protection against allegations.

The team spend some time talking about whether they should revisit their policy on safeguarding; for instance, perhaps ask parents for written permission to help their children in the toilet. The team also talk about whether Alastair or Joe could be more vulnerable to malicious allegations than the female practitioners. Nobody is entirely comfortable with where this discussion is going. Then Shoshana interjects with, 'Remember the Four Diamonds! We're trying to find a solution. But we've hardly talked about what exactly is the problem.'

Pause and reflect

The discussion takes a different direction and Alastair says, 'I think protecting the children should be top of our list. The problem shouldn't be to protect us.' Corinne adds, 'Are we really supposed to plan children's personal routines around the most unpleasant interpretation that anyone could make of our care?'

The team reframe the problem for discussion as how to be even clearer about their approach to nurture. They need to address, but not be overwhelmed by, a very different approach to safeguarding. They start with the written material from Alastair's course pack. He uses a highlighter pen on the phrase 'a reasonable person' in the sections flagging up how actions could be misinterpreted. Siobhan points out that this 'reasonable person' must be presumed to understand the details of life with young children.

Questions

1. In what ways might the Meerkats team continue this discussion? What are the issues and what might they decide to do?
2. Can you see the elements here of a lose–lose dilemma, which they avoid by going back to what really matters?
3. Can you recall issues in your own practice, not necessarily about safeguarding, in which you and your colleagues maybe rushed to a solution before being clear about the problem?

Facing dilemmas

Some problems are especially troublesome, because it seems that any of the possible options bring unwanted consequences. It then seems that there is no way forward that does not bring additional problems. Yet doing nothing is not an option. The way out of a dilemma is to take a deep breath and logically go through the options and their full consequences.

- What are the expected consequences of each option? Are you overlooking anything?
- Are any negative consequences that serious? Given the need for a decision, are some consequences more important than others?
- In a choice between two options that are equally wanted, can the negative consequences of losing one option be minimised?
- For a decision between two options that both bring possible negatives, can the positive consequences of your choice be maximised?

Two positives in conflict

Dilemmas can be a struggle between two equally wanted outcomes that cannot both be achieved. For example, Ronan has greatly enjoyed his Foundation degree course. His tutor at college is pressing him to register for the next stage

REFLECTIVE PRACTICE AND EARLY YEARS PROFESSIONALISM

and go for the Honours part. But Ronan has been really looking forward to a break from study, to uninterrupted time with his young daughters and giving his partner space for her own professional development, following their one-at-a-time principle.

Alicia has mentored Ronan and helps him consider the possibilities.

- Ronan feels the advantages of going straight on to the extra Honours year are that he will not lose the habit of study and will not risk disappointing his tutor, who has been a real inspiration.
- One advantage of time off from study is that Ronan is tired of deadlines. Also, who is more important – his tutor, who may well understand – or his partner and daughters?
- Ronan decides to talk with his tutor about taking a break and find out if there is any time limit about going on to the Honours year.

Two possible negatives

In contrast, a dilemma can present as a situation in which 'We're wrong whatever we do!' For example, Simone has supported Kim and Sadie, who run the under-twos room in FineStart day nursery. They have explored practical issues around the key person system and established regular times when each key person gets together with their key children. Theo has returned from a local workshop about use of circle time and reports that the trainer was firm that practitioners with the under-threes should start circle time, since it would help very young children with the transition into the three–fives room.

Sadie and Kim are doubtful about this advice and share their thinking in a short meeting with Simone and Theo.

- Sadie and Kim are clear about the advantages of the special times in a very small group. The babies and toddlers enjoy snuggling up close and any singing, 'chatting' or enjoying a book is within that context.
- Kim is concerned that, if she and Sadie stop the key person times, they are going against Simone's advice. But if they do not start a proper circle time, are they going against local guidance on transitions? Should they do both, even though that would overload the day?
- Simone says that they should not mind who has given what advice. What sense does it make for what they know about very young children and how you help them with any transitions?
- Theo shares his reservation about his workshop experience. Surely, it is back-to-front thinking to try to help young children with the different routine in an 'older' room by starting them on that pattern earlier?

Simone listens, as well as guides, as the three practitioners discuss what supportive transition between rooms should look like for young children. Kim and Sadie are strengthened in their rationale for key person times and Theo is seriously considering key person times with the three–five-year-olds and applying any circle time ideas in that context.

Resources

- Curriculum in Action Course Team (1981) *Curriculum in Action: An Approach to Evaluation*. Milton Keynes: Open University Publications.
- Early Childhood Unit **www.everydaystories.org.uk**
- Department for Children, Schools and Families (2008) *The Early Years Foundation Stage – Setting the Standards for Learning, Development and Care for Children from Birth to Five*. London: DCSF. **www.education.gov.uk/ publications/standard/publicationdetail/page1/DCSF-00261-2008**
- Drummond, M.J., Lally, M. and Pugh, G. (1989) *Working with Children: Developing a Curriculum for the Early Years*. London: National Children's Bureau.
- Drummond, M.J., (2003) *Assessing Children's Learning*. London: David Fulton.
- Egan, G. and Cowan, M. (1979) *People in Systems: A Model for Development in the Human-Services Professions and Education*. Monterey, California: Brooks/ Cole.
- Elfer, P., Goldschmied, E. and Selleck, D. (2003) *Key Persons in the Nursery: Building Relationships for Quality Provision*. London: David Fulton.
- Farmer, N. (2009) 'We Are All Active Learners'. *Early Years Educator*, volume 11, no 6, October.
- Godfrey, M. (2009) 'Worms Turn Into Butterflies'. *Early Years Educator*, volume 11, no 6. October, **www.bestpracticenet.co.uk/downloads/eyps/eye-v11-n6-oct09-p16.pdf**
- Learning and Teaching Scotland (2005b) *Let's Talk About Pedagogy: Towards a Shared Understanding for Early Years Education in Scotland*. Glasgow: Learning and Teaching Scotland. **www.ltscotland.org.uk/publications/l/ publication_tcm4617466.asp?strReferringChannel=search&strReferringPageID =tcm:4-615801-64**
- Lindon, J. (2001) *Understanding Children's Play*. Cheltenham: Nelson Thornes.
- Lindon, J. (2007) *Understanding Children and Young People: Development from 5–18 Years*, London: Hodder Arnold.
- Lindon, J. (2010b) *The Key Person Approach*. London: Practical Pre-School Books.
- Moyles, J., Adams, S. and Musgrove, A. (2002) *Study of Pedagogical Effectiveness in Early Learning Brief No. 363*. **www.education.gov.uk/ publications/standard/publicationDetail/Page1/RR363**
- Warden, C. (2006) *Talking and Thinking Floorbooks: Using 'Big Book Planners' to Consult Children*. Perthshire: Mindstretchers

Learning with and from other people

Best practice as a professional in services for children and families means lifelong learning. This chapter explores different routes for extending skills or knowledge and practical issues about making the most of experiences. Many ideas are also relevant for readers who guide colleagues in their continuing professional development. Suggestions include an approach to learning from different models and examples of best practice.

The main sections of this chapter are:
- Continuing professional development
- Learning from different sources
- Sharing best practice.

Continuing professional development

The concept of continuing professional development (CPD) is well established across many professions and has become part of expectations for best practice within the early years workforce. Reflective practice is part of your CPD: the continued thoughtfulness that enhances daily interaction with children and colleagues. However, CPD includes other deliberate plans to extend your current knowledge and understanding, such as attendance at training days or conferences, membership of networks, and your own reading.

What does it mean?

Continuing professional development (CPD): an ongoing process of learning, even for the most experienced professionals, through recognising current strengths, addressing areas for improvement and updating knowledge.

Personal plans for your own CPD

Continued learning within your professional life is best supported by some forward thinking about how you could, or should, develop your skills and understanding in the relatively near future.
- As a lone practitioner, such as a childminder, you may have to organise yourself, although drawing on the ideas of your network coordinator or local early years advisory team.

- Within a team, the manager should meet with individual staff on a regular basis in order to give feedback about that person's practice. This sit-down time is not instead of informal conversations; it is the opportunity to pull together what has gone well and where there is scope for improvement. See pages 156–60 about supervision and appraisal.

In either context you need to consider some specific details. A good forward plan will neither be 'more of everything' nor 'whatever I can find time to do'. Bear in mind that over the timescale you will also continue to learn in unplanned ways.

What?

Looking ahead, perhaps over the next year, can you identify three or four personal development needs?

- Perhaps the shortlist has to start with a refresher on safeguarding, or another area of practice that everyone has to attend on a regular basis. However, what else would enhance your current practice?
- Perhaps you are motivated to find out more about the concept of schemas and play patterns as a way to focus on children's self-chosen play.
- Maybe you judge you would benefit from polishing up your knowledge of child development of under-twos.
- On the other hand, your development needs may be more skills based, such as becoming more competent at writing reports or in using puppets within storytelling for the children.
- Your personal plan may be more about habits of behaviour. Perhaps you are motivated to address that you never quite manage to speak up in team meetings or on training days. You feel that you have made progress towards being a more reflective professional. However, you struggle more with aspects of being an articulate professional: voicing good ideas out loud.

Focus on what you need to learn, rather than drafting a checklist of planned tasks and events. The point is not simply to attend a safeguarding course, but to ensure that you refresh your current knowledge and are brought up to date with any changes. You could make a mental note, even if not a written one, of personal queries you want to explore: what you see as less straightforward applications of best practice in safeguarding.

How?

One route to meeting a specific development need can be to seek an appropriate training day. But that route is not the only one. Would it be a better option, or first step, to read something on this topic? Consider making a visit to another setting, if, for example, you have heard that their team has made progress in the area of practice that interests you (see page 126).

Who and where?

Think about people who will have information about training and whether a day or workshop that sounds promising is going to cover the ground that you want. Consider people who could well have good suggestions about a book or two, or a setting to visit, or at least get in contact by email or telephone for a conversation.

Who do you know, have you observed, who appears confident in the team meeting or who does not seem to hesitate to voice an opinion at a training day? Do they have any tips that you can fine-tune for yourself? Maybe a conversation with someone else, who may be your manager, helps you to develop a strategy for easing your way.

So what?

It is worthwhile thinking afterwards – making a mental note if not a written one – of what you have gained from this training day, conference, conversation, visit or reading. Has the experience met your hopes and intentions for what you would gain? Has the development activity led you to identify further learning needs? Did the strategy of making yourself a note before the team meeting help you? Do you realise that, for the time being (but not forever) you can best focus on speaking up within smaller-group discussion that is often part of a training day?

Pause for reflection

This section focuses on personal plans for CPD, but your daily practice operates within a social context. It is worth asking:

- Has this workshop or article made you think in ways that could usefully be shared with colleagues in a team or an informal professional network?
- Do you ever share what you have learned with the children, or at least explain why you were absent yesterday? It is a very positive experience for them to realise that familiar grown-ups believe they can continue to learn.
- To what extent do you find ways to share your continuing professional development with the families of children for whom you are responsible? Early years practitioners sometimes voice the opinion that 'Parents don't understand that we are trained professionals.'
- But do you show, tell and share in ways that enable parents to know how seriously you take your work and that you are far from complacent about your knowledge and skills?

The SMART criteria for goals

You are setting yourself goals for CPD and it is often worth checking your plans against the SMART criteria. This acronym is used with different key words. I have given the version I prefer, but with some of the variations. Choose what works for you; you may find a variation is more suitable when you use the SMART criteria for discussion within a team about shared goals.

Specific

You need to home in on the details of what you would like to learn and avoid vagueness. Will you be able to look back in 12 months' time and realise 'Yes I did manage to . . .'? For instance, Felicity is the newest team member of Crocus Playgroup. She admires the apparent confidence with which Natalie and Janice talk with parents and other family carers. However, if Felicity sets non-specific goals, such as 'I want to be more confident in my communication with parents,' it will be hard to judge any change. What will 'more confident' look like for Felicity? Is there much point in her feeling more confident in general if she still avoids the parents with whom she does not feel a swift connection?

Meaningful

You are unlikely to put effort into achieving a goal if you doubt that it is worthwhile or relevant. A goal can be meaningful, even if you do not relish the work to achieve it. Perhaps Kerry would prefer not to go on a particular workshop about proper business accounting. However, she is convinced that her childminding practice will be much improved if she can find an alternative to the current 'shove everything in a drawer' accounts system.

Achievable

Goals for adult development need to be feasible, attainable and such that you will be able to realise that you have, or have not, achieved what you set out to do. This letter 'A' is sometimes given as 'action-oriented' and that element is worth considering. Does this goal, as given at the moment, home in on what you are actually going to do? Any goal will need effort but it can be undermined by 'I'll try to . . .'.

At Princes Children's Centre, Ravinder is motivated to address a personal quality in her work and starts with 'I will try to be more patient with the children.' But she soon recognises that this hope is not achievable, because the actions are unclear. In discussion with Brigid, her manager, Ravinder homes in more specifically on Martin (her key child) and she is honest that she gets annoyed with the way he always wants the last word. Ravinder is keen to avoid feeling and showing her annoyance, either to Martin or any other children. Brigid suggests a specific strategy that Ravinder ensures that each day she has noticed 'three good things' about what Martin has done and has told him. There is a strong possibility that shifting her attention will enable Ravinder to be less focused on Martin's wish to have the last word.

This letter 'A' is sometimes given as 'agreed-upon'. In any discussion, such as the example of Ravinder, or a team meeting, it is crucial that the details of any goal are agreed by the person, or people, to whom it applies. Useful goals are not imposed from the outside.

Realistic

A goal has to be realistic: possible given everything about the details, the context and the people involved. Much as with children's learning, if the step to achieving this goal is too large or the conditions for success are too optimistic, then the goal as described is unwise. Different individuals are able to tolerate greater scope for not achieving a goal, or not entirely. But it is not generally a wise strategy to set goals that aim for the stars yet continually 'splash-land' in the duck pond. A habit can be established that 'We give it our best but it rarely works out.' A goal is not then a positive stretching of possibilities; it is better to be more realistic and enjoy greater success by smaller steps.

Time-bound

You will need different timescales depending on the goal: any time limit of 'by when?' needs to be realistic. An unrealistic time limit could turn a feasible goal into an impossible one. On the other hand, individuals, as well as teams, need to be aware of their attitudes to deadlines and timekeeping. Avoiding a situation when 'more time is needed' is an excuse for not having made the effort in the first place.

A CPD learning log

Part of effective CPD is your reflection on what you have learned from a given experience. It will be a positive contribution to your practice if you can give some thinking time to experiences that should, ideally, have added to your professional skills. Some of these experiences will be training days or workshops. Other experiences will be attendance at conferences. If these are large gatherings, you may have limited opportunity to talk with presenters to the whole group. However, there should be more scope if the programme includes smaller groups as workshops.

Of course, you do not want to get bogged down in paperwork. So it is a useful step to organise your CPD folder in a way that increases the chances that you will use it as a working document. As with other aspects of reflective practice, it is important that you create a format and style that work for you. I am a fan of the A4 ring binder file and it is unlikely that a full CPD log can be utterly paper-free. The binder has the advantage of being easy to reorganise and will take lightweight, transparent envelopes. This system will keep any certificates in good condition. However, if you prefer a different way to file, then ensure that you can find anything easily and that sheets do not get crumpled or torn.

You need to keep any certificates in good condition, but your CPD file is not simply a record of attendance. You need to relate the experience back into your own practice. Make your own summary notes for each training day or conference you attend. The same points apply for readers who are part of a network, such as has been established in many areas now for the growing numbers of practitioners with Early Years Professional Status.

Figure 5.1 A training workshop and chance to reflect can remind you of the power of simple resources

What have I learned?

These notes do not have to be lengthy. It might help to have some pointers:

- Today made me think about . . .
- I now know more about . . .
- I realise I need to find out more about . . .
- I would like to try . . .
- I need to talk with my colleagues about . . .

This last open-ended question refers to taking back an idea for something to do within your practice. You need to consider how a practical idea will be integrated and not simply apply someone else's technique without much thought.

A focused training experience may benefit from a different set of questions:

- What happened in this activity? What did I experience?
- If appropriate: what did I do well and what did not go smoothly?
- How did I feel about the experience?
- What did I learn from all of this?
- What will I do differently next time? What are my reasons for 'doing differently'?
- Do I need further support or resources for next time? How can I access help?
- Based on what I learned this time, what is my next step in this area of learning?
- What are my reasons for thinking of this direction?

REFLECTIVE PRACTICE AND EARLY YEARS PROFESSIONALISM

There is no need to take the above list of questions as a given that should not be changed. Look at them, maybe try them out and adjust the wording in ways that work for you. Do not add lots more questions; in fact, some suggested questions for a CPD learning log are shorter than this list. The questions are there to provoke your reflection and not to form a daunting schedule. It is better to reflect more deeply, guided by a short list of questions, than to end up thinking and writing less in order to get to the end of a long list.

Within group provision the whole team needs to benefit from training days, conferences or network meetings that one or two practitioners attend. Some settings have established as usual practice that time is allocated in team meetings for summary highlights from these days. It will be easier to pull together a summary with some guiding questions. You can also share what you have learned by referring to handouts that you were given on the day. But, again, your colleagues will benefit from your time in reading the handouts and marking them up for key points of interest.

Learning from different sources

Early years practitioners, like any other professionals, can learn from a wide range of sources. Chapters 6 and 7 cover ways you can learn directly from your colleagues. This section covers external sources of learning, including attendance at specific training events and extending your knowledge through reading.

Training courses

These CPD experiences can be of different types. The suggestions in this section arise equally from my own years as a trainer and from listening to feedback from early years practitioners about their specific and general experiences of training.

- Early years practitioners should be offered a range of opportunities for local training days or shorter workshops. Your pattern of attendance should be linked with your awareness of how you need to extend your skills and the input of a senior colleague, who is most likely to be your manager.
- The senior team is responsible for reading the details of any courses, for instance in the programme organised by your local authority. It is not good practice to send practitioners on courses without consideration of how the experience will enhance their professional learning.
- If there is a less than perfect fit, the course may still be valuable. However, the practitioner needs to know that, for instance, this training day about guiding children's behaviour does not claim to cover the impact of disability on how children behave. If, as a senior practitioner, you judge there is a gap in the local training programme, then address the issue with the early years team.
- If you are a more senior team member, then you will organise your own pattern of attendance, but maybe still with suggestions from fellow professionals.
- If you work in a group setting, then your manager may organise in-house training. In this kind of event a specialist in early years, or other relevant

professional area, comes to your place of work. This experience may be a closure day, planned with warning for families, when the entire staff group is freed up to be part of the training.

Realistic expectations

You will make the most of any training by being active in the experience. As a senior practitioner, you support that active outlook on learning within your team.

- Certainly, any practitioner should know in advance on which training they are booked during the next programme. Before you attend a day, workshop or conference, read any descriptive materials about the day.
- The format of advance material varies but, at the very least, you should have a title for the day and some broad aims. You can think ahead about what you hope for from the day, while remaining open-minded about the detail.
- Participants can realistically hope to emerge with some ideas that are directly applicable to practice. However, it is not usually appropriate to expect focused advice about individual children or families with whom you work. Nor is it professionally appropriate to share details of children, families or colleagues within an open training day.
- No trainer, however experienced, can give very specific advice about individual children or families they do not know. Trainers talk generally and practitioners have to make appropriate links and adjustments, taking ideas back to their setting for further discussion and thought.
- It is a different situation if a series of workshops is set up for delegates to bring examples from their practice and the boundaries of confidentiality are very clear. It is also a different situation if an early years consultant, or other professional, spends time with you in your place of work. They are then able to observe the child and make informed suggestions, as well as follow up that suggestion and support you in the implementation.

Direct involvement on the day

During the training day or workshop, the trainer has the responsibility to organise and resource the experience, to facilitate discussion and to contribute his or her own ideas. However, participants have a responsibility; trainers can only do just so much. Again, as a senior practitioner you need to address ways in which any staff do not make the most of training days they attend.

Within any training day, workshop or conference, participants have a responsibility to behave as active learners.

- Listen and contribute in ways that are comfortable to you, but be ready to go at least a little outside your comfort zone.
- Ask questions in a timely way and give the trainer/presenter a chance to answer, plus the option to check and get back to you later in the day.
- If you cannot see or hear clearly from your position, then tell the trainer as soon as possible. Certainly do not wait until the final evaluation form to raise a practical issue that it would then be too late to redress.

- Perhaps the content of the day is not at all what you anticipated. Check your advance material and ask, sooner rather than later, when you will be covering this issue or approach. However, the trainer cannot change the programme for the day if you, or maybe your manager, expected something very different from what was described in the course outline.

Some training days are very practical and set out to share a considerable amount of 'what you could do' with generous amounts of literally hands-on time with different resources. However, some days are balanced more towards 'Think about what you do'. On days designed to support reflective practice, it is not professional to complain, without good reason, that 'It wasn't at all practical' or 'Didn't tell me anything new'. Maybe a day was so removed from early years theory and practice that effective connections were just about impossible. However, perhaps it was a day in which the hard work was reflecting about what works with children and why.

Early years experts do not always agree and some trainers may advise a different pattern of practice than others. It is professional to raise contradictions and ask this trainer for a more detailed rationale for their recommendation or interpretation of best practice on this occasion. It is not a professional reaction to sit quiet, yet complain later about 'people telling me different things'. A professional trainer should be ready to explain and should not take offence at being asked to address conflicts over advice or apparent mismatches.

Take another **perspective**

Etiquette for training days and conferences now has to include aspects of technology. A trainer usually covers the main issues, but it is useful if managers anticipate ground rules, when they realise some staff may not foresee a problem.

It is legitimate to ask participants to switch off mobile phones, for texting or voice calls. Trainers understand if a participant needs to take an emergency call, in which case you leave the room, even if the call is predicted to be short.

The only reason to switch on technology is if it is part of the training day itself, or you prefer to make notes onto a hand-held PDA or laptop.

It is not acceptable to record – by sound or visually by taking photos – without first asking permission of the trainer or conference organiser.

Links back to your practice

Most training days and conferences will provide supporting notes and these come in different styles.

- Some will be paper copy of the overheads that guide the presentation that you hear. The advantage then is that you do not have to write at speed to get your own version of the overheads.

internal search facilities varies between websites and some are frankly rubbish. Larger sites usually have an email address. I have experienced a good rate of reply to courteous 'Where is it?' queries for reports or papers that I know exist somewhere on a specific site.

- The worldwide web is a breathtaking resource, but an open search will bring up a wide variety of materials. Some information is not more reliable just because it has been repeated in a long list of sites. National organisations will be reliable within their remit, but will not claim to cover all angles.

Primary and secondary sources

Ideally, you should go back to an original report rather than depend on a summary written by someone else. You should read a much-referenced book rather than depend entirely on someone else's choice of the most important points. Practitioners who are studying need to return to frequently quoted research for details of methods, results and practical implications. However, everyone has limited time, and some original materials, such as journal articles, are hard to obtain. It is inevitable that you need to find trustworthy secondary sources.

Reliable literature reviews of an area of practice can be extremely helpful. Busy practitioners, advisors and trainers can get an overview when they do not have the time to access even a small proportion of the original sources. If you are studying, a good literature review – such as Trevarthen et al. (2003) for practice with under-threes – can give you the scope of an area and guide you towards references that it would be wise to follow to their original source. Reviews may be online, for example Desforges and Abouchaar (2003) and their coverage of studies of partnership with families. You may also get extensive coverage of an area in a book, such as Eliot (2009) and her substantial review of research studies into differences between boys and girls throughout childhood.

Sometimes secondary sources are not very accurate. Perhaps a writer's own perspective is laid very heavily over the original ideas, or a vital part of a project has been overlooked by secondary sources who are more interested in another angle. Reinterpretations or misinterpretations then 'travel on', appearing to be part of the original source. A gap develops between what was first written and how concepts are later used. You need answers to questions like 'Who says so?' and 'Did they say/write that?' Reworking of ideas is not necessarily a problem. Some very good ideas that are attributed to Lev Vygotsky are actually further developments by thoughtful writers such as Jerome Bruner (Lindon, 2012a).

What does it mean?

Primary sources: the original book or article, going back to what this writer actually said or the details of a research report.

Secondary sources: summaries, critiques and descriptive references to a writer or research.

What is the evidence?

Reflective practice, supported by critical thinking, is not exclusively about questioning oneself. Best reflective practice also includes posing questions to others. Sometimes this communication is face to face and sometimes more as you imagine asking these questions of a writer or group of authors. Any book, article or online review needs to be read thoughtfully and the following questions may help.

- What are the main points here? Do I understand them from a single reading or will it be useful to go through this source again? Are there any terms that are unclear; are they explained somewhere? If not, can I check for a definition elsewhere?
- If the stance is that 'Research has proved that . . .', have I been given enough information to check this out if I wish? If the writer says, 'Studies show that . . .', are there proper references, which I can follow up easily?
- Is the approach more of 'This is a wise (or unwise) way to behave with young children'? Then what support is given to justify this assertion; what kind of further information or explanation? Does it make sense?
- What have I learned from what I have read? Sometimes you will have learned something entirely new. Sometimes your reading brings a fresh perspective to an approach or idea with which you were already familiar.

'Experts' will disagree sometimes

In any area of practice it is unlikely that everyone with expertise will completely agree. You will encounter different standpoints over what research has said, even what the same study actually showed. In early years practice, direct advice varies about significant issues such as touch and safeguarding (Lindon, 2012b) or the most appropriate reaction to children who want to weave pretend weapons into their imaginative play (Lindon, 2001, 2012a). Total agreement will never happen, especially in the many 'swampy zones' of practice (discussed earlier on page 35).

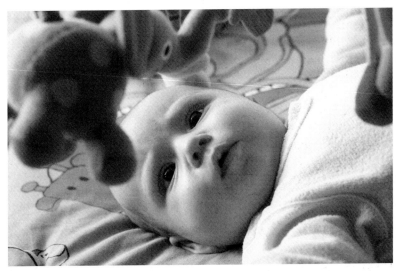

Figure 5.2 Babies' brains are very active but some 'Research shows... ' claims are not accurate

The aim of reading, like other forms of CPD, is not that it always delivers new ideas of 'what to do'. Sometimes your reading will bring a deeper understanding of why a familiar activity is so positive for children.

For example, I have long been committed to singing and the use of music with babies and young children. But while I was writing this book, I read an article by Goddard Blythe (2009) in which she described songs and nursery rhymes as a special kind of speech. She explained, in ways that I had not fully understood, how the pace, tone and lengthening of individual sounds work so well for children. Goddard Blythe also suggested that the communication of babies and very young toddlers can be seen as a special language that has more in common with music and mime than with speech with recognisable words. I found this to be a valuable concept that made me think.

Anyone in an expert position has the responsibility to give a listener or reader enough information to follow this person's line of reasoning. Ask yourself:

- Am I being asked to accept a point of view and/or to reject another one?
- What support is being given by this writer or presenter?
- If writers or presenters criticise another approach, theory or actual writer, how good a case are they making? Can I access that material to check what was actually said or argued?

Anyone listening or reading has the responsibility to do some thinking and not simply complain that 'experts' should get in line, so they can tell 'us' what to do. There are justifiable grounds for frustration if you, or the colleagues you support, are actually being given contradictory advice from within the same advisory team, or on different days of what should be a coherent training programme. It is important to raise this contradiction with someone senior in the local team.

It is also important to be sure that a given trainer or advisor did actually promote this approach. I have been involved in a number of tracking-back operations, especially on apparent 'bans' on cuddling or other forms of friendly physical contact. In some cases, anxious practitioners had misunderstood or generalised from a specific comment to reach a general prohibition. But on some occasions the search reached one or more trainers who were advising how to relate to very young children with minimal physical contact, in the name of child protection.

Pseudoscience?

With constant repetition, some ideas and the practical applications pass into the 'everybody knows' zone of minimal challenge. It does not matter how often a core idea is repeated; it is still appropriate and professional to ask, 'What is the support for that advice?'

For instance, some practical applications from research about early brain development have been very positive. However, some discussion of sex differences in early brain development has been based on the claims of one or two authors, whose interpretation has been significantly challenged (Eliot, 2009). Early years practitioners should be thoughtful about how their practice and any unchecked assumptions affect boys as well as girls. Yet a considerable amount of 'boy-brain' explanation has gained acceptance through continued repetition. The cycle needs to be broken with requests for a reference that will provide evidence of the claim. On the other hand, some writers have been loath to consider any lessons from research about brain development, arising from disdain for the scientific model from which they are derived.

Some practical advice can be sound, despite the shaky research foundation. The courteous professional challenge of 'Who says so and on what grounds?' is still necessary. Otherwise, as Goldacre (2009) points out, the developers of a complex programme seize ownership of sensible, basic recommendations on the spurious foundation of 'Research proves that . . .' their specific model is the best or only right way.

All children need regular physical activity and those of school age need plenty of breaks within a more structured day. Howard-Jones (undated, about 2008) supports Goldacre's analysis that there is no basis for claims that neural mechanisms can be influenced by specific physical exercises promoted by some 'brain-based' commercial programmes. Howard-Jones's summary is, 'The pseudo-scientific terms that are used to explain how this works, let alone the concepts they express, are unrecognisable within the domain of neuroscience' (2008: 15).

Children need a well-balanced diet of fresh food and simple drinks, including water, and they benefit from having regular meals, especially not skipping breakfast. Important nutrients are best delivered through actual food rather than supplements, unless children have special nutritional needs arising from a chronic health condition. Again, both Goldacre and Howard-Jones challenge the claim that Omega-3 (fish oil) supplements will boost children's academic performance in school, or their more general intelligence. There is no reliable research that supports this claim. I recommend reading Goldacre (2009, Chapter 8) on how not to do research, with the specific example of how Durham gave fish-oil capsules to a considerable number of adolescents.

The public prediction at the start of this enterprise was that the supplement would boost the overall GCSE results. Apart from anything else, it is impossible to judge the genuine effect of any special intervention if those involved have their expectations firmly managed at the outset over what the results will be. Goldacre reports that, in fact, the local GCSE results became even less favourable. I propose a psychological explanation for the apparent negative impact of doling out supplements in this way. It is possible that the Durham adolescents – and maybe their parents as well – believed the claims about powerful pills. Perhaps the young people decided that, given the fish oil in their system, study for their GCSEs was optional. This is a possible interpretation.

Making sense of research

There is a considerable body of research about children, from different theoretical perspectives and following different methods (Lindon, 2012a). Such research has increasingly offered practical implications for practice, rather than a more academic approach of knowledge for its own sake, or to prove a theoretical position. Additional questions arise when you are reading about research. What may you need to ask of a research team or a writer who has presented a narrative or case study as support for a perspective or recommendation? These issues are well discussed from different perspectives by Schaffer (1998), MacNaughton et al. (2004) and Goldacre (2009).

Some specific questions now follow, but they are gathered around a main theme: that it must be possible for anyone who is interested to find out and understand what was done and how. This basic requirement applies whatever the theoretical stance or the research methods of an individual or team. Only on this foundation can you come to an informed basis for accepting, or disputing, the main interpretations and conclusions.

What were the aims of the research?

Research based on the empirical, scientific model should start out with a hypothesis: a clear statement of what the research has been designed to explore. Good research in the more empirical tradition is designed so that explanations or patterns of cause and effect can be reached as reliably as possible. Some research plans can be relatively open-ended, but in that case it is not acceptable to swing back to avowed aims once the results are clearer, and revise any predictions in line with what now appear to be the results.

Research undertaken on a more subjective basis nevertheless has to be planned in ways that are transparent and justify the analysis and interpretations that follow. Equivalent clarity is needed in open-ended, more narrative studies. What are the researcher's aims in assigning the time to this exploration? It has to be possible to disprove, as well as prove, the predictions and expectations of any research team. Whatever the chosen method of research, it is useful to ask 'Is there any way this study could have overturned the researcher's existing convictions?' If the answer is, 'No', the study may still be of interest. However, readers need to recall that it was designed to (what I like to call) the BISS protocol: Because I Say So.

Any key terms have to be explained and given a working definition for this study. This requirement applies whether the results will be amenable to numerical analysis, that is, *quantitative*; or the approach is *qualitative* in that it is more descriptive. If the aim is to explore 'child-initiated play', what exactly does that phrase mean here? Research reviews that bring together many studies sometimes struggle with different, or unclear, working definitions of the same words. For instance, Desforges and Abouchaar (2003) describe the challenge of comparing studies which use words that mean something different in practice by 'parent involvement' or 'home learning'.

Any research report should acknowledge the bias and concerns of researchers. It should be easy to understand the philosophical, theoretical or policy context in which the research was planned and undertaken. Such information should be within the main body of a report – not hidden in references or obscure footnotes, which then need to be tracked. Part of this honesty is to be clear for everyone about any practical concerns that motivate the research. Any vested interests should be obvious, either from the source of funding, or other interests of the researcher(s). Goldacre (2009) discusses a range of examples where research design, analysis and/or interpretation were unduly influenced by what the key players, including the funding body, wanted to find and prove.

What does it mean?

Quantitative: analysis of the results of an experiment or observation in terms of numbers, percentages or further statistical analysis.

Qualitative: analysis of observational material in terms of descriptive themes or patterns.

Note. It is not a stark either–or choice; some studies combine both methods.

What methods were used?

It should be easy to understand what a researcher or research team actually did. Transparency or honesty about methods is a hallmark of reliable research. However, such information is also crucial for anyone to judge practical recommendations arising from the work, or to make direct comparisons between teams who allegedly studied the same topic. Details of methods as well as findings should be open to scrutiny.

Where and when was this study done? Time and place matter because the context may have influenced the results that emerged. Older studies do not necessarily come with a 'Use before' date stamp. But it is appropriate to reflect on changes in society that could affect sensible interpretation. For instance, a 1970s study of young children's attitudes about ethnic group will reflect the social circumstances of the time, as well as what may be enduring insights into cognitive and emotional development.

What methods did the researchers choose? Did they make assessments of any kind, on what instrument and what are the advantages and drawbacks of this approach? Is this a measurement tool that can be independently accessed? Is it easy to obtain a copy of this measure? If this study goes on to analyse findings in a numerical way, was this measure developed in a thorough way that justifies a quantitative approach? It is unacceptable simply to add numbers to a measure and then 'do some statistics', even of the simplest kind.

In the classic experimental design there is a control group, which does not experience the special intervention. However, normal life does not operate like a scientific laboratory and research teams do not have the right – nor should they – to direct children and families in ways that suit the research plan. For instance, by the late 1990s most young children attended some kind of early years provision before entering formal school. The 'home only' sample found the Effective Provision of Pre-School Education (EPPE) research included disproportionately more children from minority ethnic groups and disabled children. The comparisons between the group early years provision and 'home only' were possible only through use of sophisticated statistical techniques. If you ask, as I did, the EPPE team are happy to provide references to research papers explaining the model. They are a tough read for non-statisticians, but the information is made available.

A quantitative study has to be systematic: the data are collected according to a clear plan, explained in the research report; methods are not altered at whim. Even the best-laid designs do not always go to plan. In fact, some reports are especially useful when a research team is prepared to explain what went wrong and what they learned. Perhaps several nurseries agree to participate in a special programme to enhance children's physical activity. Unexpected results lead to discussion revealing that only one nursery implemented the programme as promised. The explanation and justification for patchy implementation from the other nurseries raise important practical issues and assumed priorities.

Who was involved in this research and how did they select children, families or early years settings? If different groups of people were sought, are there other ways that they differ in addition to the main point of interest? Will this additional difference distort the findings and what can be done? How many individuals were involved? A small-scale study can be valuable, but only if any limitations are acknowledged. Study of a single day nursery may offer useful insights but is not a secure basis for statements about 'day nurseries' in general. A study that looks only at children over three years of age cannot offer practical suggestions about practice with under-threes, nor be presented as a study of early childhood.

An equivalent level of transparency is necessary for methods that focus on descriptive narratives or case studies. How did this observer decide who to watch and when? Did the observation happen at particular times of the day? How were observations recorded and how did this method affect the sense that was later made of the information? An action research model deliberately encompasses the likelihood of change over time. This flexibility needs to be documented so that it is easy to follow what MacNaughton et al. (2004) call 'the research trail'.

What was done with the information?

Whatever their chosen methods, researchers then do something with their information. Again, it should be clear in any report how the researchers, supported possibly by the statistician of the team, organised what was found.

Some research generates information in a numerical format, whether that is observations of frequency of defined behaviour or assessments that can legitimately be given a score. The data are then quantitative and some form of analysis will be done on the figures. The mathematical operations may range from basic adding up or percentages through to highly complex statistics. There are strict mathematical rules for use of different statistical methods. A basic rule also is that it is unacceptable to go on extensive fishing expeditions in the hope of finding something. The more tests you run, the greater the chance of coming up with an apparently significant finding by sheer chance.

Acceptable qualitative research also follows a clearly stated pattern of how the researchers made sense of examples. If the examples are gathered in some pattern, is it clear how the categories were chosen?

What sense was made of the findings?

The details of the study will be relevant to the possible conclusions that are drawn. For instance, can you track easily how the researchers have reached their conclusions? If they make practical suggestions or recommendations, can you see obvious connections between what the study found and the links now being drawn with practice? How do they deal with any findings that do not fit? Are they acknowledged or dismissed as oddities because they do not agree with the study team's assumptions and beliefs?

Are there other ways that results could be interpreted, whether this information is numerical or a descriptive narrative? A learning story may be analysed and interpreted in line with a particular theoretical framework. In your judgement, do the details of the narrative justify the interpretation being presented? Is it a good fit, or are descriptions stretched to be consistent with the concepts?

It is uncomfortable when research challenges prevailing wisdom or an 'Everybody knows' certainty. However, there are serious risks when a research team, or their funding body, is committed to finding a particular result, or highly invested in not getting particular results. This bias can also affect formal or informal reviews of an area of interest. Responsible review and professional discussion do not select on the basis of evidence that is welcome – known as cherry-picking the research. You certainly have to be very sure of your ground if you imply that the opposition's methods are full of holes that undermine their conclusions but your side's methodology is beyond reproach. It is a measure of responsible professionalism and national policy making when commentators take seriously a well-constructed study that has generated inconvenient results.

Sharing best practice

The impetus for change sometimes arises from good ideas encountered elsewhere. Any practitioner or team no matter how good their practice, should be open to continued professional development and learning.

Integrating ideas into your practice

Promising ideas can emerge from a range of sources:
- You may read about an approach in an early years magazine, book or online.
- Ideas may be shared within a training day or by attending a conference.

- Some events, local or national, are set up to enable practitioners to hear about practice elsewhere, and to share their own insights and approach.
- You may exchange views in your local network or forum. The growing networks of early years professionals encourage exchange of professional views, as well as offering training opportunities from outside speakers.
- Some early years practitioners organise visits to other settings: within their local neighbourhood, further away nationally and occasionally in an organised trip to learn about practice in another European country.

Whatever the source of the ideas, you need to reflect on the content and not simply take an approach wholesale and add it to your practice. You, and your colleagues, could usefully consider questions such as:

- What exactly did this other practitioner or team describe? Do I need to have more information to apply the idea in a sensible way to my daily practice?
- Are there important points, potential pitfalls that I need to understand? What needs to be in place before I make this change?
- Do I understand the reasons why they took this approach? I also need my own reasons, not simply that somebody else thinks this approach is a good idea.
- If I work with colleagues, especially if I will guide the introduction of this new or different approach, I need to be able to explain clearly in my own words.
- Am I allowing for good practice that I already have? It is unwise to change my approach just for the sake of change. How will this idea or method fit with what already works well for the children, and families, here?
- Are there details that mean the idea, although promising, needs development before it will be applicable here? What was the age of the children in the other provision? What range of families? Do the children in my provision have different or special needs that mean I need to adjust what is still a sound idea?
- Was the other provision different from mine in important ways? It does not mean the idea will not work at all. But how do I allow for my pattern of work, indoor and outdoor spaces or more limited budget?

Visiting other provisions

There are a considerable number of early years settings across the country and some are located within the same neighbourhood. One potential way to extend ideas and understanding would be for practitioners to visit one another in different settings. There seem to be several reasons why visiting is an infrequent approach to continuing professional development and a source of ideas for constructive change.

Limited spare time

Time is undoubtedly an issue. Early years practitioners in full-day care have limited time to fit in going to see what is happening further up the road, let alone some distance away. Practitioners working in sessional provision often finish their paid work to transfer immediately to family obligations. Time needs to be well spent and experienced practitioners and managers are likely to want to be sure that they will observe best practice.

Trust

Practitioners in a team, or individual childminders, need to feel secure that informal observations of their practice will not be repeated to other people, out of context. Practitioners may also be uneasy that visiting fellow practitioners may focus more on what is not going well rather than good practice. This concern that most, or any, observation will find faults is a running theme that has been discussed elsewhere in this book, for instance about peer observation (page 187).

An additional issue about trust arises because some settings, or individual childminders, feel that they are in direct competition in their neighbourhood with other providers. Why should they share ideas or approaches that currently give their provision an edge over competitors? These feelings cannot simply be dismissed as paranoia. Some private and voluntary settings have seen their children and families disappear to children's centres, located with scant attention to existing sessional or full-day care in the area.

A sense of collaboration

A great deal will depend on the local atmosphere and the extent to which the early years advisory team are able to build a sense of shared purpose and genuinely mutual support. Practitioners and teams are unlikely to continue in what they feel to be a one-way experience of learning and sharing ideas. It is a different situation if you are the named mentor for a less experienced practitioner (more from page 155). But even in that situation, mentors often gain from their need to reflect in order to be an effective support.

Grenier (2010) made the following comments about the welcome that his team experienced when they visited other settings. Perhaps for understandable reasons, other practitioners were loath simply to send hard copy of explanations of how they worked. Other teams were, however, happy to show and explain in depth to fellow professionals who had organised the time to come to the setting. The Kate Greenaway team decided to put their Core Experiences approach online in a wiki format. The aim of this approach is to share knowledge and experience in the spirit of collaboration. You can look at their materials on **www.coreexperiences. wikia.com** but also use the links to read the wiki principles. Users are asked to share in their turn, to invite others to benefit from their ideas and not to use any online wiki materials for commercial gain.

Key issues around 'time', 'worth the time' and 'trust' are often resolved when practitioners are in a situation in which they have time to get to know each other. Henry (2010) describes a management programme in which visits to one another's settings were recorded formally as part of the accredited process of the course. Course members were able to gain specific ideas from each other, some of which could be implemented with few, if any, changes. Other gains resulted from watching the normal day in another setting, which was somewhat further along the route in a practice development. One such example was establishing free flow between the indoor and outdoor environments.

There has been considerable enthusiasm for learning from the innovatory practice of early years centres in the Reggio Emilia region of northern Italy. The best responses to this holistic system, with a distinct back history, is to understand the details and then to consider carefully how the ideas could improve or enhance practice back in the UK. Thornton and Brunton (2009) offer this approach by sections on 'Reflections on the Reggio Approach' throughout their descriptive account of what happens in the centres.

Marianne Valentine's 1999 report for Learning and Teaching Scotland (revised edition in 2006) dedicated about half of the booklet to an explanation of the Reggio approach. But the second half was an analysis of what the Scottish early years education system could learn from Reggio. The differences between the Reggio area and Scotland were described, along with the insights from Reggio that could make a significant impact on improvements in the Scottish context. Valentine wrote of the need to adapt a pedagogical approach from elsewhere, that the direct application of Reggio to Scotland would be ill-advised, but that 'we can, in the words of Carlina Rinaldi, seek to *translate* what we learn from Reggio educators' (2006: 25) (the same sentence was in the 1999 edition and italics were in the original). The report goes on to focus on the need to challenge beliefs that treat early years education as important only in so far as children are being prepared for the demands of formal schooling. Key points for reflection and practical application are drawn from the Reggio outlook on time, the physical environment, use of space and serious thought about the role of the adult in early childhood settings.

The Learning and Teaching Scotland (2005b) paper about pedagogy makes a significant, general point about respect for the context in which early years practitioners apply their craft. Valuable ideas and insights can be gained from alternative approaches and pedagogical thinking. However, it is not responsible simply to take ideas and insert them into existing practice elsewhere, without reflection. With specific reference to Scotland, the paper stresses not only the importance of considering the context in which pedagogical issues arise, but also showing respect for existing social–cultural traditions where you currently apply your practice. The message is that reflective practitioners and those who advise and guide them should be open to positive ideas whatever the source. However, that open-mindedness should also include reconnecting with overlooked best practice within the historical traditions of one's own culture. The careful message is that good ideas do not necessarily, or only, come from hundreds or thousands of miles away.

Practitioners visiting other countries that have a distinct approach to provision will benefit from preparation as well as a sound base of knowledge. For instance, all the nurseries in Italy are not like the Reggio model. Maureen Lee (personal communication and 2009) describes the visit to Viborg in Denmark by a group of early years professionals in order to learn more about the Danish forest school educational movement. The value of the trip was threefold: thinking and preparation before the visit, the details of the experience in Viborg and reflection on return home. The visit was judged to be especially beneficial because the Danish hosts had organised a programme combining the rationale for the outdoors approach and generous time spent in different types of kindergarten, not all of them located in a forest.

The reflective questions suggested earlier can be useful for any visits, including those in other countries. The international perspective adds that extra opportunity to consider:

- What inspires me about this different system and approach? What can I take back and make my own?
- Are there real differences between my situation and here? What implications does that bring – not excuses for making no changes at all?
- Am I assuming that someone and somewhere else have all the answers; is this really likely?
- How have I been provoked to revisit what I think of as normal, obvious, not worth questioning?
- What do I hold dear in terms of values and priorities? Do I revisit them, not necessarily for change but for a stronger foundation of 'why'?

The English early years professionals on the trip to Viborg realised that not all went smoothly in the Danish settings. Some of the group were less inspired by the indoor environments of some of the kindergartens. An excellent system elsewhere is not necessarily best in every aspect and it is professional to feel pride in what you now realise you, and your colleagues, do very well.

Resources

- Desforges, C. and Abouchaar, A. (2003) *The Impact of Parental Involvement, Parental Support and Family Education on Pupil Achievement and Adjustment: a Literature Review*. London: Department for Education and Skills. **www.education.gov.uk/publications/standard/publicationdetail/page1/RR433**
- Eliot, L. (2009) *Pink Brain, Blue Brain: How Small Differences Grow into Troublesome Gaps and What We Can Do About It*. New York: Houghton Mifflin Harcourt. Access a presentation at **http://fora.tv/2009/09/29/Lise_Eliot_Pink_Brain_Blue_Brain**
- Goddard Blythe, S. (2009) 'All About Movement and Music'. *Nursery World*, 3 December.
- Goldacre, B. (2009) *Bad Science*. London: HarperCollins, **www.badscience.net/**
- Henry, L. (2010) 'Open the Door to New Ideas'. *Nursery World*. 28 January.
- Howard-Jones, P. (undated, circa 2008) *Neuroscience and Education: Issues and Opportunities*. London: Teaching and Learning Research Programme, **www.tlrp.org/pub/commentaries.html**
- Kate Greenaway Nursery School and Children's Centre (2009) *Core Experiences for the Early Years Foundation Stage* distributed by Early Education. Also information on **www.coreexperiences.wikia.com**

- Learning and Teaching Scotland (2005b) *Let's Talk About Pedagogy: Towards a Shared Understanding for Early Years Education in Scotland.* Glasgow: Learning and Teaching Scotland, **www.ltscotland.org.uk/publications/l/ publication_tcm4617466.asp?strReferringChannel=search&strReferringPageID =tcm:4-615801-64**
- Lee, M. (2009) 'International Networks', *Early Years Educator.* 11 (6) October.
- Lindon, J. (2001) *Understanding Children's Play.* Cheltenham: Nelson Thornes.
- Lindon, J. (2012a, third edition) *Understanding Child Development: 0–8 Years.* London: Hodder Education.
- Lindon, J. (2012b, fourth edition) *Safeguarding and Child Protection: 0–8 Years.* London: Hodder Education.
- MacNaughton, G. and Williams, G. (2004) *Teaching Young Children: Choices in Theory and Practice.* Maidenhead: Open University Press.
- Schaffer, H.R. (1998) *Making Decisions about Children: Psychological Questions and Answers.* Oxford: Blackwell Publishing.
- Thornton, L. and Brunton, P. (2009) *Understanding the Reggio Approach: Early Years Education in Practice.* London: Routledge.
- Valentine, M. (1999 and second edition 2006) *The Reggio Emilia Approach to Early Years Education.* Glasgow: Learning and Teaching Scotland, **www.ltscotland.org.uk/resources/r/genericresource_tcm4242154.asp?strReferr ingChannel=search&strReferringPageID=tcm:4-615801-64**

Working together in reflective practice

Effective early years practitioners operate best within a community of learners, even if this is a very small community. Some thoughtful practitioners will spend most of their time with children and without adult colleagues. However, many practitioners work within a group setting and are in a daily working relationship with fellow practitioners, who can directly support each other.

The main sections of this chapter are:
- The context of support
- Skills for effective communication
- Direct support for colleagues.

The context of support

Many early years practitioners are part of a staff group, which may or may not operate as a coherent team. If supportive teamwork is well established, then a nursery or other kind of centre can feel like a harmonious community, in which reflection and discussion are a shared undertaking, as well as personal.

Most childminders work as sole practitioners in their own home. Yet an individual childminder still needs to see learning, and reflection on learning, as an enterprise shared with the children and their family. Best practice will be supported when childminders take advantage of opportunities to participate in a local network. Whatever your working circumstances, the fruits of your reflection need to be expressed through practice, and so have an impact on the children, as well as your direct colleagues or local fellow practitioners.

A community of learners

The self-evaluation approach in Scotland is presented through the *Child at the Centre* guidance (HMIE, 2007). The process of self-evaluation is described as a joint enterprise for the well-being of children and their families. The guidance refers to: 'reflection as a community of professionals'; 'a community of learners'; and 'a collegiate culture' (pages 4:05 to 4:07). The guidance recognises that a process of self-evaluation will not flourish unless there is an atmosphere of support, of working together towards common goals and a perspective on being a professional that includes continuing to learn.

Early years practitioners operate within a social, cultural, political and economic context. You have direct control over some aspects of what affects your practice and minimal control over others. Bronfenbrenner (1979) developed an ecological model within systems theory (Lindon, 2012a) to illustrate the complexity of individuals and social groups. This model is discussed in the context of managing change in Chapter 7. Take a look now at Figure 7.1 on page 164 as a reminder of how different social groups and communities rest within a broader context. Practitioners can make a significant difference to the atmosphere in their place of work, whether this location is your own home as a childminder, or a group setting.

Figure 6.1 Any team needs a consistent approach to valuing and following children's interests

A harmonious community?

This concept fits well with the increased focus within early years on the importance of warm, personal relationships with children and families. Positive relationships – one of four key themes within the first Early Years Foundation Stage framework (2008) – can only evolve within a harmonious nursery, school or club community. There is an intellectual harmony because adults share consistency about their approach (Rich et al., 2005, 2008), and a commitment to address any contradictions. But there is also an emotional harmony of commitment to children as individuals, whose well-being is the top priority. The same points apply to provision that serves older children and adolescents.

- Any group setting becomes more like an institution when approaches are determined by 'It's health and safety policy. We have no choice.' A group that commits to working as a harmonious community gives time to 'Is this health and safety policy really working and in whose interests?'
- Institutions tend to operate with a fixed hierarchy, creating differential status for adults and for children. Such settings often also have differential status for adults, depending on their professional background and qualifications.
- A whole nursery, school or club approach becomes more like a community when there are genuine opportunities for everyone to be heard. Practitioners behave as responsible grown-ups and the atmosphere is democratic: all members of this community have rights and responsibilities.
- In some settings, all practitioners work effectively as a team. Everyone is equally involved in reflection on policy and practice. Managers carry additional responsibility, but this role includes listening and showing active respect to the views of the team.
- Children and their families observe the visible signs of a harmonious atmosphere between practitioners – or the lack of one. Positive relationships within the team set the tone and give a clear message about communication, trust and honesty.
- In settings that operate as a harmonious community, practitioners show respect for partners in the life of the children: their family, other practitioners involved over the same period of time and the provision from which a child is moving. Practitioners make strong efforts to understand children's previous experience and to create continuities. Practitioners express a genuine interest in children's life outside their hours with them (Lindon, 2009).
- In contrast, settings that operate like an institution have minimal interest in children's life other than their role in this place. Family life and the input of other early years provision is seen exclusively through the lens of what 'we need you to do for us'.

Working as a team

Within a group setting, the culture of the organisation can work in favour of reflective practice or undermine that possibility. The concept of what is, and is not, working as a team has much in common with the ideas of a harmonious community.

A group of people working in the same place do not automatically become a team. The key characteristics of team working are confidence that you are in a shared enterprise, with common values and principles and easy opportunities to contribute ideas. Reflective practice will struggle to flourish in a staff group if the atmosphere is not that of a team. There will be too many blockages: that the manager only pretends to ask for ideas; that 'nobody tells us what is happening'; or that one sub-group of staff is definitely lower on the hierarchy. Practitioners who feel sidelined or belittled will decide that any claims of 'We're all a team here' are empty talk. They will not hazard themselves in reflective discussion and are likely to view any new ideas, like peer observation (see page 187), as covert methods of criticism.

A continuing experience of trust is crucial for managers to build and maintain a genuine early years team. Trust that supports team working is created through experience for everyone that colleagues are:

- *Reliable*: people follow through on their commitments, and that includes the most senior practitioners. If problems have arisen, team members let each other know promptly.
- *Consistent*: colleagues can be depended upon to give their best. The quality of their practice does not vary with their mood, with personal problems outside work or whether they have warmed to a child, parent or room partner.

- *Honest*: they will express feelings and opinions openly, yet constructively. Team members are not left to puzzle out what is happening or are not told about concerns or reservations until it is too late for them to do anything.

In a team, individual practitioners realise that they are in a relationship of interdependence: what one individual does in their work will affect other team members, to a greater or lesser extent.

- Thoughtful practitioners consider the likely impact of their actions on colleagues and consult within the team when there is any doubt.
- Managers need to know about and be able to call on the full range of skills within the group. Having common ground in a team does not mean that individuality is lost. In fact, it can undermine thoughtful practice if team members become so similar that they do not take time to question an approach with which everyone agrees.
- Teams only work well when each member is explicitly valued and their contribution is clearly seen to be used within working life. In multidisciplinary teams, managers have the responsibility to show active respect for all practitioners, regardless of their professional qualifications. If practitioners themselves defer to one or two colleagues – as a matter of course – then this situation needs to be addressed.
- Reflective practice and critical thinking in a team will be undermined if the hidden agenda is that practitioners with one kind of qualification are judged to be better informed – again, as a matter of course. Any team needs to respect the special knowledge or understanding of individuals.
- A group that is very dependent on regular volunteers needs to offer involvement in discussion about practice in the setting. Without this sense of genuine participation, there is a risk that resentment caused by not feeling valued will create a sour atmosphere. Volunteers may feel disrespected if, for instance, they believe that a manager makes a greater effort to inform service users, such as parents, than the regular volunteers.

Personal and professional

Effective support of any kind for colleagues has to rest not only on their current knowledge and understanding, but also on personal aspects about their approach, feelings and current state.

Personal issues or concerns

Best early years practice operates within a nurturing environment for young children. That atmosphere and duty of care also apply to the adults involved. There is limited point in pressing ahead with experiences to promote reflective practice when a practitioner is weighed down with serious, non-work problems.

- It is legitimate to say in general that 'personal problems should be left at the door'. Minor aggravations and frustrations should not colour a practitioner's day with children, or their communication with parents.

- It is unprofessional for any practitioner to start a day in a bad mood because of something that has happened at home, or on the journey to work. However, some personal anxieties are very hard to put to one side within the day.
- Thoughtful team leaders are aware of individual practitioners and ready to consider how to help when personal troubles appear to be affecting work.
- However, early years provision, clubs or schools are not therapeutic communities for the staff. A responsible manager has to consider to what extent a practitioner's personal distress is taking energy and attention away from the children – and what is now the best way forward for everyone.

A hierarchy of needs

One way of looking at personal needs and professional development is to use the pyramid model of the hierarchy of needs developed by Abraham Maslow (1943), which he proposed as an explanation for human behaviour. The ideas have been extensively applied to adult behaviour at work. However, Maslow discussed children in the key 1943 paper and the model also offers insights for the behaviour of the younger generation (Lindon, 2012c). Maslow came to be seen as the founder of humanistic psychology, with his focus on well-being and peak experiences. The main idea of the pyramid model, shown in Figure 6.2, is that needs in the lower levels take precedence over higher levels. People cannot move into what Maslow saw as the uppermost level of self-actualisation unless they are reasonably satisfied within the other four levels.

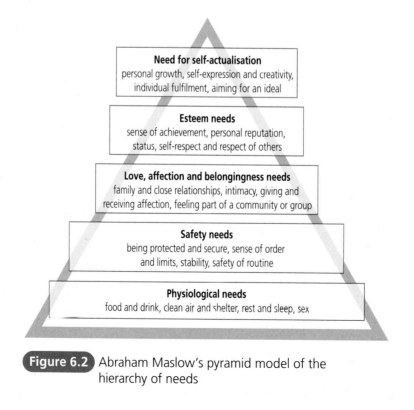

Figure 6.2 Abraham Maslow's pyramid model of the hierarchy of needs

REFLECTIVE PRACTICE AND EARLY YEARS PROFESSIONALISM

At the base of the pyramid, the human biological and physiological needs are dominant. If these needs are met, at least to a reasonable level, then human behaviour is influenced by a drive to be safe and feel protected. In a safe enough environment people have spare energy to acknowledge and strive towards affectionate relationships and a sense of belonging. Then, when people feel secure in this way, they have a firm basis on which to build the sense of competence that supports secure self-esteem. Finally, this emotional security enables people to strive to fulfil their personal potential in individual ways.

Applications to practice with children

This model offers insights for professional life and the possibilities of developing reflective early years practice. Here are some possibilities to consider.

The basic need states at the base of the pyramid dominate and will exert an observable impact on behaviour when they are not satisfied. Practitioners are unlikely to be able to think more deeply about their work if they are anxious about basics, such as having a home. Nor will they be in a positive state if serious worries – or possibly a young baby – keep them awake at night or if practitioners are ill-nourished. Managers or senior practitioners have to decide what is, and is not, their business, and adults' eating habits are by and large their own responsibility. However, practitioners who are on an unwise diet – for weight loss or just seriously unhealthy eating – may be physically and intellectually compromised and their practice with children may suffer. Early years practitioners should also set a visual good example to young children about eating and drinking.

Practitioners have a right to safety and a sense of basic well-being. Some early years provision, after-school clubs and schools are located in genuinely unsafe neighbourhoods. The whole team needs to be confident that appropriate steps are taken to ensure their safety at work and in the surrounding area. These same teams may offer a service to families who are under significant stress and serious problems may erupt through the behaviour of adults or children.

Feelings of safety are not only about physical security. It is difficult to find the emotional energy to step back mentally and think about practice if daily working life is dominated by the bullying behaviour of colleagues. Even highly motivated practitioners feel drained if their ideas are belittled on a regular basis, or they have to operate in a sour atmosphere. Under these circumstances a staff group is not operating at all like a team and the conditions have not been created for a harmonious learning community. The practitioner, or senior team, is responsible for tackling this disruptive situation. However, in some cases the manager is the source of many of the problems, or feels incapable of challenging the dominant staff. Given a choice of alternative jobs, a keen and reflective practitioner will leave if it becomes clear that very little will change.

So long as practitioners can relax and are not distracted by the basic needs of nurture and of physical and emotional safety, they will have energy spare for satisfying the need to be part of a social group. Commitment can grow and a sense of shared effort for the well-being of children and learning together as adults. Under these circumstances, practitioners are more likely to believe reassurances that the different approaches to reflective practice are not covert attempts to find fault. A sense of belonging is not only important for children's well-being, but also for adults. Other than very small nurseries, early years group provision will have some divisions into rooms, most often by the age-banding of children. Heads of centre need to foster not only the commitment to the smaller unit of a room, but also a sense of social commitment to the whole centre. What happens across a centre needs to be consistent with shared values and to rest on respect for what colleagues do with different age groups or services under the same roof.

On a secure base, early years and other practitioners are more able to build their confidence in a reflective approach. This sense of achievement and professional self-respect has been observable in thoughtful individuals and teams, before recent developments that have focused on the value of critical thinking as such. Abraham Maslow placed self-actualisation at the top of his pyramid. Commentators have sometimes challenged the concept that personal growth is necessarily a 'higher' level. Certainly within any professional life there is a balance to be considered. Personal goals for self-expression and fulfilment may be met within working life, but not at the price of taking attention away from the children or families. Some creative endeavours flourish in non-work time.

Early years practitioners are likely to be more supportive to young children when they feel a boost to their self-esteem through the work. If practitioners are not interested day by day, then they are unlikely to create an atmosphere in which children become engaged and keen to learn more. However, any personal wishes to learn more in this direction have to develop within the values and core goals of work with children and families. Adult enthusiasm to develop this experience, or promote that activity, has to rest on more than the practitioner's strong motivation. Is there evidence that children's interests point in this direction, or that parents would genuinely welcome this opportunity?

Attitudes towards the job

Another way of approaching personal outlooks and professional development is to gain some perspective on how individual practitioners regard their job. Lucas (2007) reported on research by Amy Wrzesniewski, who explored what work meant to different people. She acknowledged that the basic idea of three possible orientations came from previous work by organisational psychologists. However, Wrzesniewski looked in much more detail at how a person's outlook could affect their behaviour at work. The concept is that people take one of three broad orientations to their paid work.

1. The first approach is to focus on the work as something the person would not do without payment and the main motivation is financial. The outlook is basically 'I come in. I do my job. I go home.'

2. A second possible approach is to focus on the job as a career. In this case, the person wants to establish how to progress within this line of work. The main motivation for work is to advance through the occupational structure. Different positions need to be a stepping stone to other roles.

3. The third broad orientation is to regard paid work more as a calling. This person gives their energy and commitment because the work is personally fulfilling. The main motivation is the satisfaction of doing this kind of work and doing it really well.

Amy Wrzesniewski's studies were undertaken in the USA and in a range of occupations. People could fall into any of the broad categories in any job. Someone in a professional occupation could regard their job exclusively as a means to earn an income and be resistant to developments that required extra effort or changes in established patterns. On the other hand, someone could be in what would be classified as an unskilled or semi-skilled job, yet feel confident that their work made a difference to other people, and so was worth doing well. It is worth thinking about how these three broad orientations could affect early years practitioners, and how individuals may react to encouragement towards reflective practice. Here are my thoughts; see what you think.

It is possible that practitioners with the first orientation could be resistant to greater thoughtfulness about their job. A reflective outlook requires more effort and can indicate that change is needed. This invitation to inject reflection into existing practice may not be at all welcome and practitioners may object to perceived disruption of established patterns. It is easier to carry on as before: 'We've always done it this way,' 'What is the problem?' or 'Just tell me what to do and let me get on with it.'

- Careful support may bring some practitioners around and allay their anxieties. The clear message will also be that there is time to learn a more reflective approach. However, the shift is non-negotiable, because thinking about what you do and the impact on young children is definitely part of the job. The focus is not new, since thoughtful practice was always best early years practice.

- The encouragement may fall on fertile ground if early years practitioners have been self-protective and lack confidence in their role. A more reflective approach could make the days more interesting, since all the small details matter. Within a staff group, some practitioners may respond well. Others, as in any line of work, may resent the threat to what they view as an easier life and decide to leave.

- The stance of 'I just do my job' sometimes arises from the authoritarian style of a manager. Practitioners are accustomed to being treated with disrespect, as people whose ideas are not welcome and whose minor challenges are interpreted as mutiny. Change may come about when such a manager leaves. Alternatively, someone else with authority may respond to the messages emerging from deeply unhappy practitioners. An outside advisor or consultant may accept the task to create more of a team than a group of staff who follow orders given out by the person in charge.

Practitioners taking the second or third approach to work may be more responsive to the development of reflective practice. Early years practitioners who are motivated by building a career are likely to be alert to current issues for best practice. However, this orientation will not operate in the same way as within a hierarchical business organisation. Working life within early years provision has never offered a lengthy, vertical ladder of promotion. More experienced practitioners working with larger nurseries or centres may move towards the position of deputy or manager. However, career progression within early years has sometimes meant the shift into related fields such as advisory work or family support.

There is good reason to argue that in early years the career and the calling orientation possibly merge for many people. Certainly, a key issue for the growing number of practitioners with Early Years Professional Status and/or degrees is that increased experience and qualifications do not inevitably open new doors in a career progression of increased seniority. Many of the practitioners with whom I spoke as I was writing this book were using their increased understanding within their current post. Supportive managers have made serious efforts to offer different and additional responsibility to their early years professionals (EYPs), sometimes developing useful projects within the setting.

It is most likely that issues around reflective practice within the two orientations will include ideas like those given below:

- The realisation that reflective practice, and all it means, is now an integral part of what is regarded as best practice for early years. So practitioners who envisage some kind of career progression are likely to be motivated to develop their skills in this area. They realise it matters and their ability to show critical thinking and support for others in this direction will demonstrate commitment and appropriate experience.
- Early years practitioners with either broad orientation could well be motivated by the interest that can be sparked when they look carefully at what happens within their work with children and families. Thoughtful practitioners will need to keep a strong hold on the reasons for reflection: to improve experiences for children. The main focus in a practical line of work is that the reflection has observable, positive outcomes: thinking leads to doing.

Accounts of encouraging serious reflection, like that of Mary Jane Drummond (1996), show that once the serious thinking starts, there is no return path. This message also comes from the new generation of EYPs and practitioners who have studied for their degree. The teachers with whom Drummond worked described excitement and new insights. But they also shared the emotional discomfort of having previous certainties questioned. Some described their loss of any peace of mind and the uneasy realisation that they would never be easily satisfied again; they would always think and question. It is important not to lose sight of this aspect to developing reflective practice. Practitioners who care deeply about their work are likely to question how they operated before this opportunity to reassess their approach. As well as support for the intellectual side of critical thinking, there needs to be support for the emotional consequences of disrupting established patterns for individuals who regard their work as considerably more than 'just a job'.

Skills for effective communication

Part of the working role of more experienced and senior practitioners is to guide colleagues towards greater reflective practice. Practitioners with a greater understanding of what is meant by reflective practice will need to recognise and talk through common misunderstandings and any sense of unease.

Sharing the reflective approach

At least some of the practical issues outlined in Chapter 1 will arise in any group. Experienced practitioners need to recall what it felt like for them in the earlier stages of learning to reflect: the stage of conscious incompetence (see page 71). Senior colleagues will fail to be helpful unless they can explain what now seems 'obvious' to them. Genuinely reflective practitioners hold tight to the knowledge that insights and choices are not 'just common sense' to everyone else.

Part of your role is to explain what is meant by a reflective practitioner.
- You could offer examples of what you have found useful and it will be effective to raise specific examples of how this practitioner, or a room team, has been thoughtful in the past. Perhaps at that time the good practice was not explicitly described as 'reflective practice' or 'critical thinking'.
- The more senior team members need to offer a walking visual aid of a reflective practitioner in action. Guiding colleagues is one of the anticipated roles of practitioners with Early Years Professional Status, regardless of whether they are the manager of a setting.
- You aim to highlight the advantages of being reflective: the more positive experiences for children and, often, greater interest and satisfaction for practitioners. Yet you are willing to be realistic: that, of course, reflective practitioners do not sit around thinking all the time and fail to act.

Practitioners who are involved in further-educational experiences, such as a degree course, have sometimes looked at ways to share with colleagues.
- Ideas have included finding a way to share an assignment with a less than enthusiastic room colleague, bringing that person alongside and inviting their experience.
- Other practitioners have looked for ways to pass on what they are learning to colleagues in manageable amounts. The aim has been to share and to create a sense that 'we all gain from my time away'.

- Undoubtedly, reflective practitioners sometimes need to be sensitive to any gap between their level of enthusiasm and the position of their colleagues. It can be a delicate balance between maintaining the impetus of what you have learned and are sure will improve team practice, and not creating too great a leap for everyone else.

You also acknowledge and deal with perceived 'Ah but's and reservations.

- The very common concern is that reflection in its different types is aimed mainly at finding fault, criticising people in a negative way. Uneasy practitioners are unlikely to feel reassured until they have sufficient experience of reflection to be confident that the process has to be constructive.
- Another common objection is summed up with 'If it isn't broken, why try to fix it?' Certainly, it would be disruptive if practitioners wanted to bring about continuous changes for no good reason. However, the underlying issue is often that practitioners want reasons not to contemplate any change.
- You are responsible for creating an atmosphere that provides fertile ground for reflective practice: the trust which enables colleagues to observe each other and to give constructive feedback within a team.
- The ideas behind your practice need to be revisited. Even very good practice needs a team who can articulate their reasons for choices and priorities. You need to be able to explain clearly to new team members who will sometimes bring different assumptions about what is normal practice.

Make the connection with. . . **boundaries for practice**

Best practice still operates within some boundaries. Practitioners who are more at ease with critical thinking will lead colleagues to reflect on some of the 'myths and legends' in practice that are the source of 'We have to. . .' or 'We're not supposed to. . .'. Reflective practitioners need the confidence to make a courteous challenge to what is, or appears to be, a poor choice within early years practice.

Ideas will often enter a team from an external source. Sometimes these ideas and approaches will be refreshing and useful; sometimes they will be contrary to sources of information from elsewhere. A reflective and professional team needs practitioners who are willing to check 'Who says so?' and 'Who else supports this view?' An approach of courteous challenge is appropriate in training days and the more general approach can be 'Where did you read/hear that?' It is also fair that any stated boundary of 'You shouldn't be doing that' usually also needs an answer to 'What should we be doing instead under those circumstances?' as well as a fair request for reasons underlying the 'shouldn't'.

It is an integral part of early years professionalism that practitioners should be familiar with the relevant guidance for their provision. 'Who told you that. . .?' and 'Where, in the EYFS, does it say you have to. . .?' are examples of key questions. A reflective practitioner needs the tracking skills to combine with the questioning and to be active, not passive, in their practice.

Constructive communication

Colleagues need to be honest with each other, yet express that honesty in a constructive way. Blunt negative statements – 'because you need to know this' – are hard to take well, even for the most confident practitioners. On the other hand, continual and unsupported positive statements are not necessarily very constructive either. Many aspects of working well with other people benefit from an understanding of how to offer, and to receive, constructive feedback. The term 'feedback' is most accurately used in the situation where someone has asked a colleague (or anyone else) for their opinion (Lindon and Lindon, 2012). Within a professional context you would not usually hold back until specifically asked for your opinion. So, the discussion in this section is about constructive comments within a team.

Figure 6.3 You also show children respect by listening to them

Expressing constructive comments

Being genuinely constructive in your comments to colleagues is a technique in the sense that there are basic ground rules to follow, but these are not complicated. However, this form of communication needs to be authentic. It is not a technique in the sense of a limited format of words, or an approach that is devoid of feelings.

The two key points for reflection before speaking out loud are:

- What is the evidence (the support, my observations) for what I would like to say?
- How can I make what I say as useful as possible to the other person?

You do not spend ages thinking each time you speak with a colleague, although sometimes your reflection will make a potentially sensitive comment more constructive. Think of these two points more like a habit of communication to establish for yourself.

The other two issues to bear in mind are that the person on the receiving end of your comment needs to:

- Be able to understand what you say and what you mean. These two are not always the same, as summed up in 'I've heard every word you said. But I still can't work out what you think was the problem with how I . . .'.
- Accept and be able realistically to do something as a result of listening to your informed opinion.

When you express your views, you need to focus on what has happened and on your reactions – positive or negative. Vague comments are not useful in helping others to do better, nor in honestly expressing any concerns you have. Being told 'You communicate well with the children' is pleasant, but the words do not say much about actual practice. Vague negative comments may make people feel that they should change, but in what way? All of these points hold whether your colleague has specifically asked for your opinion or not.

- Useful professional communication focuses on what someone has done or not done: how exactly this person behaved. The emphasis on description rather than stark judgement makes comments more useful, as well as easier to accept.
- Give a specific, ideally a recent, example of what you mean, whether the message is a compliment or clear suggestion that change is needed.
- Avoid words such as 'never' or 'always'. They are rarely true and tend to lead the person on the receiving end to react in a defensive or actually hostile way. If you are sure about an observational 'never', say it as 'I have never seen you . . .'.
- Focus on what a practitioner has done and avoid statements that are about their personality or personal style. Negative labelling such as 'You're insensitive to the children's needs' is an interpretation. The exchange is likely to be sidelined into argument around 'I'm not an insensitive person. That's just not true.' It is then harder to return, in a constructive way, to examples that raise a genuine concern about this adult's behaviour.
- In a similar way to a positive approach to the behaviour of young children, you need to reflect before you speak to this colleague. What did she or he do, or fail to do, that leads you to the shorthand of 'insensitive'? Describe the behaviour with a specific example and avoid the label.
- However, again much as with children, positive labels can undermine or restrict a fellow adult. A colleague may initially welcome comments dominated by the

general positive that 'You are always alert to children's interests.' But what next, if there are few or no examples?

- Useful comments need to be actively constructive, such as 'I think you are really alert to children's interests. I noticed how you listened to Nick's excitement about the holes he had found in the garden. You supported him, and the other boys, in their search and wondering about what could have made these holes.'
- Constructive comments do not automatically imply that this practitioner needs to change. However, good practice is often further strengthened when a practitioner can learn what it looks like 'from the outside'.

A secure basis for comments

Constructive communication rests on a secure foundation of what you have actually seen and heard. Your opinions can be valuable, but they have to be presented as a view, and not become muddled within the more factual observation.

- Useful comments focus on what you have observed and an honest expression of your viewpoint. There is focus more on 'what' than 'why'.
- Sometimes people guess at the reason for someone else's behaviour because it seems to soften the criticism, such as, for example, 'I'm sure you didn't mean to ignore Tasha, but . . .'.
- However, this is rarely helpful because it is based on assumptions. This guess deflects attention from the main point: the observation that 'Tasha tried three times to speak up in circle time and you interrupted her words each time, once when you called across to Ben (a practitioner).'
- If possible reasons or intentions could be relevant, then that discussion needs to continue with a specific exploration of possible reasons. You ask open-ended questions such as 'What did you have in mind when you . . .?'
- Your opinions can be useful if they are honestly communicated, with examples, as your own perspective and not as if they are absolute facts. This part of the conversation, or supervision session, needs to be distinct from your observation. A personal opinion should be expressed honestly as 'I think' or 'I feel'. You can follow with 'because . . .' or 'Here's how I've been looking at this incident . . .'.

'Positive' and 'negative'

Over time within a professional relationship with colleagues, constructive comments will include compliments and what might be experienced as potential criticism. Constructive positive and negative comments need to be offered with genuineness and supported by examples.

- It is disheartening if colleagues – whether within a room partnership or a mentoring relationship – spend considerably more time on what could be significantly improved.

- Sometimes there is a great deal of ground to be covered before an individual's practice will be at a more acceptable level. Then it is very important that the support towards change, for instance within a coaching relationship (page 151), has broken down a long journey for learning into smaller steps.
- The implications of a coaching situation are that feedback will be part of that process. The person giving the feedback needs to be able to identify progress, which will be more possible when the goals are not overambitious. (Look also at SMART, page 107.) Equally, there is an increased chance that the practitioner being guided towards improvement will be more able to reflect and identify those positive changes.
- A brief conversation may focus on a particular event. If the working relationship has been constructive so far, then there may be no necessity to add a positive comment to the current conversation. The input is constructively critical – with the meaning of identifying a focus for change. Otherwise, a balance is advisable, given through a rounded summary.
- It is important to remain self-aware of your own style in giving feedback or unsolicited comments. Suppose that you frequently start with the positives and then move on to what is less good practice. Then colleagues, or someone you mentor, may begin to feel that complimentary remarks are less than genuine. They are used to pave the way to comments that challenge existing practice.

Pause for reflection

Everybody has a personal style. But we tend to be unaware of our own verbal mannerisms until they are mentioned by someone who has the opportunity to observe us.

Until a nursery manager pointed it out to me (very constructively), I did not realise that I used the word 'interesting' to lead into comments about practice that I wanted to question. Apparently I often said something like 'It's interesting that you . . . Can you talk me through how you decided to . . .?' I appreciated the manager's observation and do not, I believe, now use the word anything like as often in that context. Apart from anything else, I did not wish to lose 'interesting' for times when something had provoked my interest!

Have you been made aware of some of your own mannerisms and habits?

Constructive comments will not always be welcome – in any working relationship. There is no certain way to stop colleagues becoming defensive, but you can increase the chances that they will listen and consider what you are saying. Sometimes, other people's feelings about your observation will be strong enough to make it hard for them to listen. Avoid repeating yourself and instead focus on your colleague's feelings, working to understand how the emotions have become so strong.

Team members' reactions will be influenced by their previous experiences of discussion and what they have been told is 'feedback' or 'constructive criticism'. Perhaps some practitioners in a group have worked in another setting where 'being honest with each other' was a byword for personal attack and refusal to give any supporting examples, 'because that's just the way I feel'. In contrast, practitioners who have experienced considerate and observational comments can be shocked by another group in which meetings or supervision sessions are a hurtful free-for-all.

On the receiving end of comments

There is a shared responsibility over professional communication, because good working relationships also depend on how people react to what is said to them. Managers and senior practitioners have a special responsibility to model good practice in receiving as well as offering constructive comments or requested feedback. The role of a more senior team member is also to be gracious about comments that could have been more sensitively expressed.

First of all, you need to pay attention to what is being said to you. This simple guideline is the one that is probably most often broken. You cannot possibly understand a comment, nor decide whether it is useful or fair, unless you keep quiet and listen. Allow the other person to finish, resist the temptation to interrupt and justify yourself. Work hard to quieten your inner thoughts about what you are going to say in reply.

- You need to make the effort to understand what has been said to you. Suspend, for the moment, any conclusion over whether the comment is justified. Make sure that you understand the view that has been expressed.
- You can reflect back or briefly summarise the comment, to check you have understood. You might say, 'You felt I coped well with queries in the network meeting.'
- Ask open-ended questions to help you to gain more information or clarification. You might ask for more detail about 'How I handled the question from Kay – because I really felt under pressure at that point in the meeting.'
- If the comment is vague, then ask for an example of what your colleague (supervisor or mentor) means, an instance of 'Something I did recently . . .'. Asking for an example or putting questions to the other person are both with the aim of understanding what has been said. They should not be in words or a tone that implies 'Prove it!'
- It would be unprofessional for other people to become irritated just because they have been asked for something more specific. If they struggle for an example of a colleague's patience with children, or impatience, then they need to observe more carefully to support what is offered as informed commentary.

Listening carefully to comments can provide thinking time – so long as you consider the details and not how you might argue about or justify what you did.

- You may be comfortable to talk straightaway, but equally sometimes it is appropriate to say, 'I'd like to think about that.'
- Further reflection often occurs afterwards, especially if the comments raise new issues about your work. Your peace of mind may be disturbed, because this observation leads you to re-evaluate an aspect of practice about which you had previously felt very sure.

- Even if a colleague's comment was not expressed constructively, there may still be value in what was said. Think over what was said, trying to put aside how it was expressed, and perhaps consult one or two colleagues. If you are a senior team member, then poorly expressed comments will flag up a professional support issue for this practitioner.
- Seeking other opinions needs to be done positively, such as 'I'd like to hear your view on . . .' or 'I'm trying to understand . . .'. Avoid any sense of making your colleagues take sides with 'But I do write clear reports, don't I?'

People are usually most concerned about how criticism will be taken. Yet some people respond to positive comments in such a dismissive way that colleagues regret paying them compliments. If this pattern is established in any group or network, the result is discouraging for everyone. Certainly a team leader should not set the wrong tone with any sense of 'Everyone should be doing that, anyway!' An appropriate reaction to a compliment is simply to say 'I appreciate that' or 'Thanks for telling me.' You might follow this with something specific like 'I'm glad you think I handled the complaint calmly.' Being pleased is not the same as being boastful and a strong sense of pride in your work is a positive quality for an early years practitioner. Modesty may lie behind comments such as 'I ought to have done better' or 'I thought I made a right mess of . . .'. Yet this reply disagrees with the person who has been so encouraging and borders on being discourteous.

It is a good habit to ask for feedback from colleagues on a regular basis. You do not have to wait for a colleague to express comments on some part of your work; you can invite their views. In a supportive team atmosphere – a harmonious community of learners – brief constructive exchanges become part of daily interaction. Longer exchanges are part of supervision, mentoring or the coaching relationship – all discussed later in this chapter.

Using skills of communication

Neither mentoring nor supervision is an ordinary conversation; both are a focused type of interaction. The specific skills of communication needed in this aspect to practice have much in common with the core skills of basic counselling (Lindon and Lindon, 2007).

Active attention

An effective mentor, or someone leading a supervision session, needs to listen and to look. You need to hear what your colleague is saying and notice how they communicate. Your attention to listening also sets a good example to the other person, who needs to listen actively in their different role within the supervision relationship. Active listening is hard work, because all your attention is on what the person is saying and you need to hold back on your ideas or suggestions. However, you do need to say something; it is disconcerting if someone just listens and looks, even if they make friendly 'Uhuh' noises.

Reflective listening

One helpful pattern of response is to reflect back to the other person what you have just heard. You may repeat some of the other person's words, but with the hint of a question in your tone. For instance,

- 'So, you're still puzzled about . . .'
- 'If I've got it right, you think the main problem is . . .'

Your own reflection on practice will be fuller if you recognise what you are feeling, as well as the logical processes of thinking, reasoning and problem solving. When your role is to support, guide and advise someone else, feelings cannot be overlooked. However, you do not want to imply that you know, for certain, what someone else is feeling. You will usually mentor someone you already know. If not, then part of the early relationship is to become familiar with each other. So it can be appropriate to reflect back the feelings they show, as well as what they say in words.

- 'You look really pleased with how the first parents' group went.'
- 'You looked doubtful when I asked about your reflective learning diary.'
- 'You say you feel "overwhelmed" by continuous questioning of your practice.'

Sometimes, you will be more tentative:

- 'You looked rather sad when you talked about the end of the project. Is that how you feel?'
- 'Could it be that . . .?'
- 'I get the sense that you feel daunted about . . . Would it help to talk about . . .?'

Getting more specific

Sometimes it is useful to restate what someone else has said in a way that places them at the centre. Many people use their words, at least sometimes, to distance themselves from what is happening; their 'I' becomes lost in the words they say.

- Perhaps your colleague is describing difficulties in the relationship with a room partner. She says, 'It's so annoying when Damian interrupts my conversations with a parent.' You can reflect back, by saying, 'You get annoyed when Damian . . .'.
- The situation may also be described in terms of what the other person should do: 'Damian should stop being so thoughtless.' You may reflect back along the lines of 'You'd like to find a way to tell Damian . . .' or 'You'd much prefer if Damian . . .'.
- Sometimes there are blockages from the use of the words 'can't' or 'should'. The statement of 'I can't tell him outright' becomes 'You find it difficult to talk with Damian about this.'

Sometimes you will hear plenty of concrete examples as a colleague expands on what is going well or what is less straightforward. Reflective practice is supported by a high awareness of specific instances, and sometimes you need to bring examples to the forefront. Maybe you hear a run of general comments like 'Lately I run out of patience so easily' or 'My room partner is disrespectful to the children.' You need to make the direct invitation of 'Can you give an example?' or 'Tell me about something that happened recently.'

Summarising

It can be useful to make a brief summary of 'Where we've got to . . .' or 'I think we reached this point . . . What do you think?' A good summary is brief and includes not only the information you have heard, but also a flavour of the emotions that have been expressed. It is definitely useful to summarise the main points, if your colleague is moving to another focus for discussion, or at the end of today's session.

Careful use of questions

As well as active listening, both parties within a mentoring or supervision relationship will benefit from thoughtful use of questions. It is up to the other person to decide which questions they want to ask you or pose to themselves in a process of thinking out loud in your presence. As the supervisor or mentor, you need to be thoughtful about the kind of questions you offer.

The more useful questions are open-ended rather than closed. This distinction will be familiar from good-quality communication with children. You ask questions when it feels appropriate to invite your colleague to explore and explain. Keep the questions to a minimum; otherwise the mentoring session will turn into a question-and-answer session. At times you may ask:

- 'Would you like to say some more about . . .?'
- 'What happened then?'
- 'How did you feel about . . .?'
- 'What made you decide to . . .?'

Questions that start with the word 'Why' tend to be less useful. Even within a positive working relationship, the word 'why' seems to require a justification or a very good reason.

- Instead of 'Why did you get so cross with yourself when . . .' you could ask, 'What do you think led you to be so cross with yourself?'
- Instead of 'Why do you think Renee is disrespectful in her communication?' you could ask, 'In your view, how does Renee's pattern of communication show disrespect to the children?'

Sometimes you need to ask a question because you are confused. Perhaps you have become lost in your colleague's narrative and any contribution will now be guesswork. You need to be honest and say, 'Can you take me back to what you said about . . .?' or 'I don't understand the bit you said about . . .'.

Cautious use of personal experience

You may have specific ideas or insights to share with your colleague. However, until you have listened well, you do not know what will be useful. If it does seem appropriate to contribute a personal experience, then this example must be closely connected with what your colleague has said. Keep it brief, with the aim of shedding light on the current discussion. Ensure that your narrative does not take over from what your colleague needs and wants to discuss.

Making connections

A supervision or mentoring relationship should last over time, so it becomes appropriate to support your colleague to make meaningful connections. This contribution could include the following aspects.

- Past successes, which this practitioner may be overlooking in the current confusion.
- Bringing a good idea from previous sessions into the current discussion.
- Raising possible contradictions in a constructive way. You are not telling the other person she is 'inconsistent'; your aim is to help her revisit ideas or beliefs that do not seem to connect.
- Helping practitioners to see patterns in how they approach their work or this kind of event: 'You seem to find it easier to . . .' or 'Thinking back to . . ., I'm wondering if you find the situation more difficult when . . .'.
- In a complex situation, practitioners may be helped to reflect on the range of choices open to them, including options that they have not considered. In some cases, it helps to bring to the fore the different aspects of a dilemma when either option seems equally attractive or equally negative.

Direct support for colleagues

Experienced practitioners should behave as a positive role model. A great deal can be learned by motivated practitioners working alongside more experienced colleagues who are willing and able to share the what, why and how.

The coaching process

There is a difference between being a good role model within the flow of the day and specifically modelling an approach to someone else. Sometimes this more focused approach is needed and the process is called 'coaching'. This word used to be applied only to physical training, but is now widely applied to the process of sharing skills with another adult. Through the coaching process, you help someone else to become competent in areas in which you are already able. Within the professional context the coaching relationship may not be all one-way. Experienced practitioners may gain from a coaching session from a less senior colleague, who nevertheless is more competent in this aspect of the work.

A specific focus

The coaching process homes in on a particular skill or area of knowledge. It is a focused process that is different from being generally helpful and supportive. In order to be an effective coach with anyone, you have to be aware of what you actually do. You need to recapture what it felt like before this area of skill became more automatic and obvious to you. What can seem like 'just common sense' to an experienced practitioner can be confusing to someone who is at the early stage of learning, or who has never really thought much about how they react to children.

Look back at page 70 for the discussion about cycles of learning and reflective competence. In brief you need to be clear in your own mind:

- What do I do in this situation with a child? A parent? In a team meeting?
- What are my reasons for doing it this way?
- Can I break down what I do into smaller, more manageable steps?
- Can I recall what helped me – without assuming that this approach will be the right one in all the details for this person?

Effective coaching is a blend of helping someone to understand what they could do and then standing back to let them learn through practice. The one-step-at-a-time approach to professional development is respectful and can be adjusted to colleagues at different levels of expertise. Not everyone will be excellent at everything, but everyone can aim for a personal best. A good coach considers 'What will it take to enable this person to flourish?' and offers:

- manageable steps to challenge the other person but not to overwhelm
- supported practice, with moderate pressure to try, and expressed confidence that they will learn
- encouragement, patience and constructive feedback
- conversations to review progress and set new steps for a skill that will take time to be achieved in full.

Tell, show and do

You have several options for how to transfer your skill or understanding to that other person. It is unwise to assume that just one method, especially different forms of 'telling', will do the job entirely. It will also be wise to allow for the personal learning style of the other person. Look back at page 68.

- You can tell and explain, especially when it is crucial that the other person takes on board important information. Ideas may be communicated through conversation, but some ideas or information may be best in a written format, if only for a reminder.
- Some individuals also really like to make their own notes or memory joggers. Just talking or handing over written material is unlikely to work unless the other person is both motivated and already reasonably able in this area.
- It is frequently important to show as well as to tell. Ideas often need to be demonstrated in action. You may be able to take opportunities that arise spontaneously, but sometimes you need to create a situation. Be clear about anything that is non-negotiable: any aspect of this skill or approach that is not genuinely open for choice.
- Coaching usually involves a process of tell, show and do; the other person needs supervised practice. Transfer of skills means that ideas and actions need to pass from the usual behaviour of one person to that of another. The person whom you are coaching needs to practise, to do something, either by taking the opportunities that arise or through your invitation of 'Now you try it.'
- Safe coaching does not set people adrift before they are confident. Sometimes the more experienced person is alongside, ready to help but avoiding taking over or stepping in unnecessarily.

Provide regular feedback

In order to help other adults through the coaching process you need to offer constructive feedback on how they are doing (page 144). Feedback should be expressed clearly (for this person), be encouraging yet honest and highlight what they are actually doing, or not yet doing.

- It may be important for this practitioner, who sets himself very high standards, to be reminded 'You only had to check with me once this time. You are so close to not needing me beside you.'
- You could share your observation of a practitioner who is learning to use puppets in storytelling. Perhaps you comment on how the children looked very engaged and joined in the story with minimal prompting.
- You may also comment that the practitioner still looks uneasy about even quite short silences. You discuss ways that she could let a friendly silence continue for a short while, since this pause is probably the children's thinking time.

People can gain from their mistakes so long as constructive feedback places the experience firmly as an opportunity to learn, rather than one of frustration and regret. It is unhelpful to be told 'You're doing fine' when you are struggling. However, you explore errors more through the consequences than a blunt 'That was wrong.' Obviously, you stop someone before they make mistakes that will have serious negative consequences. If you are coaching someone in how to use tools, you step in with 'Hold on a moment. Can I show you again how to . . .', before they do themselves an injury.

Scenario

Princes Children's Centre

Harriet, the deputy of the centre, is confident and competent about getting up in front of other people, whether it is the whole centre team, other professionals or events for families whose children attend the centre. She became enthusiastic about public speaking at secondary school and has taken every opportunity to improve her skills and use technology as and when this option is appropriate for the occasion. Harriet has no problem in taking the lead in these situations. However, she and Brigid, the head of the centre, have become aware that Harriet's competence is being used as a justification by some team members for not improving their own skills.

Kitty really should be the person to talk at the next Parents' Evening about the 'Everyone can do maths' workshop. Kitty has developed the plans and she has already shown a sensitive approach to helping fellow adults to challenge their own 'maths gremlins': anxieties that get in the way. However, Kitty is very resistant to talking to the group and keeps saying, 'But Harriet is just so good at making presentations. I'm sure to mess it up.' Harriet and Brigid decide that now is the time to coach Kitty in the skills to make a short presentation.

Harriet plans several coaching sessions with Kitty, with the aim that she will speak for about ten minutes during the next Parents' Evening. They start with support for Kitty to decide on the main points she wants to communicate. Kitty experiments with speaking from memory, decides she needs a few written notes and homes in on her preferred format with four overheads on the laptop.

Kitty tries out her plan at the next team meeting and her colleagues offer constructive feedback.

- They agree that Kitty's main messages are coming across clearly and the overheads support what she is saying.
- Ravinder makes the suggestion that Kitty should keep looking at the audience and not turn back to look at the screen. Kitty agrees to line up the laptop, so she can see her material on that screen.
- Brigid suggests that Kitty removes her apologetic start of 'This is my first ever presentation, so I hope I don't mess up.' Brigid's advice is that there is no advantage in 'flagging up' inexperience in this way.
- Kitty herself then recalls feeling irritated in the audience when a presenter repeatedly said, 'I hate using microphones' and generally claimed to be inept with technology. Kitty makes minor adjustments to her talk and vows to keep looking at the audience. On the evening, she feels she has done well for a first attempt. She lost her place on one point but found the flow again. She started to look back but caught herself and faced the audience. Kitty feels that speaking in public could well get easier now.

Questions

1. Have you supported a colleague, or been coached, towards a new skill?
2. What helped that process? Looking back, what might have been more helpful?

....

What does it mean?

Coaching: the process of supporting and guiding another person to become more competent in a specific skill.

Mentoring: a one-to-one professional relationship, in which a more experienced individual supports and advises another person, with reference to all aspects of practice and with attention to well-being.

Mentoring

Another approach to supporting thoughtful professional development is for practitioners to be assigned a mentor. This mentoring role operates within a one-to-one supportive relationship through regular meetings between two practitioners, one of whom is more experienced than the other. The mentor may well be supporting more than one practitioner in this way but would meet them separately. The mentoring relationship is more holistic than that of coaching, which focuses on specific skills. A mentor should have an additional focus of taking care of the well-being of a colleague, as that person passes through significant changes of CPD.

- Practitioners on long courses such as a degree or the Early Years Professional Status track are expected to be assigned a mentor, who is fully involved in working with young children and families.

- This relationship is often between members of the same team, but not always. The mentor may be at a more senior level in the team, often the manager or deputy, but not necessarily.
- Practitioners of similar seniority, but different roles, are able to share their different perspectives and offer support to each other. This type of peer mentoring can be effective and may operate in more informal ways.
- In some cases, it makes sense for an external person to be asked to commit the time to mentor. Childminders need to seek a mentor from within the local early years structure.

The aim of the regular meetings is for the mentor to listen and be an informed sounding board. But their role is also to offer their contributions based on their experience. Mentors should support colleagues, or practitioners from outside the immediate team, towards greater awareness of their practice and to step back. The mentoring role is sometimes described as a 'critical friend', meaning constructively critical, with the underpinning of friendly support.

If there is a choice of possible mentors, the aim is that both practitioners feel able to work cooperatively together. Mentors need to assign the time for regular meetings and ensure they are well informed about the issues that the practitioner brings to the sessions. A mentor is not a substitute for a good course tutor, but complements that role with time for personal discussion, which a tutor is unlikely to be able to offer to every student.

Mentoring is a working relationship and, through using relevant skills of communication, the mentor makes a difference to the professional development of the other practitioner. However, it is important that managers who mentor members of the team keep the mentoring sessions separate from staff performance appraisal. The mentoring session is led much more by issues that the practitioner wishes to raise and not by the focus on performance that is integral to the appraisal process.

Scenario

Kerry, Accredited Childminder

Kerry is in the middle of gaining her Early Years Professional Status. Simone, an early years consultant from the local authority, agreed to be her mentor through the process. In this session Kerry raises a practical problem from running the support group for childminders at the weekly drop-in. As a sole practitioner, it has been a challenge for Kerry to find an aspect of her practice in which to show competence in working closely with fellow professionals.

The support group is currently in an awkward phase. A core group of a dozen minders are now at ease in talking about issues in their practice and much better at listening before offering advice to fellow practitioners. However, three people have newly joined the group and open discussion has 'stalled'. One of the newcomers is very outspoken and Kerry has observed the 'regulars' exchanging some sharp looks. After the last meeting, one childminder complained privately to Kerry that the established group should have been closed to new arrivals.

Pause and reflect

Simone talks through the issues with Kerry, to consider the separate issues.

- Is it even feasible now to make the group closed, when the original assumption was that it would be open?
- Kerry realises also that they did not discuss, at the outset, whether this group would meet for a fixed number of times. With hindsight, she realises the initial set-up of the group was too vague.
- Kerry considers what needs to happen within an open group when 'new' childminders join, such as sharing the confidentiality ground rules, which were agreed in the very first meeting.
- Simone also invites Kerry to reflect on the choice she made in the last meeting – not to intervene when the 'newcomer' dominated a discussion about advice to parents on night waking.
- Was she motivated by a wish to enable a new group member to feel at home? Or was she uncomfortable, lacking a strategy, to break into the flow of a fellow practitioner who showed no signs of stopping?

Questions

1. A mentor listens, but is also able to guide. What could Simone suggest for Kerry's consideration?
2. What could Kerry learn from raising these practical issues with Simone?

Supervision

Supervision is a continuing process within a setting and individual supervision sessions should be offered on an equal basis to all practitioners in the team. In contrast, mentoring is most usually a time-bound working relationship, focused on increased competence or offering guidance through a process of study or qualification. In practice, elements of mentoring can merge with a reflective form of supervision, as well as include elements of coaching.

Setting up supervision

A regular supervision session enables practitioners to discuss detailed aspects of their practice. They have time to reflect on what is going well and developments that may have taken place since the last supervision session. They can also raise issues that they currently find problematic: with children, families or relationships with other practitioners. Some basic rules apply to any kind of supervision:

- The meetings need to happen on a regular basis, and not be fitted in 'as and when'. Time is an issue in any kind of provision. However, each meeting needs to be long enough for practitioners to feel at ease and take time to express something that may not be easy.
- The supervision session is a confidential professional exchange and should happen somewhere quiet, with the door closed. The person offering

REFLECTIVE PRACTICE AND EARLY YEARS PROFESSIONALISM

supervision, often a senior practitioner, sets the expectation that these sessions are not interruptible. Other team members do not come into the room, unless there is a crisis, and someone else answers the telephone.

- Supervision is an ongoing process in which both parties are likely to return to the same or similar issues again. If you offer supervision, you should keep brief, confidential notes, enabling you to return as appropriate to what someone said last time. If you offer supervision to more than one person, it is essential that you keep the individual tracks separate and clear in your mind.

- If you are receiving supervision, it is your choice to keep notes of any kind. However, it would almost certainly be valuable to get into the habit of gathering your thoughts after a session. The supervision experience is also likely to be more productive if you are ready to talk about issues. Bring anything appropriate, like your observation of a child or notes from a home visit.

- Although supervision is an ongoing process, it can be helpful sometimes to pull together strands for the other person in an interim summative way, especially if an issue seems to be resolved, or is unlikely to arise again for some time. It can be useful to suggest some sense of 'Have we reached the point where . . .?'

- Individual issues remain private to the individual session. However, senior practitioners offering the supervision need to be alert to issues that have broader implications and discuss that aspect with this practitioner. Uncertainties around practice may need a more general airing in a team meeting or inconsistencies within a room team need a scheduled time with the other practitioners to problem solve.

Figure 6.4 Supervision can be the time to talk about whether lively can become too rumbustious and who thinks so?

A supervisor needs to show active listening and other skills described from page 149. The aim is to be non-judgemental, in order to encourage the other person to voice feelings, as well as actions. Supervision should be a collaborative process in which the person being supervised feels confident to choose a new strategy, or offer to take on a different role in the setting. Supervision will not work in a positive way if a supervisor sees the session as a time to be very directive about what the other person should do. However, in the supervision relationship, as in any aspect of early years practice, there needs to be clarity about core values and elements of practice about which there genuinely is no choice. A supervisor should express a clear judgement, supported by reasons, if the practitioner's choices are demonstrably poor or unsafe practice with children.

Supervision is not a 'telling' session, in which the supervisor directs the other person. The aim should be to create a calm and safe environment, in which it is possible to do productive talking and good thinking. However, supervision sessions can slip into a routine of limited feedback on performance, information on training needs and direct advice. The drawbacks to this more one-way pattern of communication have led to discussion around the idea of reflective supervision.

Finally, supervision is not the same as appraisal, which is a time of summative assessment, pulling together the different aspects of an individual's practice. The appraisal review brings together positive changes since the last review, clarity over directions for improvement and discussion about the best way forward for the continuing professional development of this individual practitioner.

Reflective supervision

The Zero To Three organisation in the United States has explored in detail an approach to supervision of early years practitioners, which they call 'reflective supervision'. Their ideas are a valuable way to think more deeply about the supervision process as a whole. The aim is not to have two kinds of supervision running in parallel.

The papers on the Zero To Three website describe supervision as an important support for reflective practice and so place the process firmly within the relationships established within any early years provision. Familiar, trusting and still professional relationships need to be established between the adults in any provision. Zero To Three proposes that supervision should be understood as a 'relationship for learning', with regular opportunities for collaborative reflection between the person giving and the person receiving supervision. This focus highlights how the supervisor needs to understand a practitioner's current understanding or confusion, including how he or she feels.

Supervision as part of reflective practice enables individuals to take time out from busy normal life with babies and young children, or older ones. It is the opportunity to think out loud, to voice possibilities and almost immediately to say, 'No, that's not it. It's more that I . . .'. Expressing thoughts and feelings about your work can be therapeutic, in the general sense. The qualities needed in a reflective supervisor are similar to those of the counsellor in a counselling relationship: empathy, genuineness and emotional warmth (Lindon and Lindon, 2007). However, reflective supervision is not personal therapy; it is focused directly on the experiences that arise within your practice. Individual doubts and concerns, plus the impact of your own earlier experiences, are significant. They are discussed with a view to improving practice for the benefit of the children.

Weigand (2007) describes his professional experience of this process of receiving this kind of reflective supervision, and gaining insights into his approach as an early years practitioner. His agreed focus with his supervisor was to explore Weigand's own feelings about experiences with individual children. The sessions covered events with young children, including those individuals that Weigand was able to admit to himself he found irritating. His supervisor suggested a shift in reflection of those experiences from 'knowing what to do' towards 'knowing how you are'. The key point was that the adult's emotional reaction – of frustration with one child's usual behaviour and comfort with the strategies of another child – had a direct impact on the practitioner's behaviour, the immediate interaction and the ongoing relationship with the young boy or girl.

Weigand chose to focus on behaviour in his supervision sessions and he describes the benefits of time to re-experience events through relating what happened and separating what the child did from his own adult reaction. He revisited the feelings and thoughts in his own mind and the consequences for how he typically behaved. With this awareness came the simple but crucial insight that the young children did not simply act on their own volition; they reacted to how he behaved towards them. Weigand sums up that the key change for him from reflective supervision was an increasing ability to be 'in the moment' with a young child: to focus on individuals and what they were doing, alongside awareness of the child's likely feelings, thoughts and intentions.

Catherine Croft (personal communication, 2009) describes how she has used the approach of reflective practice. She used an action research model to explore support for practitioners in their key person role. A central key concept within the research was that it was not possible to support and safely contain the feelings of very young children if the adults have limited scope for expressing their own reactions, for instance when a child, or parent, is visibly distressed (Elfer et al., 2003; Manning-Morton, 2006).

The project started with a professional day in which early years practitioners were encouraged to acknowledge and explore their own feelings about being a key person. Adults were invited to consider their own emotional journey, with the theoretical underpinning that personal experiences are valuable material for developing best practice. Practitioners within this day used visual methods for bringing emotions alive, including small-world play as a means to express issues around the key person system and children's emotional needs and behaviour.

As part of the action research, Croft interviewed practitioners and offered reflective supervision to four individuals. The supervision sessions were further supported by her observations of children and their key person within a normal day in the room. Croft used the Tavistock observation method, in which factual observation is supplemented with clearly distinguished elements of the observer's own emotional reactions, and carefully worded comments about a child's possible feelings in a given situation. Practitioners commented that they felt more able to notice and express some of the emotional issues for children and adults, because Croft, as their supervisor, had brought matters to the surface, through sharing her observations. It became more possible to disentangle adults' feelings from those of the children and to support practitioners to move beyond their first reaction and interpretation of a child's behaviour.

What does it mean?

Supervision: regular meetings between individual practitioners and a more senior team member in order to discuss issues within the work, what is going well and any problems.

Reflective supervision: sessions in which there is special emphasis on re-experiencing emotionally significant experiences in practice, in order to examine the meaning of those events and how this understanding can enhance practice.

Appraisal: a process of summative assessment in which an individual's performance is reviewed, with judgements about relative quality in different aspects and indicators for areas of improvement.

Resources

- Bronfenbrenner, U. (1979) *The Ecology of Human Development*. Cambridge, MA: Harvard University Press.
- Croft, C. (2009) *How Can a Reflective Model of Support Enhance Relationships between Babies, Young Children and Practitioners?* MA dissertation in Education in Early Childhood: London Metropolitan University.
- Department for Children, Schools and Families (2008) *The Early Years Foundation Stage – Setting the Standards for Learning, Development and Care for Children from Birth to Five*. London: DCSF. **www.education.gov.uk/publications/standard/publicationdetail/page1/DCSF-00261-2008**
- Drummond, M.J. (1996) 'Teachers Asking Questions'. *Education 3-13* volume 24, no 3, 8–17.
- Elfer, P., Goldschmied, E. and Selleck, D. (2003) *Key Persons in the Nursery: Building Relationships for Quality Provision*. London: David Fulton.
- HM Inspectorate of Education (2007) *The Child at the Centre: Self-Evaluation in the Early Years*. Livingston: HMIE. **www.hmie.gov.uk/documents/publication/catcseey.pdf**
- Lindon, J. (2009) *Parents as Partners*. London: Practical Pre-School Books.
- Lindon, J. (2012a, third edition) *Understanding Child Development: 0–8 Years*. London: Hodder Education.
- Lindon, J. (2012c) *Understanding Children's Behaviour: 0–11 Years*. London: Hodder Education.
- Lindon, J. and Lindon, L. (2007) *Mastering Counselling Skills*. Basingstoke: Palgrave Macmillan.
- Lindon, J. and Lindon, L. (2012) *Leadership and Early Years Professionalism*. London: Hodder Education.
- Lucas, E. (2007) 'Harnessing Performance' in *Professional Manager*, September, pages 22–25. More about the ideas of Amy Wrzesniewski on **www.bus.umich.edu/Positive/Pos-Research/Contributors/AmyWrzesniewski.htm**
- Manning-Morton, J. (2006) 'The Personal is Professional: Professionalism and the Birth to Three Practitioner'. *Contemporary Issues in Early Childhood*, volume 7, no 1.
- Maslow, A. (1943) 'A theory of human motivation', *Psychological Review,* 50, 370–96. Download from **http://psychclassics.yorku.ca/Maslow/motivation.htm**; also try these online sources **www.teacherstoolbox.co.uk/T_maslow.html** and **www.businessballs.com/maslow.htm**
- Rich, D., Casanova, D., Dixon, A., Drummond, M.J., Durrant, A. and Myer, C. (2005) *First Hand Experiences: What Matters to Children*. Clopton: Rich Learning Opportunities. **www.richlearningopportunities.co.uk**
- Rich, D., Drummond, M.J. and Myer, C. (2008) *Learning: What Matters to Children*. Clopton: Rich Learning Opportunities.

- Weigand, R. (2007) *Reflective Supervision in Child Care: The Discoveries of an Accidental Tourist.* Access this and other articles on **http://main.zerotothree. org/site/DocServer/ZTT28-2_nov_07.pdf?docID=7244**
- Zero to Three Best Practice with Infants and Toddlers, with section on *Reflective Practice and Program Development.* **www.zerotothree.org/about-us/areas-of-expertise/reflective-practice-program-development/**

The process of managing change

A professional habit of reflection will often lead to small, although still important, changes in your daily practice. However, some teams and services also go through a process of significant change that involves revisiting values and assumptions, as well as changing actual practice. This chapter covers the issues of managing change, major as well as relatively minor, and the contribution of methods of self-evaluation.

The main sections of this chapter are:
- Managing change
- Self-evaluation within the team.

Managing change

This section focuses on understanding the process of change, which can productively start from within a team and is not always provoked or imposed by external forces. If you make changes through active choice, your positive motivation works to support the process and deal with unexpected problems.

Early years change agents

Anyone involved in guiding change needs to recall the immediate and broader context in which they are working. Figure 7.1 uses the ecological model developed by Bronfenbrenner (1979) as a reminder of the circles of influence on what happens within any given early years provision, school or out-of-school facility. Change agents need a clear sense of the source of information when practitioners believe they 'must', 'should' or 'cannot' do something within their daily practice.

Early years services and professionals have experienced waves of change since the 1990s. Much of this change has arrived because of national changes to the broad framework in which practitioners are expecting to operate. Other changes have been led through national initiatives that created new types of provision, such as the significant growth of children's centres. Required new change has sometimes arrived well before it is feasible to evaluate whether the last change has stabilised or been beneficial. Positive change can definitely be viewed as progress. However, discussion around managing change becomes more complex, because some changes are unsettling, unwelcome and at best neutral overall in their impact.

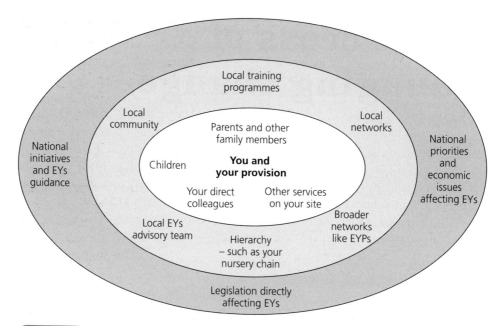

Figure 7.1 Change within a social context using the ecological model of Urie Bronfenbrenner

What does it mean?

Change agent: an individual who has the responsibility to identify the need for change and to manage the process of change towards identified goals.

Managing and leading

Traditionally, when change has occurred, managers have led that development within a setting. The person in charge of a service or provision can, of course, be desperate to avoid any change whatsoever. The difference between being a manager and being a leader was discussed on page 4 and needs to be revisited here in the context of managing change.

- The role of manager is focused on the present and the short term. Managers use past experience as a basis to monitor and control all the organisational systems that ensure that work goes smoothly. Organisations need good managers who ask 'How?' and 'When?'
- The role of a leader is to focus on the future, to take a longer-term perspective and to bring improvements to the organisation, by harnessing the commitment of the team. Leaders are willing to challenge the status quo, to ask 'Why?' and 'So what?'
- The tasks of managing and leading cross over when changes are necessary within a medium-term time span. At this point, the skills needed are to consider the capabilities in the team, possible flexibility and opportunities for

change by changing aspects of the current way of working. The role of leading a team in this situation is described as transactional or situational leadership.

- Leaders need an image, a vision, of how the current situation could change, and how a long-term prospect of change will transform the organisation or service. Change that encompasses innovative changes of direction, or a complete reorganisation around different key principles, requires a transformatory form of leadership.

Within an organisation one person might blend all these roles, although nobody will guide an organisation through significant change without the commitment and hard work of the rest of the team. Leadership is essential but so is management. The process is called 'managing change' because organisations really need people who keep focused on the short term, who manage a significant change step by step. A visionary leader may be less strong on the daily detail, although I have known some early years and school leaders who have successfully combined both sets of skills.

Different change agents
The position of the Children's Workforce Development Council is that practitioners with Early Years Professional Status are expected to be agents of change within their provision. This role is possible only if EYPs – or other professionals in a similar role – have an understanding of the process of bringing about change in their setting and also that they are in a position of authority. EYPs will not necessarily be the manager of a setting. However, they need to be regarded by colleagues as someone who has the right to take the lead, have a clear guiding role and that they have the full support of the senior team.

EYPs are not the only change agents within the early years services. In some cases, external, independent consultants support change, because they are specifically invited by a team leader to be involved on a short- or longer-term basis. I work in this way within my own consultancy business. A range of early years advisors and consultants work within the local authority team to support and guide provision within the area.

Understanding the process of change
There is a considerable amount of research about the factors involved in successful organisational change, much of it drawn from study of change within commercial organisations. Some aspects of business life do not apply to the early years workforce, any more than to other parts of the public sector. However, the majority of the lessons from organisational change are directly relevant to provision for children and families, because people are involved.

Argyris and Schön (see page 34) moved away from the approach of scientific management, which focused on human behaviour, but discounted the social and emotional factors in how people behave. Argyris and Schön were key figures in creating the foundations of an approach through human resources. A full understanding of the process of change, of what will ease the flow and what will block it, encompasses a grasp of systems and organisational structures. However, any realistic framework of change never loses sight of the fact that individuals operate within those structures, along with their ideas, past experiences, feelings and mental maps.

The scope of change

Valuable change is not always a huge overturning of what already exists. It is useful to consider three broad levels of change. In practice, these often merge.

Routine changes

Routine changes are the regular and necessary adjustments to usual work practices and procedures. If you work with someone else, daily conversations guide who is taking responsibility for what, even if you have a general shape to the day or session. Today, you may need to reorganise slightly so that you can have more than a swift conversation with Lily's mother. Perhaps the usual walk to the library needs to be amended, because a road has been closed. Routine changes are not inevitably easier than more significant change. Minor problems can highlight larger issues that need resolving. Maybe it becomes clear that a colleague resists taking their turn with the lively games out in the garden. Perhaps the nursery manager is so uneasy about any local trips that a closed road is seized as an excuse not to go out at all this week.

Figure 7.2 Children learn a great deal through play, but do you value how much they also learn through real-life experiences?

Improvement changes

Improvement changes are more about enhancing current practices and adjusting procedures when they have strayed too far from what was originally agreed. Perhaps in theory, a centre has a supervision system but during recent weeks many scheduled times have been cancelled at short notice. What is happening and how can an important part of centre life be re-established? Maybe the newsletter for parents is mainly working well and the content is well received. But somebody needs to take responsibility for ensuring that text does not slide out of the boxes. After last month's embarrassing wrong word, the final draft must not only be spell-checked but also read for meaning.

Improvement changes may emerge from a series of routine changes and the related reflection and discussion. For instance, minor adjustments to the daily routine of who will set up equipment outdoors raise questions about why the adults make all these decisions. Children are looking out of the window, trying to direct the practitioner in the garden. Then they reorganise equipment when they are allowed outside. So why not make setting up the garden a joint enterprise?

Innovative changes

Innovative changes will profoundly influence the way that provision operates. Significant change may be imposed by external forces, in the outer layers of the model shown in Figure 7.1, such as changes in legislation or government initiatives. However, an individual provider or group will have to rethink their provision if there are major changes in the range of children and families who typically attend. For instance, some playgroups and nurseries have had to rethink what they offer when the age of their youngest children dropped from rising threes down to very young twos. A small reduction in the youngest age could be addressed through improvement changes. However, best practice, in the thoughtful teams, brought a more innovative form of change: rethinking about routines, personal care, equipment and adult habits of communication (Lindon, 2012d).

The Early Years Foundation Stage brought the requirement that every setting in England had to establish a key person system, which enabled personal, sustained relationships between the named practitioner and key children with their family. Many settings had developed a full key person system, when this approach was a firm recommendation. Those teams continue to consider how the system works and any further improvements. However, managers who previously chose to ignore the recommendation, or find reasons why it was not possible, were then faced with a non-negotiable requirement, necessitating innovative change in organisation and equally important changes in attitudes (Lindon, 2010c).

Pause for reflection

Julian Grenier, head of Kate Greenway Nursery and Children's Centre in London, described their experience in saying that 'the best way for practice to evolve and improve is from the ground up, rather than in response to central Government prescription and guidance' (Grenier, 2010: 2). The Kate Greenaway approach has been to develop practice by taking the Early Years Foundation Stage into account, rather than believing that another new framework inevitably required extensive changes in practice, policies and procedures. Grenier sums up the problems as: 'Revolution in early years practice seems to mean spending one decade clearing out all the play equipment and bringing in the literacy hour, and then struggling to reintroduce play the next. That is why I would favour evolutionary change every time' (2010: 3). I agree; three cheers for that perspective.

Despite written reassurances that the EYFS mainly brought together what was already regarded as good practice, many groups and sole practitioners, such as childminders, were sure that wholesale change must be required. Uncertain professionalism is stoked by a stream of guidance documents as well as a series of actual changes in the framework for early years experiences. Sadly, even excellent practice can risk being diluted or sidelined, with the anxious outlook that existing practice obviously cannot be good enough, or else why would there be all these additional guidance documents?

Early years provision in England faces another period of potential change when the revised EYFS comes into force in September 2012. The final version is not available at the time of writing (late 2011). However, the proposed revision (see website link below) includes some reorganisation of areas of learning and development and a contentious approach to ensuring that young children are to be 'school ready'.

www.education.gov.uk/consultations/index.cfm?action=conResults&consultationId=1747&external=no&menu=3

Comments

1. Wherever you work in the UK, what approach have you taken in your own provision when new initiatives and guidance emerge?
2. On reflection have you, or some of your colleagues, been overanxious about the need for complete, revolutionary change?
3. How can you apply the ideas of evolutionary change to your situation?

How are people affected by change?

Practical research and observation highlight that on balance:

- It is easier to change the situation than to change a person's behaviour.
- It is easier to change someone's behaviour than to change their attitudes.
- It is easier to change a person's attitudes than their personality.

This ordering does not imply that the first option is easy, as such. Making changes within the context of how people behave is hard work and a relatively long-term process. The point is to highlight where you best put your efforts in the steps of bringing about change.

When appropriate, change agents put most of their energy on focused change in the situation and towards clear-cut expectations of what people will do or not do – their behaviour. Where there is a stark choice over good practice, you do not spend a great deal of time in unproductive discussion around attitudes and preferred outlook. The focus is on how the other person is now expected to behave.

For example, Katy (the manager) realises that Syreene, a student who is new on placement with FineStart, believes it is acceptable to use her mobile phone during her time with the children. Katy is not interested in discussing with Syreene that 'everybody' answered their mobile in her previous nursery (located on the other side of the town). Nor does Katy try to dispute Syreene's claim that 'I can keep an eye on children and text at the same time.' Katy states firmly that in this nursery mobile phones are placed in your locker and she explains clearly why children deserve your full attention. Katy decides to pass the information about the other nursery to Simone, an early years consultant with the local authority.

Scenario

Daleside After School and Holiday Club

Alicia, the club leader, reviews the year with Ronan, her deputy. Twelve months ago they recognised the limited progress that had been made in encouraging practitioners to talk on a regular basis with parents. Sheila, who has worked with Daleside since it opened ten years ago, was especially firm in her view that informal conversation was a waste of time, unless parents had to be told about their child's 'behaviour problems'.

Alicia and Ronan decided they would change the situation and introduced a club logbook. At the same time they revisited the key person system, which had always been part of club life. Each practitioner made professional notes in their own logbook and was expected to talk, however briefly, with the parents of their key children at the end of each day. Alicia and Ronan offered regular support, including explaining highlights of the day that should be shared. These brief conversations in the team were also the way to address what was actually a problem and how to raise it with a parent.

Zainub and Katya grew in confidence as they built up experiences of informal, non-problematic conversations with individual parents. Sheila remained convinced that some of her key parents were 'easy' to talk with and some were 'difficult', rather like their children. However, she was willing to make notes in her logbook, which gave Alicia the opportunity to discuss issues in detail with Sheila each day.

For almost two months, Alicia was prepared to make the final decision about what Sheila's key families needed to be told, for example the decision about what was a minor and resolved disagreement between Jof and his best friend Simon and what was a more serious issue about the dismissive language that Jof used towards the girls in club. Sheila was able, on reflection, to consider that Jof's offhand remarks to Becky, in particular, were possibly a misplaced attempt at expressing fondness.

The logbook system encouraged all team members to allow that there were at least two people in any 'difficult' situation. Even Sheila became less swift to announce that a parent 'should' react in a different way and more willing to adjust how she raised genuine problems from the child's day. By mid-year, some of the broader practice issues were being raised in the team meetings. One idea was that children themselves needed to have affirmation for what had gone well and how they were managing in situations they found less than easy in club life.

Questions

1. In your practice have you, or your team leader, brought about useful change by altering the situation?

2. Do you currently face a practice problem that you are attempting to resolve in ways that require a practitioner to become somebody different from who they are?

Another way of looking at change is that there are four broad areas that can be the focus of change within your practice or entire organisation. Each area poses a different type of demand on individuals for adjustment and reflection. Some programmes of change aim deliberately to affect more than one of these broad areas. Alternatively, some unexpected consequences of the change process may affect an area that was not within the expressed intentions of the change process.

- *Behavioural*: a need to change what people do, or how they currently work day by day. This focus may be on skills and any gap between existing skills of individuals and what is now needed for their work.
- *Psychological*: a focus for change on current values, beliefs or attitudes; also perhaps opinions, and feelings about the nature of the job or the organisation.
- *Social*: a need to change the pattern of working relationships within the group – between senior and less senior staff, between peers and with external professionals or agencies. Relationships matter to people, so changes in the social network of work can be experienced as disruptive. Equally, a change in social relationships may bring about improvements in a team, as new pairings work better together or support each other's skills base.
- *Cognitive/intellectual*: a focus on acquiring new knowledge relevant to the work, or which could change the nature of the current role. Knowledge and how it is applied may also connect with the need to extend individuals' current skills base.

Individuals are active within any process of change and a wide range of factors can enter that affect the personal outlook on change and inclinations to be supportive, resistant or actively obstructive.

Personal feelings of security or insecurity

Individuals may experience personal feelings of security or insecurity and not only within the context of work. Some individuals may generally feel unsure of their position and even minor changes can feel potentially threatening. Then individuals feel psychologically unsafe and do not welcome any shifting of what already feels like an uncertain foundation. Additionally, individuals within a staff group may have different outlooks on the nature of their work, such as the distinction between paid work as just a job, a career or a calling (see page 138) and their outlook may affect willingness to change, especially if significant effort is involved.

The prevailing beliefs about any change

What are the prevailing beliefs about any change, not only within this social group, but also the culture or subculture in which this proposed change will operate? Is potential change viewed as refreshing or disruptive? Is change seen as a means for improvement, or more of a criticism of the existing situation? The prevailing outlook in this organisation, or this part of even a small setting, will moderate how individuals feel about change, until they realise the views of their colleagues.

The level of trust in the source of the change

What is the level of trust in the source of the change – whether this source is the known manager of the setting or the (possibly) less familiar hierarchy of the nursery chain? If there is distrust of management, or other groups who are central to this change, then individuals and staff groups are more likely to consider that the change will benefit somebody other than themselves. Without trust, there is a greater chance of suspicion about hidden agendas within the stimulus for change. Look again at Figure 7.1 to remind yourself that change may arise, or be believed to originate, from very different sources.

Past experiences of change

Past experiences of change will affect reactions to the current proposals. Previous experiences may be within the current organisation or from other jobs. These memories flavour reactions to the current proposed changes and can work in a positive or negative way. Individuals who are resistant to change do not necessarily lack confidence or a sense of personal security. They may have experiences of badly managed changes, or a clear memory of expressed goals for a change that proved to be dishonest. On the other hand, positive experiences can lead people to be well disposed towards the current initiative and to have some understanding of what is involved in the process of change.

How change is introduced

The way in which change is now introduced will be significant. Imposed and prescriptive change, with minimal discussion and time to adjust, will alienate the most positive of individuals and teams. Change can, and sometimes does, have an element of limited choice, for instance that particular legislation will require specific kinds of non-negotiable changes, or that this statutory guidance will apply from a given date. However, a sensitive introduction and honesty about what is required, given alongside available choices, are more likely to settle concerns or resistance arising from lack of information. However, even the most resilient and enthusiastic of individuals are worn down by a long sequence of changes. The temptation to label yet another change as 'flavour of the month' is hard to resist when one change is never given sufficient time to become established before another reorganisation, review or total overhaul of practice is started.

Specific concerns about consequences of change

Specific concerns about the consequences of a change may increase wariness or resistance. Is the change likely to require a significant change in role, put your job under threat or the continued existence of the whole setting? Look back at the concepts in Abraham Maslow's hierarchy of needs (discussed on page 136). This kind of anxiety about basic well-being and security will take precedence over feelings that otherwise the proposed change could have benefits.

Steps in bringing about a change

Change will usually be a cyclical process and not a single change 'and then we're done'. However, the process takes time, even when those changes are relatively minor. Estimates of significant organisational change are that even when undertaken in the most positive way possible, the change process is unlikely to take less than two years. Early years or school teams I have known, who have been taken through a complete and major change in how they operate, had to allow sufficient time (Lindon, 2012c). The change of direction was led by heads of school or centre, who had a clear vision of the need for change, the core values and the steps in best practice along the way. The complete process took a few years and not months.

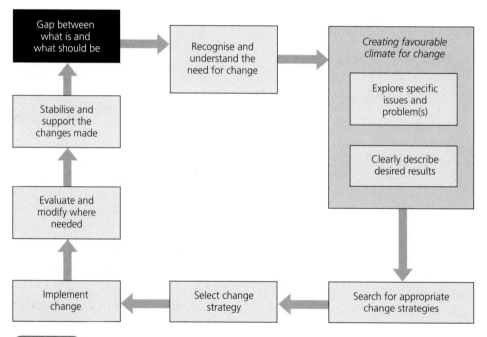

Figure 7.3 The basic steps of change

The basic steps of change are shown in Figure 7.3. The process of minor change follows similar steps to a significant change of direction, but only part of practice is being changed and the timescale can be shorter. You do not want an end point stretching into the distant future, but impossibly tight deadlines disrupt the change process. If the pressure is to fit an unrealistic target, then shortcuts will be taken, problems and resistance glossed over. Apparent changes will be on the surface and insecurely grounded and stressed practitioners will be 'just going through the motions'.

The process starts when a gap is identified between current practice and better or best practice.

- Perhaps a significant change is led by recognition that an established approach is not working well, such as how practitioners deal with children's behaviour. Despite an avowed aim of the team that 'we tune into how children feel', practitioners have developed less positive habits of nagging children and seeing them as the problem.
- A significant review may be triggered by a change of the framework in which a team has to work, such as the introduction of the 0–5 Early Years Foundation Stage in England. However, that review by the whole team may confirm existing good practice and indicate less than substantial change is needed.
- Alternatively an early years setting or individual practitioner may experience an unfavourable inspection and focused requirements to change. There is a recognised need to change, but this attitude may not be shared by everyone.

You need a full and wide-ranging discussion around the gap between the current situation and what is felt to be a possible improvement.

- A more favourable atmosphere for change, and commitment to change, will be established if the key promoters of the change are clear about the rationale. Discussion also covers 'Where are we going?' and 'What kind of outcome will show that change has been successful?'
- It is not possible to search for the more appropriate strategies for change –'how we do it' – unless there has been a thorough discussion of what you need to achieve.
- Group members are likely to feel more committed to a change when they are part of thorough discussion about how that change will unfold. The change agent has been honest about what is not up for discussion: the end results that are being sought. Full discussion is focused on sorting out the 'What?' and 'How?' of doing it.

In some ways a programme of change starts at the 'end', because there has to be clarity of 'Where do we want to end up?' The discussion now has to be about 'How are we going to get there?'. The plans describe what could be called a transition programme, or the process of getting everyone (or the vast majority) from where they are now, working towards to the defined end point. As in any problem-solving process (see page 98), there need to be well-rounded discussions about 'What might we do?' rather than seizing a strategy 'off the shelf' or following a plan that worked in a different setting.

- People's feelings matter, but the leader of an early years team needs to consider how far to postpone actual change for the sake of team members whose anxiety about anything new does not reduce, despite support. In some cases, postponing an inevitable change actually makes these negative feelings stronger, rather than allowing them to fade. Postponement can allow the highly resistant part of a staff group to become more entrenched and to develop a strategy of obstruction to a non-negotiable change.

- The approach has to be put into action, having fully discussed what is involved – who will do what, in what way, by when and where, as appropriate.
- Relevant support needs to be in place, attuned to what could be predicted as the emotional or intellectual needs of the key practitioners. Part of that support could be reminders, further explanations or a friendly presence that communicates 'We are serious about this change and we want to make it as painless as possible.'

Scenario

Greyhorse Road Early Years Unit

The nursery and reception staff at Greyhorse Road are still finding their way towards working as a combined team. This term they are working out a sensible response to feedback from a local early years advisor that the unit is not making the most of imaginative role play for the children. Chloe has made notes of their discussion and plans so far.

Wesley, the head of Greyhorse Primary, is also reviewing a whole-school approach to developing language skills, following a local study of the gap between children from the more and less prosperous sections of the neighbourhood. The EYU practitioners feel they have got stuck and invite Wesley to join them in their next team meeting. He supports them to review what they have done so far and reflect on next steps.

Chloe, supported by her colleagues, explains that in the first discussion they started with 'We need to develop the role-play area' and were sure that would meet a goal of 'creating more imaginative play to develop children's language'. They drew up an action plan to get more dressing-up clothes, develop the role-play area, organise a workable storage system and get children to tidy it up when they finish a role play.

They used the SMART criteria for setting goals (page 107), but looked back on 'S' for 'Specific' when the role-play area was not much used by children. The next step was that Pippa accepted the task to set up some possible role plays for the children. However, Pippa has brought her serious reservations to this meeting. She challenges herself and her colleagues with 'How can we say we're supporting children's imagination if I'm thinking up possible role plays? I got interested in being an explorer at the North or South Pole, and there were good ideas in this magazine. But has any child expressed an interest in polar exploration and how do my ideas connect with their current knowledge?'

Pause and reflect

Wesley suggests that the unit team have rushed to a solution without fully discussing the nature of the problem. He freely admits that the unit team's knowledge of early learning is more extensive than his. But Wesley is able to guide the discussion by relevant comments. He asks the open-ended question, 'What about the "M" for Meaningful?' His contribution leads the unit team to pose other questions, which lead them towards a different approach:

- Does it make sense to identify enhancing imaginative play as our main thrust to supporting communication skills? Why have we put the two together? Because the advisor said so? What did she actually say and does it make sense?

- How do we support children's language skills at the moment? Are we trying to plan more adult-led activities about communication? If so, why?
- Do we focus enough on relaxed, spontaneous conversation – about anything?
- Do children start conversations with us: when, who and on what subject?
- Does imaginative play only happen in the role-play corner? How much are we pre-packaging the play?
- Last week we talked about organising a travel agency, but what was the source of that idea? If it came from the children, they should be part of setting it up.

Comments

1. It is tempting to seize a solution to a problem because you feel you are doing something and making progress. But is it energy that will benefit the children?
2. Look back at the discussion on page 107 about SMART goals and about problem solving on page 98. That process is also about making changes.

Review and discussions need to highlight whether further adjustments to the plan need to be made, as well as to focus on what has been achieved and is already successful. The process is much the same as the plan–do–review cycle, familiar to many early years settings and originally developed within the High/Scope approach to early learning (Holt, 2007).

- Regular review, especially of a longer-term change process, leads into a more extensive evaluation of the change. Is the new approach well established and has it led to the positive outcomes that were envisaged at the beginning? Are any other adjustments needed? Have we missed anything? What has been learned?
- A major change has to be allowed to stabilise before there is further significant change. You need to give even minor, routine changes sufficient time to stabilise: for any wrinkles to be ironed out in what is basically a sound plan.
- A series of successful, minor changes can be part of a positive spiral that moves on to 'Now we can tackle . . .', with a confident sense of 'This is the next step and we can do this!'

If you prefer the diamonds

There is no single way to represent the process in a diagram. The four diamonds model is given in Chapter 4 to depict the steps in solving a problem. A more complex version is shown in Figure 7.4 to illustrate the process of change. Again, the visual of the diamonds communicates an information-sharing and -gathering phase (opening) and a decision-making phase (closing) to reach an agreed outcome at the end of each of the four stages.

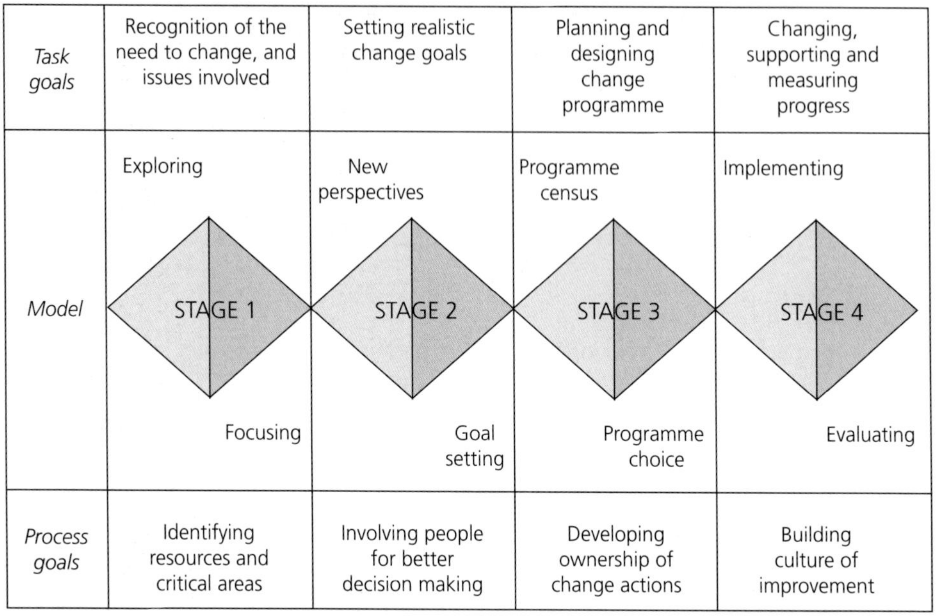

Task goals	Recognition of the need to change, and issues involved	Setting realistic change goals	Planning and designing change programme	Changing, supporting and measuring progress
Model	Exploring STAGE 1 Focusing	New perspectives STAGE 2 Goal setting	Programme census STAGE 3 Programme choice	Implementing STAGE 4 Evaluating
Process goals	Identifying resources and critical areas	Involving people for better decision making	Developing ownership of change actions	Building culture of improvement

Figure 7.4 The overall change process model

In stage 1 the team needs to explore not only the reasons for change but also identify the main issues and aspects that may be critical for successful change. Stage 2 opens up with a full discussion about the new perspective on practice – not yet what exactly will be done. This stage draws to a close with an agreement about goals, possibly using the SMART criteria (see page 107). Stage 3 is about actions, completely linked to the change goals. Stage 3 closes with commitment to what will be done, by whom, when and where. Stage 4 focuses on implementing the agreed programme of actions and evaluating what has happened. Like the visual in Figure 7.3, the change process in the diamonds model allows for recycling back to the previous stage if new information becomes available. For instance, a successful change may pose new issues that need to be resolved.

Figure 7.5 Reflection for 'boy-friendly practice' benefits girls too

The role of the change agent

When key agents for change are managers or senior practitioners, they need to keep reasonably in step with their colleagues. You need energy but also to avoid what may be perceived as overenthusiasm: being way ahead of what the rest of the group can currently manage. Practitioners who have benefited from CPD need to reconnect with the mixed emotions that are usually provoked by a shift in established habits of practice. A change agent may be a team member in the provision where change is taking place, or they may be involved as an external consultant.

Take another **perspective**

I have heard of people in the role of consultant or change agent being told that 'Your role is to get people to change, not to build relationships with them. You haven't got time to be pleasant.' This kind of directive does not fit a constructive view of managing change, or an appropriate role for a change agent.

This approach of what it means to be 'objective' confuses being over-friendly, or wanting to be liked, with the need to understand those people with whom you definitely do have a working relationship, even if your involvement is short term.

The 'Tell them and move on' approach seems also to be linked with a particular view of an early years or school consultant: someone who delivers a programme, implements the most recent initiative and gets people to reach externally determined targets and numerical outcomes. Not the definition used here.

As Carter et al. show (1984), the role of change agent is about steering towards a target, rather than operating a control knob and feeling sure that what you expect to come about will indeed happen. When you are tasked to bring about minor or major change, your working relationship is ideally amicable. Certainly you should model respect, willingness to listen and honesty about your aims and concerns. The challenge of this kind of role is to accept that everyone may not like your ideas or plans and some resistance may be expressed in a personal way. A change agent cannot afford to be shifted by a wish to convert apparent dislike into like. You are in a working relationship, not a friendship, and you need to keep the boundaries clear. Even in a welcoming atmosphere a change agent still needs to keep a level of detachment, with a clear view on the process.

Resistance to major change

It is inevitable that a significant change within any organisation, large or small, will provoke more resistance than the change agents predict. The sources of resistance are not all about people being awkward. However, some individuals may object to such an extent that their refusal to adjust at all threatens to sabotage the change process. People tend to resist change for two broad reasons:

1. They feel incapable of dealing with the change, or

2. They cannot see any benefits in making the effort to change.

Feelings of incompetence in the face of change are best dealt with by explanations, recognition that changing habits of practice is not easy and can feel very uncomfortable. Well-tuned support and constructive feedback about what will work well can ease the process. It is also important to identify when practitioners genuinely do not have the necessary skills or grasp of what is meant. Focused support, possibly through the coaching process, will be necessary under those circumstances.

Early years practitioners may feel there are no benefits for them in change – perhaps if they take a 'just a job' approach to their work. It may be possible to show personal benefits, but part of the rationale may be that this change will lead to refreshed practice that is part of this job now. However, very committed practitioners may seriously doubt that a change is for the benefit of the children. Their resistance evolves from a strong desire to stand up for children. Further explanation may allay their anxiety. However, it is important to allow that their concerns may be well founded. When the discussion goes into detail about how this change will, allegedly, improve the situation for the children, valid doubts are aired that lead to a more appropriate focus.

As change agents it will certainly help to deal with the strong feelings or contrary ideas that are expressed. Martin et al. (1984: 86) explain it helpfully with six points, to which I have added my own thoughts. You need to do the following:

● Let the people who are angry confront you and grasp their heartfelt message, even if it could be better expressed.

- Hear what the arrogant and opinionated people have to say, without being unduly swayed or letting them 'drown out' other people.
- Provide a safe place for people who feel hurt, tense or anxious. They need to be able to express those feelings without negative consequences for themselves, or with such an unpleasant result that they do not put themselves at risk again.
- Fire enthusiasm in the bored and the disillusioned – finding out something of how they have come to feel fed up and stagnant.
- Satisfy the sceptical, who may be asking important questions and well-informed 'Ah but's – even though the constant flow is rather wearing.
- Explain carefully and respectfully to the confused, who may helpfully voice the confusion of some other people who choose to remain silent.

Checklist for successful change

This checklist is not comprehensive; it is always possible to think of further issues that affect whether a significant change will be successful. Here are the main issues:

- Is the proposed change based on sound ideas? Does the proposal tackle an issue, problem or shift in approach that matters for best practice?
- Is there good reason to expect that this approach will bring about the changes that are wanted and valued? Does the overall strategy deal with all the key issues and the full impact, rather than being a quick-fix or patch-up approach?
- Is there clear support from more senior practitioners or other key people for this change? Are the responsibilities for bringing about change clearly understood?
- If the change agent is not the manager, has it been made clear that this person has his/her authority and back-up?
- Has time been given to develop and commit to a plan that is thorough and based on all the relevant information? Has an appropriate strategy been chosen that will apply to this situation?
- Are there clear goals for the change and a realistic timescale for that change, allowing for the usual workload and obligations of the team?
- Is there a support system for the change agent, who is giving time and emotional energy to colleagues throughout the process? Are there adequate resources allowing for the nature of this change?
- Has thought been given to sharing necessary information and building, or refreshing, skills before observable change is expected?
- Has there been consideration of what could go wrong, and not in a pessimistic way, in order to anticipate blocks that could be foreseen?

You will find detailed discussion of the process of change, as well as other aspects of leadership and management in Lindon and Lindon (2012).

Team leaders of some provisions can find themselves in a dilemma. From 1997 the Labour government launched a series of initiatives, regularly changing the preferred name and briefing for early years centres. Klavins (2008) offers case studies of staff in children's centres who have found themselves in the situation of inviting parents to evaluate services which would not necessarily have been the first choice of families at the outset.

Klavins highlights the potential challenge to centre leaders, some of whom describe the need to 'swim against the tide'. Genuine consultation with local parents sometimes identifies that what they would most welcome does not fit the targets which the centre is required to meet for their funding.

For instance, the children's centre package is supposed to include day care, because of the policy link with getting parents into work. However, in some communities, local families do not want to share the care of their children in this way. They may be interested to have informal drop-ins. Targets for reducing adult smoking will not be met by a centre, unless parents or other family members are motivated to address this aspect of their behaviour.

Self-evaluation within the team

Within early years provision, the process of change is now sometimes started from the experience of self-evaluation – in a team or the individual version of this organised reflection on current practice.

The case for self-evaluation

The self-evaluation guidance in Scotland is led through the concept of 'the child at the centre'. The 2007 edition made changes to create a common approach for public services in Scotland. This document provides a rationale which is a good beginning for anyone in the UK: 'Self-evaluation is a reflective professional process through which centres get to know themselves well and identify the way forward which is best for their children. It should, therefore, promote well-considered innovation' (2007: 04.05). The process of self-evaluation can therefore be part of the process of managing change for clearly understood reasons. The key questions put at the heart of self-evaluation in this Scottish guidance are:

- How are we doing?
- How do we know?
- What are we going to do now?

The Scottish schedule of questions, like the English counterpart of the Self-Evaluation Form (SEF) introduced by the Ofsted inspectorate (Ofsted, 2009), is comprehensive. So it can be useful to bear those three key questions in mind. The second question above goes to the crux of evidence: that everyone has to have more than 'We/I just do know.' The similar question that runs through the English SEF is 'How do you know?'

A strong team and provision need work; and managers need a sense of where the team is at the moment. Some general questionnaires offered for this purpose – not from the Scottish or English schedules – are rather vague. Often the missing element is an invitation to think about concrete examples. For instance, it may feel positive to a head of centre to get back a questionnaire in which everyone strongly agrees that 'I feel appreciated in this team for what I do.' But you really need the addition of 'for instance, when . . .'. Suppose there is a less than enthusiastic response to 'I feel involved in decisions about what will happen' from most volunteers in a centre where their input is crucial. Again, a manager needs to ask for examples and listen to the answers – not argue or justify.

In the same way as for individual reflective practice, a full-team approach to self-evaluation has to acknowledge the likely concerns of at least some of the practitioners involved. It is very possible that some will suspect that the aim of any evaluation process is to criticise in a negative way. Practitioners are often uneasy about the process of inspection and any framework that is linked with the inspectorate will be coloured by feelings about that process: direct experiences as well as what has travelled the local grapevine.

A great deal seems to depend on the prevailing culture of a setting and the extent to which practitioners have become accustomed to serious reflection on their current practice. Some nurseries look at summaries of peer observations (see page 187) across the setting in order to home in on team strengths as a whole and on scope for improvement. When the information is used in this way to enhance best practice for the whole team, the records can still stay with individuals. The information has been merged in a way that does not highlight particular team members. Self-evaluation then becomes a rolling process, part of normal working practices. The positive feeling from some teams is then that self-evaluation is part of striving for best practice; you do not address these questions exclusively because the inspectorate expects some answers.

Description and evaluation

The process of evaluation goes beyond description to reach supported, evaluative judgements. Self-evaluation is not about making lists of what you and your colleagues have done. There needs to be a considered assessment of the impact on the children or parents, as appropriate.

Unless you also make an evaluation, a description of all the changes you have made in your outdoor space attracts the challenge of 'So what?' What difference have your changes made to the children and what makes you sure of that judgement? This exploration may raise the best-practice question of to what extent the children themselves were involved in discussion, planning and implementation of the changes. If not, why not? And are there constructive messages about next time?

However, self-evaluation lacks secure foundations without good-quality description. A claim that 'We are successful in engaging parents in their children's learning' needs specific examples. In what way were parents engaged, how did you judge 'success' and from whose perspective? Descriptive examples answer the fair question of 'How do you know this?' or 'What makes you so sure?' Without this further information, the earlier statement is an unsupported assertion.

It is unlikely that one main approach to engagement will suit every parent or family carer. So the supportive material within a self-evaluation report will give some sense of a team that is alert to different ways to offer engagement. Or the reflection, that needs to be part of self-evaluation, successfully highlights assumptions that need to be examined.

Rating scales

One approach to self-evaluation has been through prepared rating scales. The Effective Provision of Pre-School Provision team (EPPE) used the Early Childhood Environmental Rating Scale developed by Thelma Harris, Richard Clifford and Debby Cryer (**www.fpg.unc.edu/~ECERS/**). This rating scale and others were developed and revised at the Frank Porter Graham (FPG) Child Development Institute to assess the quality of early childhood programmes in the USA using a consistent measure.

The instrument is organised into seven sub-scales covering space and furnishings, personal care routines, language and reasoning, activities, interactions, programme structure, parents and staff. The ECERS-R scale is designed for use in group provision for children from 2:6 to 5 years of age. (The 'R' stands for 'revised'.) For younger children in group provision, the FPG Child Development Institute team developed the Infant Toddler Environment Rating Scale. They later revised the measure, so it is known as the ITERS-R. The same team developed the Family Child Care Environmental Rating Scale (FCCERS-R), which is designed for childminding provision in a family home.

The EPPE project extended the ECERS-R scale to provide greater depth and additional items in four educational aspects of provision (**www.ecersuk.org/4. html**). They added literacy (opportunities for emergent writing, letters and sounds), mathematics (number and reasoning), science and environment (creative and critical thinking and understanding of the natural and physical world) and diversity (individual learning needs, valuing and respecting other cultures, gender diversity). This scale is known as ECERS-E (E for 'extended').

These environmental rating scales have been used in other research projects. However, they have also been developed as an audit and self-evaluation tool by local authorities, as a means of supporting quality improvement in settings. The elements to the approach include:

- Advisors and/or practitioners trained in using the ECERS-R scale make an assessment of current practice.
- The evaluation and numerical scores are used to guide assessment of good practice, problem areas and scope for change: a tool for quality improvement.
- Self-evaluation through the scales is sometimes used to inform the self-evaluation process for inspection.

- Local support teams use the information as an audit to focus where direct support or training is needed.
- Repeat use of the scales offers a measure of improvement, against the aspects that were identified previously. As appropriate, practitioners then learn how to use the more challenging ECERS-E scale.

Like any tool of this kind, it is necessary to be trained in how to use it and support is needed to ensure that judgements are made in a systematic way. Unlike more open-ended self-evaluation, the ECERS scales provide the brief example descriptions, set against a numerical score. Settings are assessed against their similarity to the closest description on the sub-scale. Improvement in practice is not about a literal checklist to improve the score but to understand the nature of the descriptions that attract higher scores in each case.

As with any approach to self-evaluation, it matters what exactly happens after the assessment. High scores are a reason for pride and pleasure in the team, but not a justification for complacency. Lower scores need to be discussed with a leader and the team as a basis for looking at change. Sometimes a minor adjustment to current practice will work well, but sometimes a more significant overhaul is needed of how the setting currently operates. The advantage of the specific nature of the scales is that practitioners often have a steer on how to improve.

Learning from consultation with children and families

Schedules for self-evaluation usually include something on consultation with children and their families. The point, of course, is not only do you consult; but what happens with the information; what impact does it have on your practice? What have you learned from children and their families? Even confident practitioners and teams can be taken aback if children or parents take a view that is noticeably different from that of the professionals.

Genuine consultation

There is a difference between:

- Here is a completely free choice; your preference will be followed.
- These are the limits and within those your views will prevail.
- There are really only two (or a similarly small number of) options and we would like you to suggest which one is best.
- We would like to hear your views and general opinions. We will consider possible changes and get back to you.

Figure 7.6 Practitioners need to recognise how much children can learn within their family life

Of course, there can be very different views and preferences coexisting in even a small group of children, body of parents or staff team. The challenge is to find a balance between contrasting viewpoints. It is not feasible to consult when there is no scope for choice or a decision has already been made. This situation, expressed honestly, is an information-giving conversation, a meeting or update in the parents' newsletter. You welcome questions; you are ready to explain in different ways but the decision is not open to change – if need be, with a 'because . . .'.

Pause for reflection

Consultation, with any age or social grouping, needs to be an open and honest process. Nobody appreciates being misled, intentionally or through lack of thought, by the person or people who set up what claimed to be a consultation.

- Have you experienced a 'consultation' in which you later realised the decision had already been made?
- Or there was considerably less scope for choices than you were led to believe? How did you feel on that occasion?
- Have you, maybe in your turn, been unclear about the nature and scope of a consultation you ran with children or their parents?

Consultation with children

An important first step in terms of consultation with children is to recognise that they do have views and can express them in different ways. Younger children are more able to voice opinions and preferences when they can use visuals along with their spoken language. Fajerman et al. (2000) show how young children could express clear views through using play figures and layouts of a familiar environment. The Mosaic approach (Clark and Moss, 2001) demonstrates the value of giving children cameras and an invitation to capture important places and experiences within their nursery. Warden (2006) describes a wide range of visual methods, including her Talking and Thinking Floorbooks™, three-dimensional mind-mapping and consultation boards.

Even under-fives can be vocal about what they enjoy: nice meals and picnics being a regular favourite. Younger, and older, children can also be forthright about what, in their view, should be sorted out by the adults. I have heard from more than one primary-school team who have been left in no doubt that the state of the children's toilets is unacceptable, accompanied by generous photographic evidence. Consultation with children brings a fair expectation that the grown-ups will take notice of the views that boys and girls have taken the trouble to express. Children, and adolescents, get irritated if they are asked for their opinions and then the grown-ups have gone ahead with what they appear always to have had in mind.

Consultation with parents and other family carers

In open, friendly communication, you will gather views from at least some of the parents. A suggestions box or board may bring in other views. However, some individuals will be more forthcoming than others. Settings often aim for a regular questionnaire that is sent home for parents to complete, perhaps once a year although more often in some places.

There is no single right format for such a questionnaire, but I suggest these points for guidance:

- Consider on which aspects of practice it will be useful to gain information, or changes in the provision since the last time of asking.
- It is unlikely that the questionnaire will stay the same each time, although there should be some consistent questions.
- You need to draft questions without implying that you definitely will, or could, make changes in line with every request.
- Ask questions in an even-handed way, without a wording that is loaded towards a positive response; but also avoid inviting a list of complaints.
- It is useful to have a balance between specific questions that can sensibly be a yes/no reply and open-ended queries with space for a written reply.
- You may like to have a small section that is relevant to families that have recently joined your setting. Would it be useful to know 'How did you hear about us?' or 'What made you decide to choose our nursery?'

- Simple numbers can be useful, such as a scale from 1 to 5, where 1 is the negative/unhappy/completely disagree end. A basic adding up of the numbers of parents checking each rating will give you a meaningful grasp of views. Unless you have commissioned someone to develop a sophisticated questionnaire, it will not be appropriate to do statistics on a simple questionnaire.
- Keep the questionnaire relatively short. You need a good reason to get beyond one or at most two pages of A4-size paper, with the writing in a font no smaller than 12 point and with spacing between questions.
- Be ready to talk through the questionnaire with any parents who you realise have difficulties with the written word, or whose most fluent language is not English.

Whatever the approach to consultation, you need to let families know what you have done in response to their suggestions or a clear pattern of preference.

A fresh perspective from parents

Some effective consultation emerges through group discussion. In Millom Children's Centre, Cumbria, the team reflect on their practice through the strong children's rights perspective of children's charity Action for Children. Anna Batty, the centre leader, explained to me how their 'Hear by Right' model, which is also fully adopted by Cumbria local authority, led them to explore ways to enable parent participation.

A small group of parents met with a project worker over a period of 12 weeks, with the expressed aim of helping to plan activities for local families. The centre team learned a great deal, gaining insights for their practice as a whole.

- Parents expressed the view that it was important to be told about the aim of a given activity. If a planned event was about children's speech and the importance of talking with them, then that should be clear in the promotional material. If the aim of an activity was social, getting to know each other, then say so.
- They pinpointed information that should be on a flyer or poster, for instance that an event is free. Then families do not have to ask the question and maybe feel embarrassed.
- The group welcomed honesty about the centre aims as a whole, including what the team had to do. This information made it much clearer where there were choices about what or how.
- Parents identified words that practitioners might believe were clear. But the phrases did not carry the same meaning, or were confusing, for people who did not share this profession.
- The group was very positive about the value of evaluating activities that had taken effort to organise and absorbed some of a limited budget. Their view was that asking them if they had 'a good time' did not go very far.

- They were motivated to tell practitioners what they felt they had got out of an experience and took the view of 'Don't apologise for asking us.' However, they needed a clear view of what the centre hoped an event could achieve.
- There was discussion around questions that were worth asking and a wish to have the results of any evaluation shared generally with families.

Pause for reflection

You need accurate feedback from parents and other family members about how they have experienced your service in general or specific activities. Look at the ideas summarised from the parents' planning group at Millom Children's Centre. What direct links can you make to your own practice?

It is wise to offer different routes for feedback, as well as to give parents time to think. When you have good relations with families, they may not wish to appear critical (usual meaning) or unappreciative. The Millom team is also aware that parents may wish to say something one to one, rather than in an open discussion session, for the considerate reason of not wanting to put a practitioner on the spot.

Issues expressed in a more private conversation are not necessarily about problems. They can be about feedback where small changes could make a significant difference. For instance, that parents who have a long journey to get to any event really notice if, when they finally make it, the welcome is immediate and warm. In contrast, it does not feel positive if a workshop is still being set up at the start time, or the person leading a session seems ill-prepared.

What insights would you offer to other practitioners or settings, based on what you have learned from your experience of consultation with parents?

Some early years provision, such as children's centres, combines a range of services on a single site, along with outreach services to make contact with families who may not find it easy to attend the centre. Teams need an accurate understanding of how families hear about the centre and what they have been told already (Lindon, 2009b). Reflective practice for these teams includes not only the challenges of working within a multidisciplinary team, but also a network of relationships with other local professionals and services.

Different ways of working and assumptions about referral process have to fit together. The Social Exclusion Task Force (2007) proposed the key concept of 'no wrong door', which points to the professional obligation to remove obstructions between families and services. Acceptance of different routes to necessary support is especially crucial for families who are already at risk, for whatever reason, and should not have to find extra energy to find the 'right' way to access a service.

Peer observation

Observation and feedback between colleagues have developed within several professional fields as a way to give and receive feedback from an informed fellow professional. In teaching, the objective of peer or mutual observation has been

- This learning is best supported by senior colleagues who are able to share something of the how and why, without taking over from the practitioner who is currently sharing his or her observation.
- Even the most experienced and/or senior team members should be ready to learn from colleagues. Less experienced practitioners can have a fresh approach and new ideas. They may lead their reflection through questions that more senior colleagues have ceased to ask. In an atmosphere in which people feel emotionally secure, the learning can go in all directions.

Different approaches

The process of peer observation works in different ways. Managers, with their team or an advisor, have adjusted the initial system in the light of what seems to work best in their context. Overall the system needs to work to provide good-quality description within the observation and the supported comments that offer an evaluation.

- There is always a focus on description, to provide the basis for constructive feedback. There is observational evidence to support what the observer expresses on what, in their view, went well and any reservations they may have. The descriptive material is also the basis for informed comments along the lines of 'Were you aware that . . .?' or 'When you . . . I notice that . . .'.
- There is always a focus on 'What is it like for the child(ren)?' Some approaches to peer observation have as a primary aim that practitioners – observer and observed – are able to get closer to the perspective of the baby, toddler or child who is part of this observed sequence.
- Observers may be able to point to a gap, in a constructive way, between what observed practitioners are sure they are doing and how they actually behave. Alternatively, the gap may be between what practitioners believe the children are doing and what the observer notices and can describe in the follow-up conversation.
- In a busy early years setting peer observations do not last a long time, maybe no more than ten minutes and, although made on a regular basis, may not be more than three or four times a year. The timing varies between settings and any leader needs to make an informed decision with the team about what will be a practical system. The aim is to provide valuable information, without becoming a burden.
- Practitioners may write at the time. But the approach is sometimes to concentrate on watching and listening and then write up the notes immediately afterwards. There needs to be time for discussion between the two practitioners. One approach is that the observed practitioner also has time to add a written comment to the observation, to create a full final record.

Choice of format

The focus of the observation may be determined by a schedule that is part of a quality-assurance scheme, or the details may initially come from this source. As the peer-observation system develops it is important that different aspects of practice are observed. Examples include observations of: children's personal care routines; children playing; times when adults come alongside children's chosen activities; as well as adult-initiated experiences.

- A brief layout may have some questions, but these should not be a long list; otherwise the process turns into a checklist format. Any questions are to guide the observation and encourage a breadth of description. Observers need to avoid simply 'answering the questions'.
- Some formats have a yes/no element. Some ask the observer to grade the practitioner with a short numerical scale, such as 1 to 5. Some teams and practitioners are comfortable with assigning grades, and being able to explain their reasons for the choice of score.
- It is important that practitioners understand that less than 'top marks' suggests there is scope for improvement and is not a blunt criticism of that aspect of practice. On the other hand, 'low marks', unsupported by descriptive observation, may highlight a misunderstanding of this question about practice, or possibly a colleague who habitually 'marks down'.
- Practitioners who regularly give grades on the higher or lower side of a scale may, of course, be able to support their view with the observations. But they may work to a general bias of being positive, or else a belief that they must show a colleague that there is significant scope for improvement. A manager, or other senior practitioner, remains very involved in the process of peer observation and can therefore deal with any practical issues.
- Staff from some settings, with whom I spoke, found that practitioners were not resistant to peer observations, as such. But they found the process of giving 'marks' raised their level of discomfort and undermined the process. In this case, all the settings in the local authority had started with the same format for peer observation. Some had removed the numerical part of the schedule and others had continued with it.

Learning from the observation

The discussion after an observation should evolve into a two-way discussion. Patterns vary, but generally the written peer observation would then stay with the person observed. It forms part of a personal record to guide their continuing professional development.

Practical issues may continue to arise, even when a manager has taken care over the introduction of peer observation. When there is an observer, there is always the possibility that practitioners will 'be on their best behaviour'. The question arises of whether what has been observed is representative of typical behaviour for this practitioner. There is a good chance that as peer observation becomes a normal part of life in this setting, practitioners will become less self-conscious, or keen to create a good impression. However, 'best behaviour' is not always best practice. The SPEEL research (discussed on page 88) found that the sequences that practitioners chose to have filmed as part of a reflective dialogue quite often showed over-directive communication in interaction with children.

There will always be a time gap between peer observations. The next observation may highlight a change in how this practitioner behaves. Perhaps there is a noticeable positive shift in how the adult communicates with young children and the feedback can describe something of this change. On the other hand, there may be a less positive change between peer-observation times. Constructive feedback leads through the description and does not leap to conclusions about why. However, perhaps a practitioner is weighed down with a personal problem, or a change in staffing has created an unhappy dynamic in this room.

It is possible that practitioners may want to reflect further on some feedback that surprises them or challenges a belief about what they do and the impact on the children. Taking time to think is a positive part of reflective practice and should not be a way of avoiding the implications of constructive criticism. Peer observation is part of the whole approach to being reflective about early years practice and so it does not stand alone.

Broad impact of peer observations

It takes time to establish peer observation with the associated skills, and to deal sensitively with any reservations within the team. Once everyone is reassured about the aims of the process – to improve practice and not to catch people out in a negative way – some general benefits are often noticed.

- The advantage of a mixed pattern of peer observation is that normal team practice becomes an expectation that colleagues can comment on the practice and views of others, even the more senior team members.
- An additional benefit of regular peer observation is that practitioners become familiar with being watched, in a supportive way. They may also be more at ease when an outsider is in the room, whether this person is an early years advisor or an inspector.
- There can also be a positive, general effect when practitioners have become accustomed to talking in detail about what is happening and how experiences are most likely to affect the children.
- Some team leaders felt their staff were more able to explain, again perhaps to an inspector, the reasons behind an approach or the rationale for the practitioner's decision for dealing with a particular situation.
- There is also a good chance that practitioners' skills are sharpened with regard to observing children. The habits of careful description of peers can support a greater awareness of considering what children are doing and taking care to support interpretations or conclusions – the whole process of 'What leads me to say that?'
- Peer observation will be at a scheduled time, so that the practitioner can be freed up temporarily to observe a colleague. However, an increased comfort in watching and learning from each other can lead to friendly informal communication. There seems to be a good chance that colleagues notice what has gone well, or that maybe it would be worth finding at least a brief time to talk about a practical issue within the room.

Some team leaders ensure that they spend time in each room on a regular basis. Practitioners then do not think the leader only appears when there is something awry with practice. This time is sometimes informal, just a friendly presence. But sometimes a team leader will go into rooms on a regular basis with a notebook and feed back immediately to the practitioners.

Resources

- Argyris, C. and Schön, D. (1974) *Theory in Practice*. San Francisco: Jossey-Bass.
- Argyris, C. and Schön, D. (1978) *Organizational Learning: A Theory of Action Perspective*. Reading, Mass: Addison-Wesley.
- Bronfenbrenner, U. (1979) *The Ecology of Human Development*. Cambridge, MA: Harvard University Press.
- Carter, R., Martin, J., Mayblin, B. and Munday, M. (1984) *Systems, Management and Change: A Graphic Guide*. London: Harper and Row.
- Clark, A. and Moss, P. (2001) *Listening to Young Children: The Mosaic Approach*. London: National Children's Bureau.
- Department for Children, Schools and Families (2008) *The Early Years Foundation Stage – Setting the Standards for Learning, Development and Care for Children from Birth to Five*. London: DCSF. **www.education.gov.uk/ publications/standard/publicationdetail/page1/DCSF-00261-2008**
- Fajerman, L., Jarrett, M. and Sutton, F. (2000) *Children as Partners in Planning: A Training Resource to Support Consultation with Children*. London: Save the Children.
- Grenier, J. (2010) 'Planning Around Core Experiences'. *Nursery World*, 4 February.
- Holt, N. (2007) *Bringing the High/Scope Approach to Your Early Years Practice*. London: Routledge. See also **www.high-scope.org.uk**
- Kate Greenaway Nursery School and Children's Centre (2009) *Core Experiences for the Early Years Foundation Stage*, distributed by Early Education, also information on **www.coreexperiences.wikia.com**
- Lindon, J. (2009) *Parents as Partners*. London: Practical Pre-School Books.
- Lindon, J. (2010b) *The Key Person Approach*. London: Practical Pre-School Books.
- Lindon, J. (2012c) *Understanding Children's Behaviour: 0–11 Years*. London: Hodder Education.
- Lindon, J. (2012d, third edition) *What Does It Mean To Be Two? A Practical Guide to Child Development in the Early Years Foundation Stage*. London: Practical Pre-School Books.
- Lindon, J. and Lindon, L. (2012) *Leadership and Early Years Professionalism*. London: Hodder Education.
- Maslow, A. (1943) 'A theory of human motivation', *Psychological Review*, 50, 370–96. **http://psychclassics.yorku.ca/Maslow/motivation.htm**; also try these online sources: **www.teacherstoolbox.co.uk/T_maslow.html** and **www.businessballs.com/maslow.htm**

- Moyles, J., Adams, S. and Musgrove, A. (2002) *Study of Pedagogical Effectiveness in Early Learning Brief No. 363.* **www.education.gov.uk/publications/standard/publicationDetail/Page1/RR363**
- National Strategies Early Years (2008) *Early Years Consultant's Handbook.* London: DCSF. **www.nsonline.org.uk/node/132576?uc=force_deep**
- OFSTED (2009) *Early Years Online Self-Evaluation Form (SEF) and Guidance.* **www.ofsted.gov.uk/resources/early-years-online-self-evaluation-form-sef-and-guidance-for-settings-delivering-early-years-foundat**. (This address is complete, although it does not look so.)
- Social Exclusion Task Force (2007) *Families at Risk Review.* London: Social Exclusion Task Force.
- Warden, C. (2006) *Talking and Thinking Floorbooks: Using 'Big Book Planners' to Consult Children.* Perthshire: Mindstretchers.

Using further resources

Any website reference within this book was correct when checked in August 2011.

Websites

- Business Balls Useful because some key ideas for reflective practice in early years originated with organisational psychology. **www.businessballs.com/**
- Centre for Excellence and Outcomes in Children's and Young People's Services (C4EO) research and practical implications. **www.c4eo.org.uk/**
- Children's Workforce Development Council (CWDC). **www.cwdcouncil.org.uk** Qualifications structure, pathways for EYP Status
- Classics in the History of Psychology Developed by Christopher D. Green at York University, Toronto, Canada – research studies and conceptual articles with significant impact on psychology. **http://psychclassics.yorku.ca/**
- Current Education and Children's Services Research Search the database for projects in your area of interest. **www.ceruk.ac.uk/**
- ERIC or Educational Resources Information Center. **www.eric.ed.gov**
- EPPI-Centre or Evidence for Policy and Practice Information. Research reviews and information. **www.eppi.ioe.ac.uk/cms/**
- Informal Education group and Encyclopaedia of Informal Education. Not-for-profit site established by the YMCA George Williams College based in Canning Town, east London. **www.infed.org/about_us.htm**
- Learning and Teaching Scotland Useful papers and practical booklets for anyone in the UK. **www.ltscotland.org.uk/earlyyears/index.asp**
- National Educational Research Forum NERF no longer exists but access the Evidence for Teaching and Learning bulletins on **www.eep.ac.uk/nerf/bulletin/index.html**
- Teaching and Learning Research Programme Wide range of research briefings and commentaries. **www.tlrp.org/**
- The Critical Thinking Community An online resource about the approach of critical thinking in general. **www.criticalthinking.org/**
- Zero to Three Best practice with infants and toddlers, with section on Reflective Practice and Program Development. **www.zerotothree.org/about-us/areas-of-expertise/reflective-practice-program-development/**

References

Since the first edition of this book in 2010 a considerable amount of material generated within the era of the Labour government has been archived by the (current) Coalition government. Many papers and valuable guidance, for instance from the previous National Strategies team, presumably have a continued existence in some cyber cave. However, some archived references have proved impossible to find in their new location. (If you have paper copy of useful guidance from this era, hold onto it!)

Action for Children (2007) *As long as it takes: a new politics for children.* http://www.actionforchildren.org.uk/media/144001/alait.pdf

Amulya, J. (undated) *What is Reflective Practice?* The Center for Reflective Community Practice, Massachusetts Institute of Technology. www.itslifejimbutnotasweknowit.org.uk/files/whatisreflectivepractice.pdf

Anderson, L. (1997) *Argyris and Schön's Theory on Congruence and Learning.* www.scu.edu.au/schools/gcm/ar/arp/argyris.html

Argyris, C. (1970) *Intervention Theory and Method: A Behavioural Science View.* Reading, MA: Addison-Wesley.

Argyris, C. and Schön, D. (1974) *Theory in Practice.* San Francisco: Jossey-Bass.

Argyris, C. and Schön, D. (1978) *Organizational Learning: A Theory of Action Perspective.* Reading, MA: Addison-Wesley.

Argyris, C., Putnam, R. and McLain Smith, D. (1985) *Action Science: Concepts, Methods and Skills for Research and Intervention.* San Francisco: Jossey-Bass. The authors have made the entire book available online: www.actiondesign.com/resources/research/action-science

Blakemore, S. and Frith, U. (2000) *The Implications of Recent Developments in Neuroscience for Research on Teaching and Learning.* www.tlrp.org/pub/acadpub/Blakemore2000.pdf

Brand, S. (2009) *Whole Earth Discipline: An Ecopragmatist Manifesto.* London: Atlantic.

Bridges, D. (2009) '"Evidence-based policy": What evidence? What basis? Whose policy?' *Teaching and Learning Research Briefing*, February, no 74. London: Teaching and Learning Research Programme. ww.tlrp.org/pub/documents/Bridges RB74 Final.pdf

Bronfenbrenner, U. (1979) *The Ecology of Human Development.* Cambridge, MA: Harvard University Press.

Caddell, D. (1998) *Numeracy in The Early Years: What the Research Tells Us.* Dundee: Scottish Consultative Council on the Curriculum. www.waterstones.com/waterstonesweb/products/dorothy+caddell/numeracy+in+the+early+years/4611609/

Carter, R., Martin, J., Mayblin, B. and Munday, M. (1984) *Systems, Management and Change: A Graphic Guide.* London: Harper and Row.

Chapman, A. (2009) *Conscious Competence Learning Model.* www.businessballs.com/consciouscompetencelearningmodel.htm

Clark, A. and Moss, P. (2001) *Listening to Young Children: The Mosaic Approach.* London: National Children's Bureau.

Croft, C. (2009) 'How can a reflective model of support enhance relationships between babies, young children and practitioners?' MA dissertation in Education in Early Childhood: London Metropolitan University.

Curriculum in Action Course Team (1981) *Curriculum in Action: An Approach to Evaluation*. Milton Keynes: Open University Publications.

Department for Children, Schools and Families (2008) *The Early Years Foundation Stage – Setting the Standards for Learning, Development and Care for Children from Birth to Five*. London: DCSF. www.education.gov.uk/publications/standard/publicationdetail/page1/DCSF-00261-2008 A revised EYFS framework will be in force from September 2012. At the time of writing (late 2011), only the proposed revisions are available on www.education.gov.uk/consultations/index.cfm?action=conResults&consultationId=1747&external=no&menu=3

Department for Children, Schools and Families (2010) *Guide to the Early Years Foundation Stage in Steiner Waldorf Early Childhood Settings*. http://webarchive.nationalarchives.gov.uk/20110202093118/http://nationalstrategies.standards.dcsf.gov

Department for Education and Skills (2005a) *Common Core of Skills and Knowledge for The Children's Workforce: Non-Statutory Guidance*. London: DfES. www.cwdcouncil.org.uk/common-core

Department for Education and Skills (2005b) *KEEP: Key Elements of Effective Practice*. London: DfES. www.leics.gov.uk/index/education/childcare/early_years_service/foundationstage/evaluatingandqualityassurance/ai_keep.htm

Desforges, C. and Abouchaar, A. (2003) *The Impact of Parental Involvement, Parental Support and Family Education on Pupil Achievement and Adjustment: a Literature Review*. London: Department for Education and Skills. www.education.gov.uk/publications/standard/publicationdetail/page1/RR433

Drummond, M.J., Lally, M. and Pugh, G. (1989) *Working with Children: Developing a Curriculum for The Early Years*. London: National Children's Bureau.

Drummond, M.J. (1996) 'Teachers asking questions', Education 3–13, vol 24, no 3, 8–17.

Drummond, M.J. (2003) *Assessing Children's Learning*. London: David Fulton.

Drummond, M.J. and Jenkinson, S. (2009) *Meeting The Child: Approaches to Observation and Assessment in Steiner Kindergartens*. Plymouth: University of Plymouth. www.steinerwaldorf.org/bookshop_earlyyearsparenting.html

Effective Provision of Pre-School Education Project (EPPE). http://eppe.ioe.ac.uk/ This longitudinal project has followed children through primary, into secondary school and now further education.

Egan, G. and Cowan, M. (1979) *People in Systems: A Model for Development in The Human-Services Professions and Education*. Monterey, California: Brooks/Cole.

Elfer, P., Goldschmied, E. and Selleck, D. (2003) *Key Persons in The Nursery: Building Relationships for Quality Provision*. London: David Fulton.

Eliot, L. (2009) *Pink Brain, Blue Brain: How Small Differences Grow into Troublesome Gaps and What We Can Do About It*. New York: Houghton Mifflin Harcourt. Access a presentation: http://fora.tv/2009/09/29/Lise_Eliot_Pink_Brain_Blue_Brain

Evans, B. (2002) *You Can't Come to My Birthday Party: Conflict Resolution with Young Children*. Ypsilanti: High Scope Press.

Fajerman, L., Jarrett, M. and Sutton, F. (2000) *Children as Partners in Planning: A Training Resource to Support Consultation with Children*. London: Save the Children.

Farmer, N. (2009) 'We are all active learners', *Early Years Educator*, vol 11, no 6, October.

Fisher, A. (2001) *Critical Thinking: An Introduction*. Cambridge: Cambridge University Press.

Ghaye, A. and Ghaye, K. (1998) *Teaching and Learning through Critical Reflective Practice*. London: David Fulton.

Goldacre, B. (2009) *Bad Science.* London: Harper Collins, www.badscience.net/

Goddard Blythe, S. (2009) 'All about movement and music', *Nursery World*, 3 December.

Godfrey, M. (2009) 'Worms turn into butterflies', *Early Years Educator*, vol 11, no 6, October. Download from: www.bestpracticenet.co.uk/downloads/eyps/eye-v11-n6-oct09-p16.pdf

Gopnik, A. (2009) *The Philosophical Baby: What Children's Minds Tell Us about Truth, Love and the Meaning of Life.* London: Bodley Head. Also a conversational feature on: www.edge.org/3rd_culture/gopnik09/gopnik09_index.html

Grenier, J. (2010) 'Planning around core experiences', *Nursery World*, 4 February.

Henry, L. (2010) 'Open the door to new ideas', *Nursery World*, 28 January.

HM Inspectorate of Education (2007) *The Child at the Centre: Self-Evaluation in the Early Years.* Livingston: HMIE. www.hmie.gov.uk/documents/publication/catcseey.pdf

High/Scope UK (1988) *Supporting Children in Resolving Conflicts* (DVD). www.high-scope.org.uk

Holt, N. (2007) *Bringing the High/Scope Approach to Your Early Years Practice.* London: Routledge. See also: www.high-scope.org.uk

Honey, P. (2006) *The Learning Styles Questionnaire.* www.peterhoney.com/documents/Learning-Styles-Questionnaire-80-item_QuickPeek.pdf

Howard-Jones, P. (undated, about 2008) *Neuroscience and Education: Issues and Opportunities.* London: Teaching and Learning Research Programme. www.tlrp.org/pub/commentaries.html

Kate Greenaway Nursery School and Children's Centre (2009) *Core Experiences for the Early Years Foundation Stage distributed by Early Education.* Also information on: www.coreexperiences.wikia.com

Kolb, D. (1984) *Experiential Learning: Experience as the Source of Learning and Development.* New Jersey: Prentice Hall.

Learning and Teaching Scotland (2005b) *Let's Talk about Pedagogy: Towards a Shared Understanding for Early Years Education in Scotland.* Glasgow: Learning and Teaching Scotland. www.ltscotland.org.uk/publications/l/publication_tcm4617466.asp?strReferringChannel=search&strReferringPageID=tcm:4-615801-64

Learning and Teaching Scotland (2010) *Pre-birth to Three: Positive Outcomes for Scotland's Children and Families.* www.ltscotland.org.uk/earlyyears/

Lee, M. (2009) 'International networks', *Early Years Educator*, 11, (6), October.

Lepper, J. (2009) 'Social pedagogy demystified', *Children and Young People Now*, 2-8 April.

Lindon, J. (2001) *Understanding Children's Play.* Cheltenham: Nelson Thornes.

Lindon, J. (2006) *Care and Caring Matter: Young Children Learning through Care.* London: Early Education.

Lindon, J. (2007) *Understanding Children and Young People: Development from 5-18 Years.* London: Hodder Education.

Lindon, J. (2009) *Parents as Partners.* London: Practical Pre-School Books.

Lindon, J. (2010a) *Child-Initiated Learning.* London: Practical Pre-School Books.

Lindon, J. (2010b) *The Key Person Approach.* London: Practical Pre-School Books.

Lindon, J. (2012a, third edition) *Understanding Child Development: 0–8 Years.* London: Hodder Education.

Lindon, J. (2012b, fourth edition) *Safeguarding and Child Protection: 0-8 Years,* London: Hodder Education.

Lindon, J. (2012c) *Understanding Children's Behaviour: 0–11 Years.* London: Hodder Education.

Lindon, J. (2012d, third edition) *What Does It Mean to Be Two? A Practical Guide to Child Development in the Early Years Foundation Stage.* London: Practical Pre-School Books.

Lindon, J. (2012e, third edition) *What Does It Mean to Be Four? A Practical Guide to Child Development in the Early Years Foundation Stage.* London: Practical Pre-School Books.

Lindon, J. and Lindon, L. (2007) *Mastering Counselling Skills.* Basingstoke: Palgrave Macmillan.

Lindon, J. and Lindon, L. (2012) *Leadership and Early Years Professionalism. London:* Hodder Education.

Lucas, E. (2007) 'Harnessing performance', *Professional Manager*, September, pages 22-25. More about the ideas of Amy Wrzesniewski on: **www.bus.umich.edu/Positive/Pos-Research/ Contributors/AmyWrzesniewski.htm**

MacNaughton, G. and Williams, G. (2004) *Teaching Young Children: Choices in Theory and Practice.* Maidenhead: Open University Press.

Manning-Morton, J. (2006) 'The personal is professional: professionalism and the birth to three practitioner', *Contemporary issues in early childhood*, vol 7, no 1.

Marsden, L. and Woodbridge, J. (2005) *Looking Closely at Learning and Teaching… A Journey of Development.* Outlane: Early Excellence. **www.earlyexcellence.com**

Maslow, A. (1943) 'A theory of human motivation', *Psychological review*, 50, pages 370–96. Download from: **http://psychclassics.yorku.ca/Maslow/motivation.htm** Also try these online sources: **www.teacherstoolbox.co.uk/T_maslow.html** and **www.businessballs.com/maslow. htm**

McGuinness, C. (1999) *From Thinking Skills to Thinking Classrooms.* London: Department for Education and Employment. **www.sustainablethinkingclassrooms.qub.ac.uk/DFEE_ Brief_115.pdf**

Miller, S. and Sambell, K. (eds) (2003) *Contemporary Issues in Childhood: Approaches to Teaching and Learning.* Newcastle upon Tyne: Northumbria University Press.

Moon, J. (1999) *Reflection in Learning and Professional Development: Theory and Practice.* Abingdon: RoutledgeFalmer.

Moon, J. (2003) *Learning Journals and Logs, Reflective Diaries.* Dublin: Centre for Teaching and Learning, University College Dublin. **www.ucd.ie/t4cms/ucdtla0035.pdf**

Moon, J. (2008) *Critical Thinking: An Exploration of Theory and Practice.* London: Routledge.

Moyles, J., Adams, S. and Musgrove, A. (2002) *Study of Pedagogical Effectiveness in Early Learning Brief No. 363.* **www.education.gov.uk/publications/standard/publicationDetail/ Page1/RR363**

National Children's Bureau *Everyday stories.* **www.everydaystories.org.uk**

National Strategies Early Years (2008) *Early Years Consultant's Handbook.* London: DCSF. **www.nsonline.org.uk/node/132576?uc=force_deep**

National Union of Teachers (2009) *Continence and Toilet Issues in Schools: Advice to NUT Members, School Representatives and Health and Safety Representatives.* **www.teachers. org.uk/node/12506**

Nicol, J. (2007) *Bringing the Steiner Waldorf Approach to Your Early Years Practice.* Abingdon: Routledge.

OFSTED (2009) *Early years online self-evaluation form (SEF) and guidance.* **www.ofsted. gov.uk/resources/early-years-online-self-evaluation-form-sef-and-guidance-for-settings- delivering-early-years-foundat**

Rich, D., Casanova, D., Dixon, A., Drummond, M.J., Durrant, A. and Myer, C. (2005) *First Hand Experiences: What Matters to Children.* Clopton: Rich Learning Opportunities. www.richlearningopportunities.co.uk

Rich, D., Drummond, M.J. and Myer, C. (2008) *Learning: What Matters to Children.* Clopton: Rich Learning Opportunities.

Ridler, C. (2002) 'Teachers, children and number understanding', Conference paper, British Psychological Society Psychology of Education. University College, Worcester.

Schaffer, H. (1998) *Making Decisions about Children: Psychological Questions and Answers.* Oxford: Blackwell Publishing

Schön, D. (1983) *The Reflective Practitioner: How Professionals Think in Action.* London: Routledge.

Schön, D. (1987) *Educating the Reflective Practitioner: Towards a New Design for Teaching and Learning in the Professions.* San Francisco: Jossey-Bass.

Siraj-Blatchford, I., Sylva, K., Muttock, S., Gilden, R. and Bell, D. (2002) *Researching Effective Pedagogy in Early Years: Brief No. 356.* www.education.gov.uk/publications/standard/publicationDetail/Page1/RB356

Smith, M. (1996) 'David A. Kolb on experiential learning', *the encyclopaedia of informal education.* www.infed.org/biblio/b-explrn.htm

Smith, M. (2001a) 'Donald Schön: learning, reflection and change', *the encyclopaedia of informal education*, www.infed.org/thinkers/et-schon.htm

Smith, M. (2001b) 'Chris Argyris: theories of action, double-loop learning and organizational learning', *the encyclopaedia of informal education.* www.infed.org/thinkers/argyris.htm

Smith, M. (2009) 'Social pedagogy', *the encyclopaedia of informal education.* http://www.infed.org/biblio/b-socped.htm

Social Exclusion Task Force (2007) *Families at Risk Review.* London: Social Exclusion Task Force.

Tayler, C. (2007) 'The brain, development and learning in early childhood', Centre for Educational Research and Innovation, *Understanding the Brain: the Birth of a Learning Science* Part II, pages 161-183. www.oecd.org/document/60/0,3343, en_2649_35845581_38811388_1_1_1_1,00.html

Thornton, L. and Brunton, P. (2009) *Understanding the Reggio Approach: Early Years Education in Practice.* London: Routledge.

Trevarthen, C., Barr, I., Dunlop, A., Gjersoe, N., Marwick, H. and Stephen, C. (2003) *Meeting the Needs of Children from Birth to Three Years.* Edinburgh: Scottish Executive. Download the summary on: www.scotland.gov.uk/Publications/2003/06/17458/22696 or the full report on www.scotland.gov.uk/Resource/Doc/933/0007610.pdf

Valentine, M. (1999, and second edition 2006) *The Reggio Emilia Approach to Early Years Education.* Glasgow: Learning and Teaching Scotland, www.ltscotland.org.uk/resources/r/genericresource_tcm4242154.asp?strReferringChannel=search&strReferringPageID=tcm:4-615801-64

van Manen, M. (1995) 'On the epistemology of reflective practice', *Teachers and teaching: theory and practice*, vol 1, no 1. www.maxvanmanen.com/category/articles/

Warden, C. (2006) *Talking and Thinking Floorbooks: Using 'Big Book Planners' to Consult Children.* Perthshire: Mindstretchers.

Weigand, R. (2007) *Reflective Supervision in Child Care: The Discoveries of An Accidental Tourist.* Access this and other articles on: http://main.zerotothree.org/site/DocServer/ZTT28-2_nov_07.pdf?docID=7244

Index